A Place *for* Every...One

Finding My Place in a World that
Is Not My Home

wishing you the lord's greatest blessings!

Rose

ROSE GARDUNIO

ISBN 978-1-64140-226-2 (paperback)
ISBN 978-1-64140-227-9 (digital)

Christian Faith Publishing, Inc.
832 Park Avenue
Meadville, PA 16335
www.christianfaithpublishing.com

Cover Painting © 2018 by Sarabeth and Gordon Gardunio

Printed in the United States of America

This book is dedicated to:

My best friend and my truest love, Jesus,
who has never given up on me,
and to the treasures He has given to me.

To Gordon, who has patiently loved me,
even when I have been unlovable.
You were the first person to help me to understand God's love.

To Eric, who has taught me about little boys
and their lives as they grow into men.
There is a deep love and pride in my heart for you.

To Sarabeth, who renewed memories of little girls
and their lives as they grow into women.
You brought joy back to our hearts after deep pain.

To our three treasures in heaven, Heather, Matthew, and Hannah,
You have brought depth to my life, teaching me of
pain and sorrow and love and compassion.
How I long to see each one of you in person one day!

I love you all!

And I will provide a place for my people …
and will plant them so that they can have a home of their own
and no longer be disturbed.

—2 Samuel 7:10a

In my Father's house are many rooms;
if it were not so, I would have told you.
I am going there to prepare a place for you.
And if I go and prepare a place for you,
I will come back and take you to be with me
that you also may be where I am.

—John 14:2–3

Contents

Preface

I have learned to be content whatever the circumstances.

—Philippians 4:11b

The devotional book *Streams in the Desert* contains the recap of a story about a king who visited his garden, anticipating its beauty. Instead, he found most of the plants sick and dying. When he sought the source of the problem, he found them all struggling because they longed to have the attributes of another: the oak wished to be tall like the pine, the pine wanted to bear fruit like the grapevine, and the grape wanted to stand and bear peaches. Only one plant, a violet, was content. When the king commented upon this, its response was that, although small, it was sure the king had a purpose for having planted it and was determined to become all that the king had in mind—the best it could be. It realized that its purpose was to please the king.[1]

This scripture and recap explain what this book, God's book and my story, is about: my account of trying to find my place in this world—a world often cruel and heartless and definitely not my home. From as far back as I can remember, I have sought to fit in, to be a part, to be accepted, and my seeking led to many wrong paths and much discouragement. However, the Lord is faithful, and He saved me from my despair and began working, little by little, to accomplish His purposes.

As said above, this book is God's book, the story of His work in my life. I am hoping it will give a glimmer of hope to those who are hurting as I have, never able to see any purpose for their birth or life, constantly stumbling through and feeling like a failure and misfit. Because it is true, I am intending to be as honest as I can be. In doing so, I hope the readers will remember that all of us view the world through our own spectacles, our own set of lenses. We all have different perceptions because of our own unique personalities and past experiences, so what I have interpreted from certain people and/or situations may not have been what they intended to convey to me.

Thankfully, we have a kind Father who gently and patiently works with us, supplying His lenses to us so we can see more clearly and have a better understanding of His plan and purposes and the people and situations He uses to accomplish them. For He says, "For I know the plans I have for you ... plans to prosper you and not to harm you, plans to give you hope and a future" (Jeremiah 29:11). Just as Mary said, I repeat, "My soul praises the Lord and my spirit rejoices in God my Savior, for he has been mindful of the humble state of his servant" (Luke 1:46b–48a).

My main hopes for this book are the following:

1. To give thanks and praise to the Lord, who has been so kind and patient with me
2. To reveal to others the true character of the Lord that I have come to know
3. To give comfort, hope, and encouragement to those people, Christian or non-Christian, who may be struggling to find their place in this world
4. To be a voice for those who are hurting
5. To provide a better understanding of my struggles to those from my past, that they may find it in their hearts to forgive any wrongs that I may have committed against them

CHAPTER 1

The Search

So we fix our eyes not on what is seen, but on what is unseen.
For what is seen is temporary, but what is unseen is eternal.
—2 Corinthians 4:18

The most profound thought I have ever had came to me as a little child, probably elementary school. I guess I judge it as that because, even after all these years, the question still elicits the same empty and bewildering feeling within me whenever I truly ponder it. Perhaps everyone goes through the same questioning and soul-searching, but it is easy, especially as a child, to discount it when once shared and dismissed with an easy answer.

The day is still clear in my mind. My cousin Lani was in town for part of the summer, visiting her grandparents. We always had such fun playing together in her grandma's yard. There was an old apple tree to climb and a ditch that ran in front of the small yard. The garden to the east had strawberries, raspberries, and many veggies. On the west side was a small pasture that housed a horse we would feed sugar cubes. And the train tracks were just beyond the pasture, so we could hear when the train passed and blew its whistle, beckoning my great-aunt Teresa out the door to wave at great-uncle John as he went by. They had a simple life, which felt heavenly to me as a kid.

Maybe we had eaten a treat from the old icebox, some little cups of chocolate, strawberry, or vanilla ice cream, delivered earlier in the day, to be eaten with little wooden spoons. Or maybe we were resting in the shade of the tree, eating green apples, raspberries, or strawberries. Or we might have been playing in the water. I do not remember those details. But whatever we were doing, the warmth and peace of the summer day and the heavenly home prompted me to ask my most secret question of one of my favorite people.

"Have you ever wondered where you would be if you weren't here?" There, I had finally asked it!

Just as simply and easily, with no hesitation, she responded, "At my other grandma's."

It was not exactly the answer I was looking for, and it was then that I wondered if I were not truly different from most people! Not easily discouraged at that point in my life, I decided to ask another friend. We too had shared many lazy summer days growing up as next-door neighbors: reading under her apple tree, picking goodies from her garden, eating cherry tomatoes, which grew outside the greenhouse across the street, and making numerous trips to the candy store a block away. There was ample opportunity to talk and contemplate those things we were trying to figure out. Fortunately, Sandy was a bit deeper thinker than my cousin was, or perhaps I just phrased my question better. "Have you ever thought about if you weren't here, if you'd never been born?" Her response gave me hope. Yes, she had. We discussed our feelings about it, though I could not tell you what they were. It was such a relief to know someone else understood and actually thought like me!

This, however, was not the end of it for me. Perhaps my questions came, even at that young age, because I never felt I belonged here and I longed for answers about why I was—and what my part, my place, was—in this world. There seemed to be much more, much that was unseen, hidden things. I knew there was something deeper behind all of it. The clouds in the sky all held pictures to be deciphered, as did the texture on the walls in the bedroom where I awoke after having dreams full of wonder and promise. My life as a child was filled with seeking for hidden, deep things.

Books, especially mysteries, intrigued me. By junior high school, math had become my favorite subject, something requiring much thought in order to find the solution, an answer hidden in a puzzle. Following my heart, I majored in math and computer science in college, always trying to discover secrets, treasures.

Science pointed to the need to prove everything by what we could see and measure. But there had to be more. There was no way to measure love or hate or fear, the emotions, but they were no less real than the liquid in the beaker—no less real, just different.

Life had to have something beyond what most people daily took for granted, merely living and pursuing happiness. It all seemed empty, shallow, and meaningless to me.

CHAPTER 2

The Treasure

The kingdom of heaven is like treasure hidden in a field.
When a man found it, he hid it again, and then in his
joy went and sold all he had and bought that field.
—Matthew 13:44

Do not store up for yourselves treasures on earth, where moth
and rust destroy, and where thieves break in and steal. But store
up for yourselves treasures in heaven, where moth and rust
do not destroy, and where thieves do not break in and steal.
For where your treasure is, there your heart will be also.
—Matthew 6:19–21

Growing up in a small town (Salida, Colorado) in a Catholic family with an older brother and sister and two younger sisters, I learned early on about God and even attended Catholic school during grade school. So a religious foundation was established, but God seemed mostly distant and uncaring, most likely even displeased with me, at least the Father. Jesus, the Jesus in the manger at church surrounded by the peaceful blue lights of Christmas, seemed more able to understand. Somehow, His thoughts for me might even be tender. But in all the searching, it never occurred to me that there was any real connection between God and the compulsion in my heart to discover and uncover the mystery surrounding my life. I never dreamed, never fathomed, certainly never entertained any thoughts that those very passions in my heart were dear to Him and, in fact, placed there by Him.

So I struggled not only searching for the hidden but also with myself. That in itself was a mystery. Why was I such a shy kid? Elementary school was mostly a lonely time, with three friends all moving by fourth grade. Junior high in public school also began as a challenge, when a good friend decided we could no longer be friends. Thankfully, new friends reached out, including me in their group, so that the rest of junior high proved an encouraging time. High school was certainly a time of wanting to fit in, particularly to get the attention of one boy I had liked in junior high. The path to fulfill those desires brought not only pain but also confusion. The partying that took away my shyness and was so much fun soon became depressing and always brought more questions, less about the hidden than about who I was and if I would ever truly belong anywhere.

College only intensified those feelings. With a roommate who had a boyfriend and was seldom around, I found my quiet nature not very conducive to making friends. After my first year, I decided to return home and work for a year to buy a car. But returning to something that *was* and no longer *is* leaves a sense of loss and confusion also. Instead of providing a respite from the questions and pain, the desires to understand myself and find fulfillment grew daily within me. Somehow, it all seemed linked to becoming a wife and mother, my two main desires since childhood.

At that time, my older sister, Mary Kay, began speaking to me about the Lord, explaining that He wants to have a personal relationship with us. My immediate response was that I could not change. Her answer was unexpected: "You don't have to change. He will change you."

Years earlier, my best friend in high school and I had worked one summer cleaning motel rooms. Every day after work, we would read Christian magazines in the laundry room. The first seeds were planted at that point, followed by Mary Kay's. But no one, including myself, would have known that those very seeds were not only implanted but also nurtured. By spring 1976, I was discouraged with my hometown and my job. One particularly bad day, I cried out to the Lord, asking Him to come into my life, and for a husband. That began for me a new life.

For the following year, I was growing, as a baby grows in its mother's womb. I returned to college in the fall, only this time with a boyfriend of my own. May had brought Gordon, my first real boyfriend. Although heading to different colleges, hope was renewed in my heart.

October brought a visit from Gordon and bad news from home. Mary Kay and her husband, Ken, lost their sixteen-month-old son, Luke, who drowned in an irrigation ditch near their home. Our hearts ached for them. Within a month, I ended up in the hospital with mononucleosis, followed by long months of recuperation. The New Year brought depression and even more questions. What was happening? A Campus Crusade for Christ meeting in the spring beckoned me, and I shared my questions about Luke's death and about the faith I had seen in Mary Kay and Ken. No one had any answers but encouraged me to look to the Lord.

May came with a return home, and a new job, at a Christian bookstore! Who would have known? Mary Kay had arranged it, not without some struggle, as the new owners naturally did not want to hire someone who was not a Christian. I myself had reservations. Only the Lord was sure; He knew it was time for my birth. Within a few weeks, I made public my secret commitment of the previous year. There was joy, yet I struggled. The Bible said I was now a new creation, but there was certainly no evidence of that. Still I was obviously shy and quiet and found it difficult to fit in.

During the next school year, with a move to attend college nearer to Gordon, I saw there were many different beliefs within this Christian realm, and I still did not feel part. Thankfully, the Lord held me close and took my hand. "The Lord does not look at the things man looks at. Man looks at the outward appearance, but the Lord looks at the heart" (1 Samuel 16:7b).

CHAPTER 3

The House

By wisdom a house is built, and through
understanding it is established;
through knowledge its rooms are filled
with rare and beautiful treasures.

—Proverbs 24:3–4

From the start, I knew that following Him would take me to some of the hidden places I had been seeking, and though fearful, the desires in my heart compelled me on. Often since I had come to know Him, He had taken me on walks within this new kingdom. From the start, I found it beautiful beyond words. Mostly we had been on paths out in nature, through meadows and woods and beside streams, places that made the most amazing worldly sights pale in comparison, breathtaking and oh-so peaceful.

Lately, we had been seeing more houses, though not in town, but scattered here and there, some hidden. I marveled at their unique architecture and composition. Truly, they were as nothing I had seen before. We had gone many times on these peaceful walks, always returning to the house just inside the gate of the kingdom, a haven of rest, this first place He brought His new children.

One day, He asked if I was up for a longer walk, deeper into the kingdom, in a special, secluded area. Every adventure had left me with new insights and understanding. Of course I wanted to go again, and farther on. The early path led us along now familiar sites, but soon we were winding our way through mountainous areas, and though there may have been dangerous or frightening spots, I never knew, for He was with me and the path and view were stunning, ever inviting.

Though it was a longer walk than we had attempted before, we soon came to the place I surmised to be our destination, although it very much surprised me. The path led down out of many towering pine trees to reveal a most unusual scene. Before us was a gorgeous sunlit land with a huge sunken garden of fruit trees and flowers, above which was a narrow meadow with a happily gurgling stream, all encompassed by massive rock cliffs looming up before us.

Not far from the stream was a house, but mind you, not the kind of house I had been accustomed to seeing here. *This house*, though obviously with a grand design, was what I would call dilapidated, a total mess! Perhaps that is why it was hidden. It certainly did not seem to fit within *this* kingdom, whose scenery and houses were immaculate.

Though I was still getting to know my Guide, it had not taken long to decipher His tender heart and love for those in His kingdom. Though I may not have understood, I was certain I could trust Him. Surely there was a good reason for coming here, and if He saw anything wrong, He did not share it, except to say, "What do you think of this place?" and "Would you like to look inside?"

To which I replied, "The design is quite lovely, although I do not understand what happened to it, as it looks like it is in need of much repair" and "Yes, I am curious to see what is inside."

"Before we head inside, I want you to see the outside and the pretty view surrounding it."

The side we were facing was bathed in morning sunlight. Over half was windows, both the walls and roof, similar to a greenhouse, only the windows looked to be made of a special kind of glass with a rainbow tint. Unfortunately, many were now broken. On the far end of this east side was the textured part of the house, at least at the top.

The bottom was covered with beautiful slabs of rock. Unfortunately, the textured siding was cracked in many places. There was a door on the first floor, and windows with shutters, barely hanging by their hinges, decked both the first and second floors.

When we ventured around the corner to the south side of the house, the view took my breath away. The yard sloped gently to another gurgling stream, but the view that so amazed me was the majestic stone walls towering so high like a barrier against all enemies. They were so high I wondered that the sun could complete its path without being hidden. Farther on, in the distance to the west, I caught a glimpse of what looked to be a huge waterfall. Although quite far away, its peaceful sound could be heard quite distinctly.

As I turned to look toward the house, I was surprised to see what looked like a once-cozy porch with a swing, but now with many loose and missing boards. Oddly enough, there appeared to be two doors on this side, one at the back of the porch and another farther to the west, from which another room protruded, so the porch formed an L shape.

We continued around the corner to the west side, a replica of the east in every way, except that where the glass part began, there was an enclosed patio. The same kind of textured walls as the rest of the house surrounded a courtyard that became visible as we approached and looked through its iron gate. The flooring was the same beautiful rock that encompassed the house. We did not enter at the gate but continued, instead, to the north side, but not before looking down another gently sloping grassed area leading to a secluded lake. Far below could be seen a cluster of houses in a deep valley. This view too was stunning. How sad the house itself was in such bad shape because it was definitely in a perfect place!

The north side of the house was in great shape, a gorgeous wall of rock with narrow, horizontal slits of glass imbedded various places from the foundation to the roof. This house had a magnificent design. But for the obvious signs of neglect, it would have been near perfect. However, much repair would be required to fix broken windows, cracked siding, falling shutters, and splintered wood, not to mention things I may not have noticed, and the inside also. The only thing intact and strong was the rock.

Before we continued on, I looked back to the north at the dense forest from which we had come. I could now see that although this house was in a valley below the forest, it was also actually on a plateau, with sides gently sloping down to the east, south, and west.

When we reached the door on the east side of the house, my Friend gently turned the knob, pushing the creaking door open. He held it for me to enter a huge room, such an amazing room. On both sides by the windows were benches. The north wall was as beautiful inside as out with the glass slits, but also small shelves here and there, which looked to have held special treasures, many of which lay broken on the floor.

Opposite this massive wall, at the far end of the room, was a beautiful stone fireplace with a recessed cubby for firewood. On either side of the fireplace were stairs leading to closed doors above. We had not talked much on this tour, so I was caught by surprise when He asked, "Do you want to see the rooms upstairs?" When I agreed, He led me to the stairs on the right. "We'll go this way so that we can easily view both rooms." Though I did not understand, I followed obediently.

When He opened the door, once again, a surprise awaited me. This was a strange room. In contrast to the lower room, which had no furniture but was huge, this small room was packed full of furniture. There was barely a path through to the other side. But that was the least of its oddness. It looked like every piece had been hastily covered and with material of older fabric styles, so I could not tell what each piece had originally looked like. Mostly I had been observing, but this piqued my curiosity, so I asked, "Why is this room so packed with furniture?"

"Well, an enemy has been coming to destroy the house since it was built, and eventually it was decided that all the furniture should be moved, covered, and locked in this room, thinking to preserve it.

Unfortunately, the material sewn over the original will be difficult to remove when it comes time to remodel." To remodel? Hmm, He obviously still had hope for the place.

"Come this way. Let's go to the back of the room. See, it's open here, for two reasons: for access to this window looking out to the cliffs and also because it leads to the other room, which is convenient, so we don't have to return downstairs and up the other staircase." As I gazed into the room and began to step forward, He said, "Wait! We can only look into this room." Unlike the adjacent room, this room had no furniture, and no wonder why! Various places of the wooden flooring were falling in!

"What happened here?"

"This room originally had beautiful floors, but with time, they were replaced with what was thought to be a more updated, modern wood, which was not what it was supposed to be."

As we headed back through the first room, I could see that these two rooms were mirror images. Both had windows on their outer walls and full bookcases on their south walls. Separating the rooms were stone fireplaces. The view of the big room below was bright and cheerful with the sun flooding it.

Underneath each staircase were halls to the south side of the house. The Lord explained to me that the doors on either side of the left hallway led, one to a shower and the other to a bath area. We did not go in; however, as He assured me, they were also in bad shape.

Next I noticed a door to the left. As it turned out, this door led underground. One thing I knew, if I owned this house, I would never venture here! The minute the door was opened, a musty smell surrounded us. "This is the best time to come down here," my Friend said. Hmm. The only light that was visible came from a narrow rectangular glass near the ceiling. The east light now entered, so we could make our way down the winding staircase. What was this room? Just a basement for storage? No, it must be something else. There were benches around the perimeter and shelves here and there, with what appeared to be another bookcase on the west wall, a sort of oblong, oval room. It was unfinished; in fact, it looked completely ignored, with cobwebs hanging everywhere. Obviously, the owner must love books, as there seemed an abundance of bookcases.

Once upstairs, we continued into a sunny, happy kitchen with a stone hearth. The wooden cabinets were old and showed signs of wear, as did the floor. It was a welcoming place, nonetheless. The most amazing part of it all was a small room that descended from the kitchen. This faced south and must have been at one time a type of greenhouse, as many dead plants filled the enclosed area. Benches encompassed the sides, with a fountain by the window. The kitchen table looked down into this precious alcove.

The last room was one protruding to the south. There were steps down from the kitchen into this west room. The outer south wall was glass, revealing the amazing rock wall outside. In the corner was a rock fireplace. The north wall also was rock. It and the west wall had padded benches, and there was a daybed near the door on the opposite side.

This was not a huge house, but its design was fascinating and the rock beautiful and mostly intact. Everything else needed a major remodel. It was obvious it would not only be expensive to repair but would also require a great amount of time and energy to restore it to the original design.

We returned to our start by way of the other hall under the west staircase. I was facing the glass room, dreaming of how it must have been and could be one day.

"Well, what do you think of this house?"

Once again, my mind was shocked into the present. "Oh, it had to have been so beautiful at one time, but what has happened? Where is its owner? Doesn't he care? Won't he ever fix it?"

My back was to my Lord. "My dear Rose, this house, *this house*, is your house." With His words, tears filled my eyes, threatening to fall. As He gently turned me toward Him, I lowered my head, for fear He would see my pain, even as tears trickled down my cheeks. Of course, *this* was *my* house. Even here, in this wonderful land, my house was the one in major decline. Why had I not realized it from the start?

"Please don't cry. I have not shown this to you to make you sad but instead to bring you hope and joy. Your house can once again be lovely, just as you were now dreaming."

"But why? I don't understand. Why is my house *alone* like this? You've shown me many houses here, and they are all beautiful, at least, from the outside, they appear so. I know I have never seen their insides. Why is mine like this? Even the houses outside the kingdom are grander than mine. Will I never belong anywhere? Even in Your kingdom, there is no place for me."

"Dear Rose, come and sit with me. The houses you have seen are indeed beautiful. But let Me explain. When your house was first built, it was perfect and complete but, of course, unfurnished. And it was also outside My kingdom and, therefore, vulnerable to the evil influences of the enemy. Whenever someone enters My kingdom, I move his or her house here, so you see, all houses that enter My land are in need of some repair. Those you have seen so far fall into two categories: those who have allowed Me to work on their houses and those who have chosen to fix theirs themselves. The first category, whose owners have given Me permission to work, always have their repairs made from the inside out so that they are usually here a long time before their outside is finished. The second category have decided to live within My kingdom, yet they have not allowed Me to remodel their houses. Therefore, most often, they concentrate only on the outside. They are less concerned for their insides than I am. So you see, all come the same way. And yes, there is a place for every...one, every single one, in My kingdom. I have brought you here to ask you if I may begin working on your home. Will you allow Me to remodel it?"

He was willing to fix this mess? How wonderful! I certainly knew I could not! Without hesitation and with joy filling my heart, I eagerly replied, "Of course, dear Lord, of course I give You my permission."

"It may take a long time," He warned.

"That is okay. I am willing to wait and will try to be patient." Both relief and excitement began engulfing me.

"There is one more thing, Rose. While I am working on this project, I want to send you on a journey. Although I can't be with you, I will provide companions for you and will be ever close at hand. If you ever need Me, just call."

"Oh, my dear Lord, thank you. Thank you." Then I hugged Him. I *knew* He could be trusted!

"Shall we head back?" He asked. As we left the house, I looked back with joy. I remembered this Man is a Master Carpenter!

CHAPTER 4

The Journey: Spring and Summer

Along the Road

I walked a mile with pleasure;
She chattered all the way,
But left me none the wiser
For all she had to say.
I walked a mile with sorrow
And ne'er a word said she;
But oh, the things I learned from her
When sorrow walked with me.

Robert Browning Hamilton[1]

**Beginning My Journey to the High Places
And God's Answers to My Desires**

(1976–1983)

One of the first books I read after becoming a Christian was to have a huge impact on my life. *Hind's Feet on High Places* by Hannah Hurnard is the story, an allegory, of the journey of a young girl to the High Places. Much-Afraid is handicapped when she begins her service with the Shepherd and wants to be whole, like others who work for Him. When she shares her desire to go to the High Places for healing with the Shepherd, He agrees. I have always loved allegories and symbolism, so this became a favorite book of mine. But it was to be years before I realized exactly how closely my life was to mirror the adventures of Much-Afraid. I have shared our journey below.

Invitation from the Shepherd / Invasion of Fearing Relatives / Escape into the Night / Beginning the Journey[2]

The book begins with Much-Afraid already in the Shepherd's service but struggling with her obvious weaknesses. After He agrees to her desire to go to the High Places for healing, she is invaded by her fearing family before anxiously and secretly departing to look for the Shepherd late at night. When she finds Him the following morning, she begins her journey with two unexpected companions: Sorrow and Suffering. From the beginning, she struggles with her weaknesses and, though reluctantly, finds she has to accept help from her aides. Unfortunately, her physical problems are not her only challenge. She is also accosted by enemies from her family, often having to call her Shepherd. She also finds the path not always as she has anticipated and has to decide if she will relinquish her own will and continue to follow the Shepherd or return to the valley. Each time, she builds an altar, keeping a stone as a memorial of her yielding to her Lord and her continued trust.

Like Much-Afraid, I also saw my many needs and longed to be like other Christians. Although I secretly accepted the Lord in 1976, it was a year before I made public my earlier commitment. Once I did, however, my joy was evident and shared with many: Gordon, my parents, friends from college. Unfortunately, their responses were unanticipated: friends made jokes or discounted my new relationship, my parents were unhappy, and worst of all, Gordon was angry. Like Much-Afraid, their reactions not only shocked me but they also instilled fear inside, causing me to question my decision. Midsummer after accepting the Lord, I was invited by my employer's parents to an evangelical meeting in another town. This event was similar to Much-Afraid's escaping her home to leave for the High Places. Not only did I long to be like other Christians, but I was also trusting the Lord to bring my heart's desires: marriage and family.

Although there were struggles that summer, often with my dad, it was mostly a time of joy—perpetual spring, full of hope. My sister Judy also accepted the Lord that summer, and we often stayed up late discussing the new learning, most very encouraging, that was coming from our Bible reading. But I was also learning that believers should not be united with unbelievers. Was my dating Gordon wrong? This was an unexpected, unwelcome question. Because my plans for transferring schools to be near him were already underway, I continued along my path.

Fall of 1977 quickly approached, with plans to live in the dorms again, while Gordon rented an apartment close to campus. My roommate was a Christian, and I met another Christian at initiation. Although good to have Christian support, it did not take long to discover that Christians often differ on beliefs and issues. Also, when I went with my roommate to events on campus and to church with the other friend, my shyness stood out horribly. So during the year, I was learning (1) there are many different beliefs among Christians and (2) I still was not part.

This year was definitely a time of growth and questioning. When I went to the meeting the previous summer, I had given money. Shortly after, the same amount came from insurance for my hospital stay. Although it was Dad's, it seemed as if the Lord returned it, as they had said at the meeting. Going on that premise, I took my savings for tuition and gave it to charity, sure the Lord would return it. When my check to the college bounced, my parents were understandably embarrassed and angry. Many years later, the realization of my having tested the Lord came clear, as did His testing me, as the rest of the year revealed.

Meeting with Pride / Unexpected Path into the Desert / Along the Sea and Shores of Loneliness / On the Old Sea Wall[3]

Fortunately, school was going well, one of the few positives. My relationship with Gordon began that way, until problems from the previous year surfaced and culminated in our breakup in the spring of the year. Had it been a mistake to move? Once again, feelings of loneliness and isolation resurfaced. My parents were angry with me (for both the bounced check and the breakup with Gordon). There were no Christians with roots similar to mine. Now Gordon and I were falling apart. Would I stick with the Lord, who seemed to be turning my world upside down, instead of bringing me to the High Places and giving me my heart's desires? Like Much-Afraid, I encountered Pride right away. My breakup with Gordon was not unlike Much-Afraid's finding a detour into the desert, after the hardship of climbing at the beginning. She then had a time of intense loneliness walking by the sea. This eventually led to an Old Sea Wall, where hope returned, when she once again saw the mountains before her. Little did I realize that this was only the first, tiniest step in a long road leading to the High Places, that many years of pain were ahead. At this point, however, there was encouragement when Gordon and I reconciled within a month of our breakup.

When school was out, I worked at the Christian bookstore again while Gordon stayed in Grand Junction to work. This summer, unlike the previous one, was difficult with constant problems with Dad and also Gordon, who felt my pressure to become a Christian. There were also problems at work, the least expected place. Would there never be a place I belonged? My hope for escape was Gordon, who was talking of marriage and had given me a promise ring the previous Christmas.

In the fall, I returned to college. Over Christmas break, Gordon and I went to Colorado Springs to pick out wedding bands. We planned to be married the following spring. Even though I knew it was wrong to marry an unbeliever, I rationalized that, at least,

Gordon had strong beliefs in God, being the first to speak of the Lord in our relationship, always reminding me to wait and see what God's plans were. Also, he was the most godly man I had ever met, his actions reflecting what every Christian should be striving for—kindness, understanding, and willingness to help, qualities I admired and desired. Also the Lord *had* brought him to me, an answer to prayer.

Gordon and I were married in "my" backyard on May 26, 1979. The day began with rain, but the Lord kindly brought the sun in time for our ceremony. Our first year of marriage was good. Gordon had graduated from college and began working for the government the previous January. I had one more year of college, involving many math and computer classes. I graduated June of 1980 and was hired at a health maintenance organization as a data entry clerk and eventually computer programmer. Gordon and I agreed I would work three to five years so we could buy a house before I would stay home to care for our children. Like Much-Afraid, the mountains were coming closer. Soon the High Places would be a reality.

Work, however, was not easy. Many of the mostly young women had different goals than mine. My desires were not an important career or a great salary but a family and home, old-fashioned notions.

Not long after we married, Gordon and I looked into buying a house. We went with a realtor many times, only to find older homes in need of major repair and with high monthly payments. There was a place in town I loved but could never seem to find. As it turned out, my workplace was in that same area.

Spring of 1981, my dad mentioned that the sister of a friend of his died and her brothers were planning to sell her house here. Early in the summer, they came to show it to us, and it was right down the alley from work. Thanksgiving of 1981, we moved in. It was a nice neighborhood, with many retired couples and Christians, a great place to start a family, surrounded by "grandparents." We became especially close to the couple south of us, Bill and Roberta.

Spring of 1983, we anxiously began to plan our family and money situation. Shortly after our fourth anniversary, we found out

I was pregnant. When the doctor mentioned the possibility of miscarriage, it frightened me. Yet I was pregnant and due March 15, a long-awaited dream.

For my birthday that year, Gordon bought me a Black Hills Gold ring, something I had wanted for a long time. It seemed to hold special significance, as we awaited our first child, a constant reminder that the Lord does answer prayer, even if it takes longer than we anticipate. Little did I know that this ring held a prophecy and would change in the coming years.

The Lord had been good. Since 1976, He had done so much: (1) brought me into His family, (2) provided a husband for me, (3) brought us a home; and now, (4) a baby was coming!

CHAPTER 5

The Journey: Fall and Winter

Joyous Harvest—Followed by Unexpected Detour into Grief
. . . .
(1983–1990)

The Great Precipice Barrier / Ascending the Precipice / Through the Forests of Danger and Tribulation / Walking in the Mist[1]

As the fall of 1983 approached, I was nearly three months pregnant, and we planned, with Gordon's parents, to rent a cabin for Labor Day. The week before, I began to spot and then bleed more profusely. When we went to the emergency room, the doctors informed us that I was having a miscarriage. We were heartbroken. We had been so close to the "High Places." Still, I was not surprised. Of course, this was impossible. "Can't you do anything right?" These words echoing in my mind through the years, amid many failures and broken dreams, were forefront at that point.

Months later, I continued to bleed and was told to bring in any tissue that came out. Much later, our dead baby, our firstborn, was delivered while I used the restroom at work. Returning to the doctor's office the next few months, they assured me that continued bleeding was normal. Meanwhile, my body was growing weaker and more tired. Mentally, reality was hitting and hard to accept. Did this mean I would never have children, my most cherished dream?

Returning to work was hard. Many had just found out I was pregnant and kindly came to congratulate me. It was awkward to share I had lost the baby. And there I was, working closely with the computer operator, who was pregnant but sick all the time. Yet she still carried her baby. I felt resentful. She was recently out of high school, married, and pregnant. I was twenty-seven, almost ten years older than she was. Now my dreams were dashed to pieces on the rocks of life.

Depression was setting in, and my feelings were hard to conceal. In November, I asked for a leave of absence and sought help from a psychologist who worked out of his home. That winter was cold and snowy. I remember driving there in the fog of depression, unsure if I would arrive safely, not only from lack of concentration, but also from temptations to drive into something and end it all. The depression was frightening, engulfing me with feelings of worthlessness, sadness, and despair.

In testing me, the doctor determined I *was* depressed and encouraged me to delve into the past for answers to my fears, anger, and sensitivity, age-old problems haunting my thoughts. Was it my environment, my personality, or a combination? Who could say? At that point, I leaned toward blaming my dad, who had belittled me through the years, with little encouragement. Now, I am more inclined to believe the Lord made me as I am for a purpose. My name seems symbolic of my nature—vulnerable to the world, easily hurt and damaged—with the Lord providing thorns for my protection. And yes, they have been evident through the years. At that point, my anger was growing every day.

The Lord was faithful to bring encouragements the rest of the year. While in Salida for Thanksgiving, I poured out my heart to my sisters, with fears I was going crazy. Mary Kay eased my fears, sharing it was part of grief. When my sisters prayed, a dramatic turning point, the depression began to lift and a spark of hope flickered. During my leave of absence, I reread *Hind's Feet on High Places* and found myself at the Precipice Injury. Like Much-Afraid, who was terrified of heights, I struggled to ascend the precipice, overwhelmed with fear. But the Lord gently led me, as the Good Shepherd does, teaching me to rest in His Presence. Like the sun, it finally lifted the fog.

During that time, the Lord was also working in other areas. He revealed resentment I had harbored toward my dad, through the story of the unmerciful servant, who had been freely forgiven of huge debts, only to seek out one who owed him little and demand restitution. There was no condemnation from the Lord, who simply and gently revealed this, as He began to place forgiveness in my heart. Whenever life had been difficult, I had always blamed Dad—if only he had treated me better, if only he had cared. I now saw that the Lord had forgiven me for major offenses when He died. Yet I was continuing to punish my dad, even placing him in a prison in my mind, until he could pay me back. The Lord was asking me to free him (and even myself), which surprisingly was not so difficult, because the Lord had gone ahead in preparation.

We returned to Salida for Christmas. That is when the Lord spoke through the church there, a word given that someone who dearly wanted a baby would be pregnant by Christmas the following year. Could it be me? Dare I hope? Did I have courage to try again?

I returned to work after the New Year. At that time, I found new pictures for my cubicle, one of a peaceful lake and the other a golden frame with the following scripture: "Delight thyself also in the Lord; and He shall give thee the desires of thine heart" (Psalms 37:4, KJV). Once back, I wrote a letter of apology to the computer operator, explaining my jealousy. Months later, I was able to attend her baby shower, sincerely sharing her joy, as I admired her little girl.

As our lost baby's due date, March 15, approached, however, we felt great sadness, but the Lord had good plans ahead, providing a special time in Phoenix, where Gordon had class. While there, I reread *Hind's Feet on High Places* and felt comfort knowing the Lord was in control and had a plan. Around this time, our hoya plant, a gift from Gordon's grandma, began blooming for the first time.

These scriptures also brought hope: "He settles the barren woman in her home as a happy mother of children" (Psalms 113:9a) and "God sets the lonely in families" (Psalms 68:6a).

Spring of 1984 brought three new paths. First, my sister Paula, living in Denver and attending a Vineyard Church, was dating Tim, who was part of the worship team. When he and others visited a church here, he invited us to the services. Shortly after, I began attending regularly and also cell group during the week for prayer. Although the people were caring, group settings were still hard. I did love the church services, both teaching and worship, soothing balms to my wounded spirit.

The second encouragement happened in April, when Gordon and I returned to Salida, where I was baptized. My previous employers had begun full-time ministry there and made arrangements for the baptism, a blessed time surrounded by family, a time of recommitting myself to the Lord.

Shortly after this, the third most beautiful and amazing encouragement came. We found out I was pregnant and due January 8, one day after Dad's birthday! God had helped me, like Much-Afraid, to ascend the Precipice Injury. Now we were once again heading in the right direction, although I did not realize that our road was leading directly into the Forests of Danger and Tribulation, where the Lord's words of encouragement, through Much-Afraid's experiences, were to bring comfort. "A thousand shall fall at thy side and ten thousand at thy right hand; *but* it shall not come nigh thee ... He shall cover thee with his feathers, and under his wings shalt thou trust" (Psalms 91:7, 4a, KJV). "I shall not die, but live, and declare the works of the Lord" (Psalms 118:17, KJV).

This pregnancy I was feeling nauseated much of the time, a new and positive sign, since there had been none the first time. When Gordon and I went for an ultrasound at twenty weeks, we were amazed. A living baby was growing inside me, a joy beyond words seeing our little child moving, its heart beating steadily. We enjoyed Lamaze classes, practicing our part while awaiting the arrival of our special person. I was huge and feeling ready when my due date came and went. Two days later, our baby arrived. My labor was long and intense. By evening, our moms had arrived, but the baby still had not. Finally, our doctor recommended a cesarean section, much to my relief! Our baby, Eric Irvin, meaning "king" and "sea friend," was born late that night. We chose his middle name in honor of Gordon's Grandpa Irv, with whom Gordon had spent much time fishing.

Gordon and I were elated to have a healthy newborn, and a boy! Even with being so thrilled, the first days home were eye-opening. I am not sure how first parents ever survive, much less their babies. I was grateful for the help from our moms and Gordon, who took off a week. It is definitely sink or swim in the beginning, as we learn to be less selfish and do those things for which we have had little training and are too tired to do. Yet how grateful, in the midst of adjusting, we were! Looking at our new baby, pondering how he was created, engendered feelings of wonder and awe. Only the Lord could accomplish such a miracle. A year earlier, I had sat steeped in depression. Now here was a precious baby boy resting in my arms. "The Lord has done great things for us, and we are filled with joy" (Psalms 126:3). At that point, I was determined to never hurt my little one. When Eric was only two weeks old, we flew to Denver to attend Paula and Tim's wedding.

It was a victorious, much-anticipated moment when Eric began sleeping through the night at fifteen months, the same time he was weaned! Around that time, I began to feel a familiar nausea and also missed a period, an unexpected surprise as Gordon and I had planned to have our kids three years apart. As usual, the Lord had different plans. Although apprehensive about miscarriage, there was also hope, having had a successful pregnancy with Eric.

From the beginning, however, we did experience more problems than with Eric. The obstetrician who performed the emergency cesarean section with Eric performed abortions. When our doctor recommended him again, I was hesitant, sharing my dilemma at cell group. My biggest concern was what we knew from personal experience: emergencies sometimes happen in pregnancy. Having limited knowledge medically, we were dependent upon our doctor's expertise and shared beliefs when we may be too upset and lacking in information to determine the best solution. After prayer, I decided to call various obstetricians' offices to determine who did *not* perform abortions. Finding one, I was elated, until I mentioned him to our family doctor, who said he did not recommend him because of incompetency. Of course, this brought more fear to my heart, already familiar with the pain of a pregnancy gone awry.

As I prayed, I opened the Bible to the story of Esther, a Jewish woman chosen to marry a non-Jewish king. In this particular story, she found herself in a precarious position when her uncle, Mordecai, would not bow to the king's high official, Haman, who became angry and determined to kill not only Mordecai but all Jews. When Mordecai received wind of the plan, he notified Esther for help. She was reluctant, knowing she could be sentenced to death for approaching the king without being summoned. After asking Mordecai for prayer, she approached the king and, very wisely, invited him and Haman to two different banquets before revealing the truth about Haman. In the end, after Esther's revelation, Haman was killed on the gallows made for Mordecai. The story eased my fears. Esther did what was right, even though it meant risking her life. I too had to do what was right, even if it meant endangering myself or our baby. When Esther chose the right path, the Lord worked, preserving her life and the whole Jewish nation. That gave me boldness to talk to our doctor with our same obstetrician request, to which he finally reluctantly agreed. Meanwhile, I prayed for protection over the baby and me.

We went in for the ultrasound at five months and were thankful to see our baby. The rest of my pregnancy went well, though I was borderline diabetic and on a low-fat diet. Our little one was due November 8, with the cesarean planned a week before to avoid labor. On the twenty-ninth, I had an amniocentesis to determine the baby's age, though few obstetricians perform this procedure, trusting the accuracy of the ultrasound. It was long and uncomfortable and especially difficult for the technician not to poke the baby. After numerous attempts, it was over, the age estimate correct.

The next morning, our baby arrived bright and early—another boy, named Matthew Leo, meaning "gift of God" and "lion." Gordon was especially proud to have a second son, and his middle name was chosen to honor Gordon's dad. Certain the baby was a girl, I was surprised but not disappointed. When Matthew's lungs would not clear, he was quickly transferred to the nursery. But he was fine, and we were thankful the Lord had taken care of us. Matthew was chosen Harvest Baby by the hospital, who put his picture on their baby board. Eric was unsure what to think of his little brother. Being not yet two years old, he was wondering what this new baby meant to him.

Our hospital stay was special, with many people sharing our joy. Our parents stayed a few days, leaving before I was released. The second night in the hospital, a depression descended on me. Contributing it to tiredness and hormones, I did not dwell on it and was fine by morning. Later I was to wonder if it were not prophetic, as also the honor of Matthew being Harvest Baby.

In January, Gordon went in for a vasectomy, certain two children were enough. Though reluctant, I knew that God is not bound by vasectomies. He could bring us a little girl also.

That same month, Gordon had classes in Phoenix—always hard with him gone. I could so identify with Much-Afraid, who had made it up the Precipice Injury and through the Forests of Danger and Tribulation to find herself walking in the Mist, slipping along a muddy path. Truly, coming to the point of having Eric and Matthew had involved danger and tribulation, but the Lord had protected us, as trees crashed all around. I was on the path to the High Places but have to admit it was a difficult journey at this point. I felt blessed to be home with two healthy sons yet never dreamed life would be so tiring and involve so much work. Eric was active and independent, and Matthew the opposite, totally dependent. I slipped along, doing my best, knowing it would be easier once Matthew was older. Being in the terrible twos, Eric often tried me, my most common response to yell. So much for being the perfect parent. It was definitely harder than I had assumed.

The beginning of March, we traveled to Salida and on to Canon City to see Gordon's Grandpa Irv, suffering with emphysema and recently diagnosed with cancer. It was a painful trip. As we looked at Matthew and Eric, we knew that their lives had just begun, but Grandpa's was almost over. Once we returned, we anxiously awaited spring. It would lift our spirits to be outside again. Also Matthew was quickly outgrowing his clothes, the remaining hand-me-downs all for warmer weather.

Church had become especially stressful. As Gordon did not want to go, I took Eric and Matthew alone, where Eric often fought staying in the toddler room. Wednesday nights were also difficult, with Gordon watching Eric. After a few months, I left both boys but felt pressure to get home to nurse Matthew. Although hard, I felt compelled to keep going because it was expected.

Finally, spring was approaching, providing many warm days outside. Eric played on the swing set while I held Matthew and visited our neighbors Bill and Roberta, to whom we had grown closer once Eric was born. Roberta had been excited during my pregnancies, crocheting a blanket and booties in anticipation. Bill loved to bring treats to Eric, animal crackers and ice cream cones. It was wonderful having "grandparents" close, with the kids' real grandparents far away!

Walking through the Valley of Loss[2]

One of the last Sundays in March, we were at church, Eric in the toddler room and Matthew with me. During worship, the most amazing joy and peace surrounded Matthew and me. As we sang, Matthew sang too, sweet little baby sounds, heavenly notes that must have pleased God. Had I known what the following week would hold, the significance of those minutes would have had an even greater impact. That day, our pastor shared Isaiah 30:21: "Whether you turn to the right or the left, your ears will hear a voice behind you, saying, 'This is the way; walk in it.'" Little did I realize my path, like Much-Afraid's, was soon to make a major detour into the Valley of Loss—devastating, shocking, and totally unexpected.

The following Tuesday, Gordon's brother, Mark, came to visit with his wife, Diane. The next morning, March 25, was gorgeous, and we made quick plans since they had to leave after lunch, when Gordon had to return to work. Gordon and Mark wanted to golf. When we arrived at the course, we were informed that children were not allowed because of the danger of flying balls. So the guys stayed while Diane and I took the kids to the mall. A children's activity center had recently opened there. While Eric played, we window-shopped. It was Eric's first time, and I was fearful for him, praying the whole time. Of course, I had no fears for Matthew, safe in his stroller. With great relief, we returned home to meet Gordon and Mark. Once there, Matthew was asleep. Not wanting to wake him and thinking about making lunch, I placed him in his crib with his Snugli bag still on.

After everyone left, I was tired and relieved to finally sit down and read my Bible and devotional for the day while both boys slept. My devotional in *God Calling* the previous day said not to seek knowledge of the future, because God, in His mercy, veils it from us.[3] My Bible reading was 1 Thessalonians 4, verses 13 through the end:

> Brothers, we do not want you to be ignorant about those who fall asleep or to grieve like the rest of men, who have no hope. We believe that Jesus died and rose again and so we believe that God will bring with Jesus those who have fallen asleep in him. According to the Lord's own word, we tell you that we who are still alive, who are left till the coming of the Lord, will certainly not precede those who have fallen asleep. For the

Lord himself will come down from heaven, with
a loud command, with the voice of the archangel
and with the trumpet call of God, and the dead
in Christ will rise first. After that, we who are still
alive and are left will be caught up with them in
the clouds to meet the Lord in the air. And so we
will be with the Lord forever. Therefore encourage each other with these words.

That was comforting, thinking of the Lord's return. I was soon
to see a deeper significance.

Shortly after reading, Eric woke and came out. He and Matthew
shared the same room, but Matthew was still sleeping. We were heading into the kitchen for pie when the thought crossed my mind that,
although Matthew was beginning to sleep longer, he had never slept
longer than Eric and had gone in for his nap before Eric. As I went to
check on him, panic gripped me. I ran into their room, where I saw
him lying face down. My first thought was to turn his head, but as I
lifted him, I saw his eyelashes pressed tightly against his eyelids and
knew in my heart that he was gone.

I rushed to the kitchen to call Gordon. When the secretary
answered and told me he was gone to the field, I blurted out the
words, "I killed my baby." The horror inside, all my worst fears,
words from my past "Can't you do anything right?" echoing in my
subconscious, overwhelmed me. I had been fearful of the responsibility of two little boys, one a baby, and knew there would be mistakes
but never dreamed of this. The secretary assured me she would con-
tact Gordon immediately.

Meanwhile, I called Roberta. When Bill said she was at the
hairdresser's, I broke down. How prophetic the scripture a good
friend shared before Matthew's birth: "Yet you brought me out of
the womb; you made me trust in you even at my mother's breast.
From birth I was cast upon you; from my mother's womb you have
been my God. Do not be far from me, for trouble is near and there

is no one to help" (Psalm 22:9–11). Once I told Bill about Matthew, he and his son, Bill Jr., came right over. After telling me to call 911, Bill Jr. began cardiopulmonary resuscitation. After explaining the situation to the woman on the phone, she asked if Bill knew what he was doing. I felt ashamed after repeating her question. Bill knew much more than I did and was willing to help. For that, I have always been grateful.

Finally, the ambulance came. I cannot recall if the siren was on or not. Most everything is a blur now. Once help came, it was harder to think, being totally willing to let someone else take charge of a situation completely out of my hands. The police and paramedics came in. I am not sure where Eric was, probably in his high chair. The paramedics worked on Matthew as the police questioned me, following me into the boys' room. When they were done, Matthew was gone. And Bill and Bill Jr. also. My neighbor across the street had come over and was telling me to go with the policeman to the hospital and she would watch Eric.

At the emergency room, I was in a daze. Since it was cell group night, I tried to call the leader. When there was no answer, I called another friend, who promised to pray. After that (oh, the sweet comfort of God), the Lord provided a nurse from our doctor's office, now working in the deputy coroner's office. What comfort to see a familiar face when I felt all alone!

It seemed an eternity before Gordon arrived. When he first received the message, he had assumed it concerned Grandpa and had not hurried. When our doctor came in, he informed us it did not look good. What seemed a long time later, he returned to tell us that our baby Matthew had died. He then asked if we wanted to see him. We both held him, as our doctor spoke comforting words about being good parents, the only thing I remember, the one thing I wanted, and desperately needed, to hear and believe. Gordon requested no autopsy be performed, but our doctor said that it was the law in unexplained deaths and that he would call us the following day with results. Time stands still when something devastating happens. It is impossible to estimate how long we were with Matthew. How difficult to comprehend that this child, for whom we had cared almost constantly, was not ours to take home. He was not even ours to bury.

The rest of the day was drenched in God's mercy and comfort. As we were leaving the room, we were blessed to be surrounded by friends. How they knew, how they were there, I had no idea. It seemed no time had passed, yet there they were. We all reentered the room, where they prayed, so beautiful, a piece of heaven; the deep peace in the room was indescribable. All of us felt it, as if a ray of heaven was shining down upon us, a door standing open as Matthew waved goodbye. The peace was beyond words, a reminder of the peace that engulfed Matthew and me at church the Sunday before. Unbeknown to me, the door had barely begun to open that day. How unbearable to leave, but we did have to go, this time, unlike months earlier, without our baby in our arms.

Once home, friends continued to support us. After sharing our sad news with our neighbor, she returned home. One friend lent me a breast pump; another generously volunteered to pick up medicine to dry up my milk. It was comforting when our pastor and his wife came with Kleenex (and compassion) and stayed into the evening while we made difficult calls to family and friends and tried to help Eric, a two-year-old, understand. Once they left, it was a frightening time, as fears of more heartache surfaced.

After we gave Eric his bath, we fell into bed, exhausted, waking early in the morning, weeping together. I told Gordon about my readings the previous day. I was also remembering an angel card that came the Christmas after our first baby died. Three little angels, two with closed eyes and one with a bent halo, were our children, our first baby, now Matthew, and little Eric. My heart felt comforted realizing that the Lord had brought these signs before Matthew died to encourage us. Although we were caught unaware and in shock, He was not.

Throughout the following day, we played a Vineyard tape from Paula and Tim as people, food, and flowers arrived. Our cell group leaders came over with a coffee maker and donuts. Others brought meat trays, fried chicken, and groceries. People from church also came, followed by Gordon's parents, Mark and Diane, and Gordon's coworkers. The kindness was like a warm blanket of love surrounding us, a beautiful expression of sympathy and care.

Our doctor called that afternoon to confirm what he had suspected the day before, that Matthew had died of Sudden Infant Death Syndrome. He had received the autopsy report that morning and said we would be receiving a copy, something we were anxious to see, not that we would understand what even the professionals could not. We remembered our Lamaze teacher's words many months earlier: "Although none of us like to think of it, SIDS is a reality."

Later, we went to the mortuary. Our pastor and Gordon's parents kindly offered to go too, a blessing, as we had never arranged for a funeral. Once done, the funeral was set for Saturday morning at the church. Being in shock, we did not consider Eric before leaving for the mortuary. Mark and Diane had volunteered to watch him, but after we left, he had a terrible fit. We later figured it might have been because we told him Matthew was gone and could not come back. He might have been afraid that we were also going, not to return. Poor siblings of children who have died! We parents do not intend to neglect them. It is such a difficult time, and the shock is debilitating. In the meantime, our remaining children do not have the support and understanding they also need. As I think back, I feel sad for Eric. What confusion and fears he must have had. His little brother, of whom he was not always fond, was here one day and whisked away the next! That is much for an adult to understand, how much more for a two-year-old!

That evening a spokeswoman for SIDS and mother of a baby girl who had died came to see us. I voiced my fear that Matthew was bundled too much. Could that have caused his death? She assured me it was not the reason. I had also been feeling guilt for not knowing cardiopulmonary resuscitation, but she explained that it is impossible to resuscitate a SIDS victim.

The following afternoon, Friday, we took Eric to the mortuary to say goodbye to his baby brother. He signed the book with a sweet two-year-old signature, scribbles that looked like a heart, and placed a multicolored bear in Matthew's casket. That afternoon, my parents and sister Judy arrived. Two neighbors kindly volunteered places for our families to stay. Later, my sister Mary Kay and her family arrived.

The next morning was Saturday, the day of the funeral. As we prepared, I shared with Mary Kay and Judy the hope that I might be pregnant. We had done a home pregnancy test, which had been negative, but maybe it was too early. Before the funeral, our family gathered in the living room as Ken prayed. Shortly after, the hearse arrived to take us to the church.

The service was touching, the music soothing and our pastor's message comforting. He shared that we are not able to understand, but the story of Jesus and the disciples on the stormy lake is reassuring: Jesus calmed the storm, and right away they were to the place they were supposed to be. After the service, many came, speaking words of encouragement. One dear lady, Virginia, shared she believed the Lord had shown her we would have another baby. It was cold and windy at the cemetery. Little did we realize that the storm in our lives was barely beginning, and it would be some time before Jesus calmed it, yet our pastor's words were written in my heart. He also spoke at the cemetery, and Gordon thanked everyone for coming, telling them they were like family. After returning to the church for the funeral dinner, we returned home.

The following morning, Sunday, we went to breakfast before everyone left. Monday morning, we received word that Gordon's Grandpa Irv had died. I remember walking down the alley to the drugstore to buy items for our trip to the funeral. Although a beautiful spring day, I felt empty inside. As we crossed the backyard and saw the swing set, tears came. We had looked so forward to summer. This poem, which came later, expressed those feelings so well:

Oh, call my brother back to me! I cannot play alone:
Summer comes with flower and bee,
Where is my brother gone?
(Felicia Dorothea Hemans)[4]

The following day, we headed first to Salida, then to Canon City the next day. Months earlier I had written Gordon's grandparents, who were both sick, expressing my faith in the Lord. At our last visit, Grandpa shared a card with the *Footprints* poem about the Lord carrying us during hard times, a sign that he too believed and was ready to go home.[5] At the funeral, I sensed Grandpa's presence in a strong way and felt his encouragement, a consolation, knowing he had lost a son in a drowning accident. Later, he experienced another loss, the death of a boy he had befriended. If anyone understood, it was Grandpa.

Once home, we were amazed by continuing expressions of love. Many special cards were awaiting us, along with meals throughout the week. There was a definite bond of understanding with some. Our pastor's parents had lost a son at birth. My cell group leaders had lost their unborn child after a car accident. Virginia had experienced the loss of babies through miscarriage. The mother of a woman in Lamaze class wrote a precious note about losing her nephew to SIDS while she was babysitting. Another woman from church, who was working at the hospital when Matthew died, had experienced miscarriage and offered her understanding, encouraging us to attend a support group.

Shortly after Grandpa's death, I told Gordon about the letter I had sent to his grandparents. I then asked him about his own salvation, to which he answered, "I know what you do." I was elated in my pain. After that, he began attending church with us.

I was unprepared for the overwhelming anger beginning to surface. Once Gordon returned to work, it all rushed out, its target being the Lord. How could He have let this happen? First, we had gone through fears of miscarriage, then we struggled to find the right doctor, and finally, I had worked hard to change my diet. There was also the threat to Matthew's lungs after birth. We were so thankful to have him here safely. Now, supposedly far away from danger, he died? Why? My anger found its release, followed by great relief. Right away, I felt the Lord's understanding and compassion, the last of my anger toward Him about Matthew's death. The realization of how little control I had in my life brought with it a deep frustration that needed to be released, a child's temper tantrum. All those emotions needed to come out, and the Lord alone, who created us, knows that and is understanding of our helplessness and humanness.

Not only did the anger emerge full force, but in the following weeks, terrible guilt followed. I was struggling with the unrelenting question, "Did I cause Matthew's death?" My mind examined every possibility. I had been taking vitamin E because my incision had been hurting. Could that have hurt him? When we went to Salida and Canon City early in March, Mom had many samples of perfume, which Eric and the cousins had fun trying. Had that hurt his lungs, already vulnerable at birth? At the beginning of my pregnancy, Gordon and I were on the interstate when our truck was hit by rocks thrown off an overpass. Had that hurt him? Was it something at his birth?

I was washing the kitchen floor while Eric took his nap. Once again, I asked the Lord, "What caused his death?" After many tears, His answer came, a huge revelation, "All the possibilities you are considering concern the *how* of Matthew's death, but what you really want to know is *why* he died, and that is with Me." Many times I have tried to explain the profound impact of His words, proof enough they were from Him. He went to the core of my being to my real question.

A huge weight was lifted off my shoulders with the realization that God indeed is in control. *How* Matthew died did not matter. We could have been in a car wreck that day. He could have been hurt on the golf course. There were numerous ways that he could have died, and always, our human nature wants to place blame. Yet the ultimate answer was what I had known from the start and, indeed, what had prompted my initial anger at God: the Lord, in control of my life, allowed this. Realizing that brought immediate comfort instead of anger. Even if his death resulted from something I had unintentionally done, there was no way I could have prevented it. Both the scripture from Thessalonians and the angel card were signs. It was good of the Lord to provide this insight so soon. Little did I realize their need was to be forthcoming, urgent, in fact, because not only were we questioning, others were also. In days to come, many would begin passing their thoughts on to me.

What seems to happen with tragedy is that our first reaction, both afflicted and onlookers, is the same: the need to understand. The story of Job clearly illustrates this. It is easy to avoid this frightening book until tragedy hits. At that point, we can glean great insight into grief and also comfort in our questioning. All of Job's "friends" tried to tell him that he had obviously sinned and was suffering the consequences. We all try to find answers as onlookers, wanting to avoid, at all costs, the ultimate suffering we see in the afflicted. If we can understand, we may avoid their same pain. It is a self-defense mechanism.

Job honestly experienced the ultimate in being blamed for what happened to him, and he was justified in his anger. I too felt condemnation, though of a different sort. One of the first comments to me, posed as a question, was, "Is Satan taking your babies?" From the beginning, the same word was repeated from different sources, that Satan had done this evil, and if only we learn to rebuke him, we will not experience hard circumstances. My reaction was that the Bible contains numerous examples of people who suffered in their lives and were much more spiritual than I am.

Having been a math and computer science major, with logic as my favorite class, it was also difficult to accept that Satan could cause evil in the life of a believer without the Lord's allowing it. In fact, the story of Job confirms this. Unlike Job's friends, who did not understand the Lord's part in his painful experiences, we are told, at the start of the story, that Satan had to ask permission from God before inflicting hardship upon Job. Satan's purpose is to bring evil to us all, but in the life of the believer, God is in control, allowing only events that will ultimately help us.

It seems that fighting the enemy is of paramount importance. What it involves, however, is not fighting the circumstances, our natural tendency, but instead fighting what seeks to pull us away from God: anger, fear, doubts, pride, rebellion, and bitterness. Although I believed this at the time, it was to be years before I was able to stand up for that belief.

Still the Lord was faithful to bring encouragements. There were those at church who listened and prayed, reaching out to Gordon. Right after Matthew's death, we also began attending meetings with Compassionate Friends, a support group for bereaved parents and siblings. These were an enormous blessing, sharing with others who had experienced the same heartache.

Another encouragement came from a woman at church who gave us a book entitled *Within Heaven's Gates*, the story of a critically ill woman who went to heaven before returning to earth with renewed health.[6] Whenever I read the book, it brings great comfort and peace to my heart, which has often ached for our babies and our homeland.

In times of grief and extreme sorrow, we become more in tune with nature. I remember being outside soaking in its quietness and peace. It is as if a ray of heaven shines down, illuminating everything and revealing God's grace and comfort. The Lord brought me a dream, shortly after Matthew's death, of a place, a gorgeous green field with trees, a bench, and a beautiful, clear stream. As I stood marveling at the beauty, He came, beckoning me to the bench, a foretaste of heaven.

Another encouragement came from an unexpected source. Our obstetrician called shortly after Matthew's death to share his condolences. He said that he and his wife had also lost a baby to SIDS. He had known of Gordon's plans to have a vasectomy and recommended a sperm bank. Of course, my earlier hope of being pregnant had long since been dashed with the start of my period. During the summer, our pastor and his wife discussed adoption with us.

The spring and summer following Matthew's death were extremely hard. Not long after, we planned a trip to Glenwood Springs, an hour away. Unfortunately, it only brought more stress when Eric had an ear infection, a problem he had often struggled with since he was a baby. This time his fever was high, causing hallucinations, a frightening experience for novice parents who had recently buried another son. We went to the hospital for medicine and returned home still hurting.

I am grateful for Eric and truly indebted to him. Had he not been here, I would have stayed in bed every day. Each morning, bright and early, he came into our room to wake me. "Come on, Mom, get up." He was full of energy with a child's excitement for life. I dreaded each day. Being on the opposite end of the spectrum, with much to work through and no energy, the desire for alone time was apparent and needed to come soon. With the advent of summer, I decided to send Eric to preschool two mornings a week. Poor Eric. Most of the children were there all day and were comfortable. For Eric, it was the opposite. He was also struggling at church, often crying when we left him. We were so overwhelmed with our own grief we were unable to see his needs. Gordon, working on road inventory most of that spring and summer, had many alone days outside. Around this time, we received the autopsy report, and our doctor reviewed it with us. Although providing few insights, we felt relieved to finally see it.

Mother's Day was especially sad, but the Lord comforted my heart with a picture presented for the nursery in memory of Matthew. In it, Jesus is surrounded by children with this scripture underneath, "Let the children come to me, and do not hinder them, for the kingdom of heaven belongs to such as these" (Matthew 19:14), the same scripture we picked for the headstone. On its front, in one corner, is a picture of Jesus holding a baby, with vines and flowers surrounding the exterior, on back the above scripture with a lamb, mountains, and trees in the distance, reminders of a song from church: "We shall go out with joy and be lead forth with peace; the mountains and the hills shall break forth before us. There'll be shouts of joy and the trees of the field shall clap their, clap their hands." I had sung it many times to Matthew and Eric. Would we ever feel joy again?

Once again, I remembered Much-Afraid. She had been struggling along the road in the mist, fearing that she was lost, as her enemy continually tormented her. This exhausting path was followed by an even more difficult one, leading down into a deep and long valley, away from the High Places all together. She was in the Valley of Loss, sincerely confused and fearful. But she also knew comfort, as the Lord stayed close beside her on this new, unwelcome path.

As the months passed, we continued to wonder about more children. We felt we had two options: either to adopt or to have Gordon's vasectomy reversed. We approached our health maintenance organization to see if they would cover the expense of a reversal. Of course, we had signed a form at the time of the vasectomy, stating that we understood reversal was not covered. We finally decided to save Gordon's overtime money through the summer for the procedure.

Fall approached and, with it, Matthew's first birthday. We had a turkey dinner, remembering the previous Thanksgiving spent at home. We also ordered a bakery cake. But for all we tried to make it memorable, it could never be so again, because the guest of honor was absent. It would always be a sad day. That day, I realized, for the first time, this was not a dream and Matthew was forever gone. As David said, "I will go to him, but he will not return to me" (2 Samuel 12:23c). The finality of it hit me hard. The Lord was faithful, however, providing this scripture to me:

> 'For my thoughts are not your thoughts, neither are your ways my ways,' declares the Lord. 'As the heavens are higher than the earth, so are my ways higher than your ways and my thoughts than your thoughts. As the rain and the snow come

down from heaven and do not return to it without watering the earth and making it bud and flourish, so that it yields seed for the sower and bread for the eater, so is my word that goes out from my mouth: It will not return to me empty, but will accomplish what I desire and achieve the purpose for which I sent it. You will go out in joy and be led forth in peace, the mountains and hills will burst into song before you, and all the trees of the field will clap their hands. Instead of the thornbush will grow the pine tree, and instead of briers the myrtle will grow. This will be for the Lord's renown, for an everlasting sign, which will not be destroyed'. (Isaiah 55: 8–13)

The Lord, full of compassion, provided a blessing after this. Once again, Gordon had a class in Phoenix right after Thanksgiving, a special time of relaxing, in a wonderfully warm place! Eric and I enjoyed playing in the pool and watching cable television, a novelty we did not have at that time. It also brought back memories of our previous trip to Phoenix and encouragement given after my miscarriage. Although grateful for the unexpected trip, the pain of the year was not to be buried. We tried to make Christmas fun for Eric, but all of us felt an emptiness and sadness inside. It was especially trying to be around people, at church and family functions, with the tendency to cry and desire to be alone always there. Yet worship at church was healing, the Lord's Presence ever near.

Lifted to the Place of Anointing/Seeking Shelter as Floods Descend / To the Grave on the Mountain[7]

The New Year 1988 dawned, with enough money in savings for Gordon's surgery. Although scheduled for a sperm count six weeks later, he did not have to keep the appointment. On the first anniversary of Matthew's death, we found out I was pregnant, the due date around Thanksgiving. How appropriate! It seemed our path was following Much-Afraid's, as the Lord led her to a chairlift, returning her to the High Places. The next step was the Place of Anointing, with the Lord's encouraging words that she was to rest to prepare for the last part of her journey. When asked if it was almost time for the fulfillment of His promise, He said she should go forward and would soon receive her heart's desires.

Summer was just around the corner, and we were enjoying the increasingly warmer days. We were also excited, looking forward to the wedding of my youngest sister, Judy, to Tim in Denver in July. On Saturday, the thirteenth of May, we were preparing for an outing when I felt a definite discharge, which I was frightened to discover was blood. Because there had been no problems with the past two pregnancies, the thought of miscarriage was barely considered. It also seemed a gift from the Lord. Now at twelve weeks, I was once again spotting. When we went to the doctor, he thought it may be a bladder infection, giving me medicine for that. That night the bleeding increased, and Gordon called our pastor and his wife the following morning for prayer. They graciously came over, but by then, I was bleeding more heavily, and we headed for the emergency room. Our doctor confirmed it was a miscarriage, performing a D and C to stop the bleeding. He was unable to administer pain medicine due to my low blood pressure and was considering a blood transfusion. Afterward, we drove to his office for iron tablets. While I waited outside, extremely weak, my chest hurting also, I soaked in the beautiful spring day, feeling a sense of relief.

Before we went to the hospital, I had spent time in our living room on the couch facing a clock picture of a beautiful waterfall. It brought to mind Much-Afraid once again. At the Place of Anointing, she was elated when her Shepherd said she was nearing the end of her journey and the fulfillment of the promises. Unfortunately, the next step, instead of being joyful, was frightful, as she found herself seeking shelter, a storm breaking, with Floods descending and her

Shepherd gone, a time of testing. Should she give up all the promises from the past? Had her Lord deceived her? She spent the night in a cave, struggling with her fears. By morning, she knew what she and her companions must do. The storm had ended, and they were above the lip of a huge waterfall. She heard a voice telling her to jump into the abyss before them. There they found a grassy area with an altar. When she called to the Shepherd to help her make her offering, there was no answer. So she accepted the help of a priest, who bound her to the altar and pulled the root, Longing-to-be-loved, from her heart. This was the Grave on the Mountains, the place where she gave up *her* desires and accepted her Lord's will only. Remembering this brought me hope, because, unlike Much-Afraid, I knew how the book ends, with her death followed by her long-awaited desires. It seemed that my unwelcome path was that same path and soon my desires would be fulfilled.

It had been a relief when our doctor performed a D and C, remembering the sad experience of my first miscarriage, having our baby born dead at work, a trying journey that lead to deep depression. I was thankful to be spared that pain again. Unfortunately, in my gratefulness, I was also naive and unprepared for the comment of a friend, who felt we should have insisted on a transfusion to try to save the baby. Although hurt, I did not accept her judgment, mainly because of *Hind's Feet*.

Within days, the Lord brought another confirmation: the angel picture—three angels, two with closed eyes and one with eyes opened and a crooked halo. After Matthew's death, I assumed the angels signified Eric and Matthew and our first baby. But that had brought confusion, wondering if there would be no more children. Now it all made sense. Our two miscarried babies had closed eyes, and Matthew was the one with open eyes and the broken halo.

In July, we traveled to Judy and Tim's wedding. At that time, we heard that Paula, Tim, and their daughter may be moving to Grand Junction, with Tim taking position of worship leader / assistant pastor at our church! We were excited, anticipating their move.

The rest of the summer, however, proved tough. Although my miscarriage had happened a few months earlier, it was as though it had never happened at all. I found it increasingly difficult dealing with the lack of concern from others. Although I had the Lord's encouragement, this was a time of sadness and grief at the loss of our fourth child. "As a woman with child and about to give birth writhes and cries out in her pain, so were we in your presence, O Lord. We were with child, we writhed in pain, but we gave birth to wind" (Isaiah 26:17, 18a). On one hand, there had been condemnation, on the other, no understanding. I am convinced few people understand miscarriage. When a couple is in a long-awaited pregnancy, the loss of that child, at whatever point, is extremely painful. "I looked for sympathy, but there was none, for comforters, but I found none" (Psalm 69:20b). By fall, my hurt and anger were deep and flowing.

At that time, the newspaper was planning an article, introducing a support group at a local hospital for those who had lost infants—through miscarriage, still birth, or later death. When they approached our Compassionate Friends' leader for a couple to interview, we were asked and agreed. It was not until later I realized it may not have been a wise idea, with so much unresolved anger inside. When the article was released, the headline spoke of couples' need for support following miscarriage.[8] The woman who interviewed us, especially me, did not need great perception to detect my anger. In fact, she suggested counseling. It had been almost one-half year since my second miscarriage and a year and a half since Matthew died. She also seemed to think we should be past the grief. Of course, Satan orchestrated the timing to be especially difficult: Gordon left town for work for a month!

The following Sunday at church was memorable and extremely uncomfortable. Our pastor spoke of how we are all in the process of being refined, and as with gold, the dross has to be skimmed off the top as the heat is continually applied to the crucible containing the gold. What I had attempted to hide had been made known to all.

"There is nothing concealed that will not be disclosed, or hidden that will not be made known" (Matthew 10:26b).

Paula, Tim, and LaRae arrived that weekend and came with me to church. We had known from the beginning of August they were coming. Now I was a wreck, not only feeling guilt about the article, but also in trying to provide for them. Although I wrote an apology for our church newsletter and apologized at cell group, my heart ached at being the different one, the misfit.

Once the holidays arrived, my stomach was a mess. The ulcer from my freshman year of college had returned in full force, the iron tablets initiating it and this new stress confirming it.

Meanwhile, 1989 dawned, with renewed hope. Since fall, the Lord seemed to be impressing upon me a new beginning for our family. Like Much-Afraid, my hard journey was over, a time of ministering now coming. Little did I suspect that its end was not to be as promising as the beginning. But blindly, we pressed eagerly on to what seemed brighter days.

For months, our Compassionate Friends leader had spoken to us about taking over leadership of the county chapter. Both she and the core group desperately wanted a couple in the position, hoping more men would come to meetings with a man in leadership. Finally, we gave our consent after much soul-searching and a sermon at church. It seemed a natural conclusion, remembering *Hind's Feet*, the end of which was healing, followed by a time of ministering to others. Our leader was supportive, encouraging us to go to the national conference in July in Tampa, Florida.

In February, Gordon had a class in San Diego, to which he invited his parents and Eric and me. We planned to arrive a few days early to take in some sights. From the start, I had no desire for this trip, being in the midst of grief and exhausted after an especially trying fall. Even with the hope of a new beginning, there was great turmoil inside—mentally, emotionally, and physically. My ulcer had grown worse, and there were no adventurous feelings, certainly not for a big trip far from home. Later, I was to wonder if this lack of desire had not been a premonition.

Gordon's parents arrived here midweek, and we flew out the following day, arriving in the misty rain. That afternoon, Eric would not be appeased until he was able to play in the outdoor pool and Jacuzzi, to which we finally consented, although it was lightly misting and cool outside. That evening Eric began complaining about his ears hurting.

The following day, he seemed all right. It was a warm day, but there was also a cold breeze. We had a full day of sightseeing. By evening, Eric had a slight fever and again complained about his ears. After obtaining medicine from a local hospital, we were encouraged, until the following day when he could no longer keep it down. By evening, we were back at the hospital, where they performed a spinal tap to check for meningitis, with negative results, thankfully. Both Gordon and I were overwhelmed, trying to be calm on the outside, our insides full of fear and confusion. This trip was meant to be a reprieve from pain and fear. Now was something going to happen to Eric, not even a year since we lost our last baby? After they took x-rays, they decided to transfer him to the San Diego Children's Hospital in the ambulance.

That night was exceptionally stressful. With much pain for Eric, an IV was inserted into his foot. It was heartbreaking to see him suffer and to feel utter helplessness in wanting to ease his pain but unable. How can it be explained to a little child that the pain is necessary for healing? My heart was, and is, extra tender toward those who have watched their children suffer for any amount of time. In my opinion, that has to be the most terrible trial anyone can experience. After the IV was in, they set up a bed for me, and Eric quickly dozed off. In exhaustion, I drifted off too, the Lord's comforting words echoing in my ears, "The Eternal God is your refuge, and underneath are the everlasting arms" (Deuteronomy 33:27a). I fell into them, exhausted but thankful for Eric's safety.

Gordon had considered forgetting his class and returning home, what we all desired. But the doctor wanted Eric's ears to be better before we flew again, which he felt may have initiated the problem. Finally, after three days and nights, Eric was released a few days before we flew home. What joy and relief to be home and to have Eric well, though on medicine a long time.

Once home, all my emotions came out, as the shock hit: Eric could have died. I felt like a horrible mom for all the times I had been impatient. Fears resurfaced. Would he be okay? What was the Lord doing? It had been a draining trip, both mentally and emotionally, and my ulcer was much worse.

At the March meeting of Compassionate Friends, our leader announced that Gordon and I had accepted leadership. All my emotions emerged, as I shared fears of being punished for being a bad mom. I revealed nothing of our trip, however, the very thing that precipitated my turmoil.

There was little time to work through this. We had much to learn in taking over leadership. We were also in the process of preparing for my parents' forty-first wedding anniversary celebration, to be held in Salida in June. We were also looking forward to our tenth wedding anniversary in May and the Compassionate Friends' National Conference in Tampa in July. I finally went to the doctor for medicine for my stomach. Although groggy from the start, I felt it was helping my stomach and continued to take it, not realizing its profound downhill effect.

In April, we had a surprise when Gordon's brother, Mark, and the woman he had been dating, Debbie, visited with news of their marriage. Mark's previous marriage had not worked out, and we were happy for his fresh start.

The weekend before my parents' anniversary celebration, Gordon and I celebrated our anniversary. After Matthew's death, I began writing our memoirs, my latest version my gift to Gordon, who gave me a beautiful diamond, which we later attached to my Black Hills gold ring.

The reunion for my parents was a blessing. Two and a half years earlier, when Mom had come after Matthew's birth, we noticed she was confused and forgetful. Later, she struggled with common chores and eventually her handwriting and speech. At the reunion, she was still fairly well. Later, tests were run that ruled out all possible causes but the obvious, the one none of us wanted to hear: Alzheimer's. This anniversary time was one of the last we were together before she became worse. During the Mass to renew Mom and Dad's vows, each of us read a scripture Father chose. Mine leapt off the page: "Am I now trying to win the approval of men, or of God? Or am I trying to please men?" (Galatians 1:10a, b). With that echoing in my mind, the weekend came to a close.

Once home, we began preparing for our trip to Tampa Bay. Gordon's parents generously agreed to watch Eric while we were gone. From the start, we found leading the Compassionate Friends chapter much more challenging than we had anticipated. The meetings alone were not easy, but there were also other functions: need for financial support, with grant application and a yearly yard sale, topics for monthly meetings, and fillings for vacant positions. It was a relief having the core group's help, yet we felt much pressure. Hopefully, the conference would provide insights.

Our time in Tampa was hurried as we each chose seminars. It was hot and humid, but the conference was healing. Our keynote speaker, Dr. John Claypool, a pastor, lost his daughter to cancer. In his opening address, he shared his struggle with the why of her death, coming to believe that we cannot possibly understand until we are in heaven. He also shared what was helpful and hurtful in his grief. What were *not* helpful were (1) those who tried to intellectualize his grief and (2) those who tried to push him through the process. Instead, people who came bearing no answers but sympathy and a tangible gift, such as food, brought him great comfort and encouragement. What also helped him was realizing two truths: (1) He had the choice of seeing his daughter's life as an entitlement and, therefore, responding in anger or seeing her life as a gift, eliciting thankfulness. (2) His second choice was to live in the past, neglecting his family, or to see that, although his loss was devastating, he had so much left, in his wife and son.[9]

The last speaker had lost many children, a touching and heart-breaking story. Her book, which I read on the way home, subtly implemented more fears concerning Eric. Although the conference was uplifting, with its end, I felt exhausted. We were thankful to return home and to have Eric safely home too. Little did I realize that the stress of the past seven years, specifically the last, was to come crashing in upon me within a few short weeks.

Not long after this, Gordon traveled to Alamosa (six hours away) for work. At that particular time, my walls began to crumble. Satan saw me at my weakest point, all alone and helpless. The wearing down had been occurring for months, and now the attack came. He planted the idea in my mind that I had lied to my cell group leader, asking for prayer about our leadership decision, when we had already accepted the position. And that we did, but I remember telling her it was not too late to back out. It would have been embarrassing, however, since it had already been announced. The story of Aninias and Saphira haunted my mind. I feared the Lord had left me because I lied. As I share this, it seems irrational, but at low points in our lives, we are most vulnerable to the enemy's voice, and it is hard to think clearly. I was horribly upset—fearful, anxious, and confused—sure the Lord had left me, as a great depression descended on me. Calls to our pastor for prayer and Gordon's return home did not help. This was major spiritual warfare. If only I knew that the Lord was still there, I would be fine. No, not just fine, but ecstatic! It was a time of realizing that, no matter what happened in my life, I could make it as long as the Lord was with me. And realizing that it was truly Him I most desired, even above His gifts.

The following evening Gordon and I ended up at the emergency room, where I shared about the medication I was taking. The doctor checked his pharmacy book, informing us that the medicine could be the cause. He also prescribed an antianxiety medicine and an antidepressant, both of which I was reluctant and fearful to take, but finally did, with Gordon's urging. A year later, I bought my own pharmacy book and discovered some of the major side effects to include confusion, anxiety, and depression.

The following days, I repeated these scriptures: "If we confess our sins, he is faithful and just and will forgive us our sins and purify us from all unrighteousness" (1 John 1:9). "Therefore, there is now no condemnation for those who are in Christ Jesus" (Romans 8:1). "Never will I leave you; never will I forsake you" (Hebrews 13:5b). At the beginning, I asked Gordon to read Psalms.

> I cried out to God for help; I cried out to God to hear me. When I was in distress, I sought the Lord; at night I stretched out untiring hands, and my soul refused to be comforted. I remembered you, O God, and I groaned, I mused, and my spirit grew faint. You kept my eyes from closing; I was too troubled to speak. I thought about the former days, the years of long ago. I remembered my songs in the night. My heart mused and my spirit inquired. "Will the Lord reject us forever? Will he never show his favor again? Has his unfailing love vanished forever? Has his promise failed for all time? Has God forgotten to be merciful? Has he in anger withheld his compassion?" (Psalms 77:1–9)

At that point, I could bear no more and had him stop. Had he continued, the following may have consoled my wounded spirit. "Then I thought, 'To this I will appeal: the years of the right hand of the Most High.' I will remember the deeds of the Lord; yes, I will remember your miracles of long ago. I will meditate on all your works and consider all your mighty deeds" (Psalms 77:10–12).

At an appointment the following week, our doctor recommended a psychologist. Because my questioning was spiritual in nature, I sought a Christian counselor but found none. The psychologist I went to had no answers but had me write a letter to God, which expressed my disappointment and confusion, believing good was coming, only to find myself in an awful sand pit, with no easy exit.

Shortly after this, a missionary couple who visited our church spoke of helping a couple with the loss of their baby. His message was that there are times we are not going to understand, but we need to remember the Lord promised He would never leave us nor forsake us. After the service, our pastor's mom prayed for me. Although unable to understand until later, she encouraged me to put on my armor every day for protection from the enemy. Her lack of judging brought great relief.

For hunting season, we traveled to Salida once again. I was tormented with fears, especially at night. While there, Satan attacked most horribly. In the state between wake and sleep, I was terrified by his presence and subsequent attack. But this night, I saw the Lord come with His shepherd's staff, which He brought down on Satan's head, causing him to cry out as he fled, a dreadful spiritual battle, from which the Lord delivered me, a turning point in my pain.

As the days progressed, the Lord brought other resources to help with the depression, a fog that only the sun could dissipate. The more time in His Presence, the sooner it began to lift. I also read Psalms, which expressed emotions I was unable to put into words myself. Scriptures from Job and Isaiah also brought hope, and I began listening to praise music constantly. During the dreary winter, I looked out at the sunshine and later began aerobics at home.

Slowly, the Lord brought light, but other encounters were discouraging and condemning. The first was a speaker at church who shared that depression is sin. Later, a seminar on depression also had the same tone. At this time, I began in earnest to ask the Lord what *He* was saying to me, as it required great effort not to believe those thoughts were also the Lord's. "Are you trying to please God or man?" How prophetic! How truly God knows our hearts.

There had been steady, slow progress since August. Coming out of depression is a monumental task. Not only was I dealing with this new problem, overwhelming in itself, but my original problem, my ulcer, was not healed. It was a blessing when a new couple came to our cell group. He was a chiropractor and, hearing of my problem, recommended an herb for my stomach and a multivitamin. He also began adjusting Eric and gave him an herb for his chronic ear problems.

With the end of the year came a change in cell groups. The one I had attended for five years was becoming too large, and the leaders decided to split it. A couple from California, who lived near our house, had recently moved here and would lead the new group. Our leaders encouraged us to pray and make our decision before the new year. Although complicated, the deciding factor was the location. I missed the previous leaders, but it was good, a new start. "Praise be to the Lord, for he showed his wonderful love to me when I was in a besieged city. In my alarm I said, 'I am cut off from your sight!' yet you heard my cry for mercy when I called to you for help" (Psalms 31:21–22).

CHAPTER 6

The Journey: Spring Comes Again

Hope Renewed

·········
(1990–1997)

Into Healing Streams / Trying Out Hind's Feet / Up in the High Places / Returning to the Valley[1]

The beginning of 1990, the Lord began to increase my understanding, even as He lifted the depression. As spring neared, Gordon and I had a major fight. When he and Eric left, I reached the point of total desperation, the most hopeless I have ever felt. Although there had been progress, all I could see were the sand walls of the pit towering above me, with no energy or desire to climb. What was the use? It had taken so much effort to get here, and now there was still more. I lost sight of going one tiny step at a time, the puzzle concept, one I have always despised. I would much rather work at things with immediate results.

On this particular day, I immediately hit rock bottom, as clouds came in once again. I lost all hope. Why go on? I took Gordon's handgun from the closet and kneeled on the floor. As the memory returns, I can see Jesus standing beside me, protecting me. Anyone beginning to go through or come out of a deep depression should be monitored closely, because at these points he is vulnerable and may reach times of despair even after many encouragements. The road to healing is long, and it takes a miraculous intervention to break the despair. Thankfully, that is what the Lord provided. At the bottom of the pit, ready to give up, He threw down a strong rope.

My sister Paula had lent me a book by Melody Green about the deaths of her husband, Keith, and two of their children in a plane crash. After many minutes, I put down the gun and reached for the book, the lifeline from the Lord, which I proceeded to read that whole day. The story was touching, but the Lord did not speak to me until its end, when Melody shared she was approaching the beginning of the eighth year since the deaths. She said that the number 7 always signifies a completion, and 8, a new beginning.[2] Those words jumped off the page. The spring of 1983 was the beginning of our hard grief years. Now it was the spring of 1990. We *were* approaching a time of a new beginning! Hope welled in my heart.

The Lord also reminded me of *Hind's Feet on High Places,* which finally made sense. And understanding, the huge missing piece of this confusing puzzle, immediately lifted my depression. "The entrance of your words give light; it gives understanding to the simple" (Psalms 119:130). I saw that I had misinterpreted my miscarriage as the time of my death. Instead, it was the Place of Anointing, when the Shepherd told Much-Afraid she was nearing the end of her journey. She was therefore expecting good. Instead, massive storms hit and floods came, forcing her to seek shelter in a cave, where she was tempted to throw away the rocks (promises) she had collected. Were they just worthless tokens? She struggled through the night, not understanding, as the storm continued to crash outside. By morning, she knew what she must do. A voice told her to continue, to make her sacrifice nearby, at the very lip of the falls she could hear. She and her helpers for the whole journey, Sorrow and Suffering, jumped down into the abyss, where she gave up all her hopes and promises, knowing that all that mattered was to obey. After landing safely, Much-Afraid saw an altar and understood it was time for her sacrifice. She called to the Shepherd but received no answer. At this point, a priest stepped out to offer his assistance, binding her to the altar to perform the surgery. All this time, she felt totally abandoned by her Shepherd, who had always answered her calls. The priest performed the extraction of the roots from her heart, after which she fell into a deep sleep. She later woke to find herself alone in a cave behind the falls, a sweet perfume emanating from her heart. She was alone and drawn to the pool by the altar. As she stepped into the healing waters, her crooked feet became whole. She then washed her face, and her mouth was healed. This was the place of healing she had been promised! The next morning she heard her Shepherd, as she saw Him skipping on the mountains, like a hind. When he called to her to follow, although fearful, she obeyed, finding the Lord's original promise of healing totally fulfilled. When they spoke, she came to realize that He had not abandoned her in her death but was, in fact, the priest at the altar. When she looked into her heart, she was surprised to find beautiful white flowers all in bloom. She did not understand, thinking He had pulled everything out of her heart. He helped her see that the seed of love He had originally planted in her heart was now blooming in place of the human plant Longing-to-be-loved. She had indeed been healed, inside and out, to live with Him in the Kingdom of Love, helping in the healing of others. She received a new name, Grace and Glory, and was reunited with her companions, Sorrow and Suffering, who had been changed to Joy and Peace.[3]

When the Lord originally spoke of a new beginning two years earlier, I did not realize that it was the Place of Anointing. What I had been unable to see was that there would be a supreme test first. In fact, intense floods were to come, followed by a sacrifice, which ended the journey. It was a time of realizing that, more than the promises, I desired the Promiser and indeed could not live without Him. I now understood that the year of 1989, full of hope, but also difficulties, was actually the beginning of floods, which were to try my faith, eventually culminating in deep depression, my sacrifice, at which time I *felt* abandoned by my dear Lord. The year 1990 signified a new dawn: spring. The Lord also healed me, removing my root of trying to please others, leaving room for the seed of true Love to bloom there instead. Now I would live with the Lord in the High Places, eventually ministering His love to others!

Early in May, Gordon and I went on a hike, the Lord's word of spring foremost in my mind. As we walked, the wind blew fiercely, so that each step was difficult, a realization that spring is often unsettled, promising, with stormy days also. That was to help in the days ahead.

Later in May, I had a bad tooth, which needed a root canal. The final part of the procedure is the placement of the gold crown. After Much-Afraid's journey, she received her new name and a crown too. They say the Lord has a sense of humor. He awarded my crown also, another sign.

Shortly after, Gordon and I went away for our anniversary. That trip, unfortunately, also began with a fight, another storm. Gordon had surprised me, with no hint of where we were going. I dreamed of lovely Ouray or some other high place, some mountain resort. When we headed into the desert, my heart sank. At least we began to talk as we neared Moab and checked into our room at a bed-and-breakfast. That evening we looked forward to a quiet time alone, only to find the neighbors having a huge, loud party, lasting into the wee hours of the morning.

The next day was better. We rented bikes, riding close to town. The scenery was captivating and healing. Later, we went to the town park, where plum trees were sitting on the grass waiting to be planted, a reminder of our anniversary gift from Gordon's parents, a plum tree for our front yard. The trees brought back another memory, of our peach tree in the backyard, a gift for our 1983 anniversary. Another sign! The peach tree signified the happier (peachy) times of our life, 1976–1983, and the plum tree our grief years, 1983–1990. So by this time, there were three different words: (1) Melody Green's book,

(2) *Hind's Feet on High Places*, and (3) these trees. I left Moab elated, a much different spirit than our arrival!

Throughout the year, the Lord spoke many times. The stories of Job and Joseph brought renewed hope, times of restoration after hardship. In 1989, the movie *The Land Before Time* came out, with the same message, hardship hitting the dinosaurs, who traveled to the Great Valley, where life was better.[4] The same message was repeated in *The Lion, the Witch, and the Wardrobe* movie, the story of spring after an extremely long winter.[5] The book *The Secret Garden* by Frances Hodgson Burnett also has a similar theme, a time of great pain, followed by restoration.[6] That summer, we had two lilies bloom in our yard: one with three blooms and the other with seven, signifying three babies in heaven and seven years of hardship ended.

Also, Tim gave a message at church one Sunday, using the story of Paul on the stormy sea as a guide in our own frightening times. He shared that storms must first come to the church to prepare us for those that would come to the world, when we would be equipped to help.

Prekindergarten ended for Eric the week following our anniversary. The summer proved to be a good one. Gordon and I began helping with children's church. We also saw much growth in Eric, more independence: riding his bike, enjoying swimming lessons, and loving to fish.

Later on, our neighbor Ruth invited us to her cabin. The Lord provided another sign when Ruth found a beautiful cluster of flowers called Pearly Everlasting, like the new flowers blooming in my heart. While at Ruth's, we hiked, fished, ate, read, and relaxed. The boys especially had fun fishing, as Eric was developing a love for the same sport as Gordon and Grandpa Irv. When the time approached to leave, I found myself wishing I could stay another week—alone with the Lord.

Earlier, this same summer, a woman from church gave me two uplifting books: one, her story about her family, and the other, an intimate daily devotional a friend had recorded, with words from the

Lord. In that book, the main message was the need to retreat to a place of peace, a Secret Place, to commune with the Lord. After having had some heavenly dreams and going to Ruth's cabin, just such a place was beginning to form in my mind. I began withdrawing into this Secret Place, which continued to expand in the days ahead as the Lord, little by little, revealed more of it through pictures and places we visited. This is my real home in the High Places with the Lord.

The summer had been filled with healing. Spiritually, the Lord was speaking about a new dawn. Physically, my stomach was better, with vitamins and aerobics rebuilding my strength. Mentally and emotionally, I was becoming stronger, with fewer bad days. Slowly, I was able to decrease my antidepressants, being almost weaned at summer's end. Throughout the summer, we rode bikes and went fishing, much more relaxing than the previous summer.

To end the summer, Eric and I accompanied Gordon to a class in Denver. While there, I met a Christian woman who, like me, had experienced depression. While our sons enjoyed playing in the Jacuzzi, we watched and talked. What she said turned out to be prophetic, assurance of better days. When I revealed feelings of guilt, not knowing my part at church, she said our works are to believe—*that* is being obedient. She quoted the scriptures John 6:28–29, "Then they asked him, 'What must we do to do the works God requires?' Jesus answered, 'The work of God is this: to believe in the one he has sent.'" She later sent an encouraging poem about joys coming on the road ahead.

After this, school was approaching, and Eric would be in kindergarten, another initiation. In the process of deciding where he would go, we considered the elementary at his preschool, another Christian school, and homeschooling. Each had advantages and disadvantages, but public school seemed to be the direction we were headed, due to cost and the lack of kids in our neighborhood. We struggled throughout the summer wondering what to do. Then one day I opened my Bible randomly to the story of Moses. Through that, the Lord reminded me of how He had protected Moses, even as he grew up in the Pharaoh's palace, learning much that was no doubt against his own people. The Lord repeated that word other times in my reading with Eric. Through that, I came to understand that the Lord uses different paths for each of us, knowing what we need most, so that no one school is the right one for everyone. Knowing that takes away judging others' school choices.

Before school began, I went on a Christian retreat with a friend from Compassionate Friends who was pregnant with their fourth child, a joy after the death of their baby. My sister Paula, who had miscarried earlier, was also pregnant and due about the same time. I was happy for them. At the retreat, an unexpected event occurred when I forgot to take my daily dose of antidepressants, which was the end! At church that Sunday, Virginia reminded me of the Lord's promise of another baby.

Paula was due around Labor Day. While camping, we found out she had another girl. Although happy for them, it was not an easy time for us. Once home, a terrible thunder- and rainstorm hit, both in town and at our house, surely from our previous disappointments.

Once school began, I volunteered one morning a week. Eric's teacher and her aide were both welcoming, and from the start, it was a much more positive experience for Eric since he was there the same time the others were. It was also fun getting to know kids and parents and finding a friend for Eric, Mark, a fellow classmate who lived around the corner!

On Matthew's fourth birthday, the following scriptures were given to me from the Lord:

> Shout for joy, O heavens; rejoice, O earth; burst into song, O mountains! For the Lord comforts his people and will have compassion on his afflicted ones. But Zion said, "The Lord has forsaken me, the Lord has forgotten me." "Can a mother forget the baby at her breast and have no compassion on the child she has borne? Though she many forget,

I will not forget you! See, I have engraved you on the palms of my hands; your walls are ever before me. Your sons hasten back, and those who laid you waste depart from you. Lift up your eyes and look around; all your sons gather and come to you. As surely as I live," declares the Lord, "you will wear them all as ornaments; you will put them on, like a bride. Though you were ruined and made desolate and your land laid waste, now you will be too small for your people, and those who devoured you will be far away. The children born during your bereavement will yet say in your hearing, 'This place is too small for us; give us more space to live in.' Then you will say in your heart, 'Who bore me these? I was bereaved and barren; I was exiled and rejected. Who brought these up? I was left all alone, but these—where have they come from?'" (Isaiah 49:13–21)

The beginning of 1991 brought more encouragement. In March, Eric began to read! After months of learning his letters, he was now reading, the beginning of a longtime love of books for him. Gordon also made plans for his dad to babysit Eric that first week so we could go to a computer class Gordon had in Eugene, Oregon. It was a wonderful trip, traveling along the Columbia River to the ocean, then down the Oregon coast before heading inland to Portland. The last night there, we went to the mall, where I found a postcard about the myrtle tree, found in Oregon and mentioned in the Bible. The scripture is Isaiah 55:8–13, the exact verse the Lord had shown me after Matthew died.

"For my thoughts are not your thoughts, neither are your ways my ways," declares the Lord. "As the heavens are higher than the earth, so are my ways higher than your ways and my thoughts than your thoughts. As the rain and snow come down from heaven, and do not return to it without watering the earth and making it bud and flourish, so that it yields seed for the sower and bread for the eater, so is my word that goes out from my mouth: It will not return to me empty, but will accomplish what I desire and achieve the purpose for which I sent it. You will go out in joy and be led forth in peace; the mountains and hills will burst into song before you, and all the trees of the field will clap their hands. Instead of the thornbush will grow the pine tree, and instead of briers the myrtle will grow. This will be for the Lord's renown, for an everlasting sign, which will not be destroyed."

I took that as another sign, a special gift from the Lord, the very part of the song I had sung to Matthew and Eric four years earlier.

Shortly after, the Lord began to show me rainbows everywhere. One night a Rainbow vacuum salesman was here, the April calendar picture was a rainbow, and Eric received a book, *Rough Roads and Rainbows* by Ann Hibbard, saying that rainbows are reminders that God always keeps His promises.[7] The year 1990 had been a new beginning, a time of rest and healing, like a newly hatched butterfly, preceding a time of learning to fly. Although I did not realize it at first, 1991 was a time of renewed promises.

Around this time, Paula found out that she was pregnant again and due in November. My cell group leader also found out the same news. Both were worried, already busy with their families. Also, a friend of Gordon's mom was unmarried, pregnant, and unhappy. Although their feelings were understandable, Gordon and I, and even Eric, could not help feeling jealousy and sorrow ourselves. All around us, women seemed to be having babies so easily. And daily there were women who aborted their babies. I did not condemn any of them in their feelings, but it hurt to be excluded from something that seemed to happen so easily for others.

Throughout the summer, the Lord continued to show me rainbows. After the loss of our last baby in 1988 and the subsequent depression in 1989, I had finally come to the point of giving up our plans for another child. I do not remember *when*, but I *do* remember telling the Lord, "Thank You for Eric. If he is the only living child for us, I am grateful. If You *do* want us to have another child, You will have to do it, Lord, because I have no courage left to try." Four pregnancies had brought only one child, along with years of anguish. I knew the Lord understood. Also, we knew six different families who had only one child, a son. Still, during the summer, there were constant rainbows. What was God saying? Just repeating His promise of spring, or was there more?

The Lord is faithful to help us in our confusion. Throughout the summer, He brought other signs, all of which seemed to be pointing to another baby. In 1990, the Lord had spoken through our lily plants, a gift from my cell group leader for one anniversary of Matthew's death. This year, the lilies brought another message. We had three plants, one with two blooms, one with one, and the last one with two. The Lord seemed to be saying that these plants represented our two miscarried babies, Matthew, and two children here. Later, I found a stem from the woodbine with berries attached, three on one stem and four on the other. He seemed to be saying that our family would be seven, three in heaven and four on earth. Also, one night as I happened to look up in the sky, I noticed the Big Dipper, with the same sign, three stars in the handle and four in the dipper. While at the cemetery, looking at Matthew's headstone, there was the same sign, only with three flowers and four leaves. In 1990, He had lifted my spirits at the cemetery another day when, through a fog of tears, I saw a headstone with the family name Gladden on it, a promise that He would gladden my heart once again—He had, indeed, been doing that. Now there was a new word of an old promise. We *were* to have another baby! Eric brought home two separate papers from church that summer with the same thought: "God does not lie" and "God keeps His promises." More confirmation!

The end of June, Eric spent two weeks with his grandparents while Gordon and I camped in the Black Canyon. After we went to get Eric, we headed to Denver to visit Judy and Tim and Mark and Debbie. While at Mark and Debbie's, they showed us a bird's nest on the ledge of their window. When they shared there had been five babies but now only two remained, I knew the Lord was speaking again. When we returned to Salida for July 4, I noticed my mom's mother's ring lying on her dresser. Another sign: five stones. Other signs came through my wedding ring and Black Hills Gold ring. My wedding ring contains two bands, one with five small diamonds (five children) and the second with a large diamond (Jesus) and two smaller ones on either side (four in our earthly family). The Black Hills Gold ring has two gold leaves (the Father and the Holy Spirit) with a flower (seven dots) nestled between them. Part of the flower is covered (three dots, our children in heaven) by the diamond (Jesus).

The remainder of the summer held memorable times. Eric got a cat and learned how to swim. We rode bikes and went fishing and swimming. At summer's end, Gordon and his dad installed a new fence around our backyard. Afterward, we decided to fish on the Mesa. It was August, the time it seemed the Lord said I would become pregnant. As we were preparing to leave, my period began, a shock and huge disappointment. "Lord, were You promising us another baby? I do not understand."

I struggled for many weeks. When Eric started first grade, I began volunteering one afternoon a week at Love Care, a church ministry headed by Virginia, to help those needing food and clothing. One day, she shared that she and the woman who had given me the book *Within Heaven's Gates* had been talking, and both felt the Lord was soon to send us another baby.[8] When she asked if I had been hearing anything, I told her about the rainbows and how the

Lord was reminding me that He always keeps His promises. I left there on cloud nine! When I told Gordon, he casually dismissed it, saying, "We'll wait and see." We continued on our path, using birth control, both because of Gordon's reluctance and my need for the Lord to make it happen, not us.

In November, Paula and Tim had their third child, another daughter. It was a blessing for me to be present for the birth, a precious gift from Paula and the Lord, who seemed to be saying, "Your turn is next." We spent Thanksgiving in Salida. A month later, as we were preparing to return for Christmas, I was late with my period and planned to leave the pads at home. Gordon encouraged me to take them. While there, my appetite was huge. I knew. By New Year's, Gordon had to concede.

We waited to go to the doctor until January. At that time, we were not overly surprised to learn I was pregnant. I had already missed two periods and had all the symptoms. What was surprising was I was *due in August!* I also waited to share our news until past the three-month marker when I had lost our other babies. As is obvious, my faith, even after the rainbows and signs, was not as strong as it could have been. There was another reason, however, that I hesitated. It was a long-awaited and blessed time, a precious gift, and we decided to keep our secret with the Lord alone for a while. "After this his wife Elizabeth became pregnant and for five months remained in seclusion. 'The Lord had done this for me,' she said. 'In these days he has shown his favor and taken away my disgrace among the people'" (Luke 1:24, 25). We *did* tell our good news to Eric right away. His response was half-hearted: "Well, we don't know that this baby will live!" Poor Eric. He also hurt and had his own fears and doubts. It broke my heart.

In February of 1992, Gordon was scheduled to teach a class in Phoenix and invited me. While there, I wrote letters to all our families and Bill and Roberta, sharing our incredibly amazing news: I was pregnant and now past the miscarriage time! Many people here were surprised as we shared our news. My first attempt was when I donated unused pads to Love Care, where it took Virginia a minute to understand. That summer she gave me a cross-stitch kit with books and a pretty straw hat. I had embroidered Bambi pictures for both boys with their names and stats. Now I had one for this baby, which I began to sense was a girl. Although the doctor had done an ultrasound at five months, we did not want to know the sex. We did request a videotape, however, and Gordon felt sure it was a boy, but I saw no evidence of that! Still we felt the need to have names for both a boy, Andrew Gordon, and a girl, Sarabeth Joy.

Eric finished first grade wonderfully. He did well in every subject, especially reading and enjoyed many hobbies: playing with Legos, planes, and dinosaurs, fishing, and riding his bike. His summer was busy with classes: swimming, bowling, and doing art.

As summer progressed, there seemed to be more signs this baby was a girl. I craved Mexican food, unlike with Eric and Matthew, when Italian was my favorite. Also, I seemed to be carrying this baby higher. The Lord seemed to be showing me signs of three girls and two boys everywhere I looked—ads on TV, reminders of my grandma's family, and other signs. When Eric was involved with the reading program at the library, I reread *The Secret Garden*.[9] When I saw the author had another book, *The Little Princess*, I also read it.[10] The girl in that book was named Sara, meaning "princess." Could this be another sign? The biggest confirmation came one day when I walked Eric and a friend to the art center. I began visiting with a woman, whose daughter was named Sarabeth, with the same spelling. I floated home on cloud nine, sure that was the ultimate sign from the Lord.

I had been tired much of the pregnancy. Toward the end, I was huge and anxious for the birth. The delivery date was set for Thursday, August 20. Our doctor was on a trip but promised to be back in time. On Tuesday, the eighteenth, Gordon was gone to Alamosa for work. I went for my morning walk around the block and, as I neared the house, felt a familiar trickle of water emerge. When Gordon called, I told him but said not to hurry. I planned to wait patiently until he returned, not wanting to call the doctor for fear he would go ahead without Gordon.

In the meantime, Eric and I sat and read that whole day. We began and finished the book *The Silver Chair* by C. S. Lewis.[11] When Gordon arrived that afternoon, we went to the doctor. With mine still gone, we saw another in the same office, who told us that it was *not* my water and sent us home. I spent most of the night in the bathtub, water trickling down my legs. The following morning, when we returned to the doctor's, they confirmed that my water had broken (not a real surprise to us) and sent me to have my presurgery lab work done, as they planned to deliver the baby that day, a day ahead of schedule. Before we left, we took Eric to stay with his friend Mark, whose mom, Lou, kindly agreed to watch him. Why the date changed is unknown, but I have wondered if the Lord wanted this first bonding for our family alone.

Delivery seemed to take a long time. Gordon was in charge of holding a mirror for me to see. Finally, there was the head, and what a surprise! This little person had lots of dark hair. Both Eric and Matthew had been mostly bald, with light-peach fuzz. Here was the last sign. It had to be a girl! And lo and behold, Gordon burst out, "We have us a little girl!" Not only was I thrilled to have a daughter but also to know that I had truly heard from the Lord. When asked her name, we answered "Sarabeth Joy," the name the Lord had given to us, our princess, the Lord's promise of joy.

There was little time to enjoy Sarabeth because the anesthesia had begun to wear off. After the first short minutes, Gordon took her to be checked and cleaned by the pediatrician. Once she was taken to the nursery and my stitching finished, I remembered little since I was taken off to recovery. Meanwhile, in the nursery, Sarabeth was given her first bath before being introduced to her big brother, waiting on the other side of the window with Mark and Lou.

Later, they returned me to my room, where Gordon and Eric had placed a helium balloon with a rainbow and the words God Bless

You on it. How appropriate! The Lord did exactly as He had promised! The following day, Gordon bought a rainbow picture for me.

The months ahead were a blessing for all of us, especially me, having more time than the boys, who had to return to work and school within the first few weeks. Eric was disappointed to have to return to school the end of August, to second grade! God's timing is always right, although we may not understand at the time. Tears of sadness and joy came to our eyes on that first day as we watched the kindergartners, Matthew's class, many of whom we knew, heading out. But as the tears came, heartbreak at the loss of our little Matthew, who was excluded from this special event of starting school, there were also tears of gladness that the Lord had seen and understood our grief and graciously sent us another precious baby to ease that pain.

In the days ahead, I found solace in a soothing lullaby tape, *Love-a-Byes*, which eased fears for Sarabeth that sometimes tried to surface.[12] Some people have asked if I have experienced fears of losing Eric or Sarabeth. What has helped most is reminding myself of the Lord's promises in 1990 and 1991, realizing He has fulfilled the first part and He is faithful and will fulfill the last: to protect our kids. I remember telling Him in 1991, after His reminders of His promise of another baby, that I could not bear to lose any more children. He then gave me promises concerning Eric and Sarabeth, to which I have clung through the years. Because He was faithful to His other words given at the same time, He can also be trusted to be faithful to these promises, for "God is not a man that He should lie" (Numbers 23:19a) and all His promises are yes and amen! (2 Corinthians 1:20). When worries for their salvation come (as ugliness in the world increases), I cope by telling the Lord, "You got our kids safely here. I could not do it. I'm trusting You to get them safely Home."

Fall came fairly soon after Sarabeth's birth. Although tiring, our warm and gentle days were spent cuddling and listening to the peaceful lullaby tape. What a blessed time! As we cuddled, I stared into her room, dreaming about redecorating it with a huge rainbow (fulfilled eight years later).

That first year was especially busy and tiring, but I tried to spend more time with Sarabeth than I had with either Eric or Matthew. Eric, being our first experience, was challenging as we were novice parents. When Matthew came, it was much easier, having experienced a baby before, but it was exhausting also, with the busyness of both a two-year-old and a baby. Sarabeth was different, and I tried to take advantage of the times we could cuddle. For years, after she came, we remained in awe, unsure if it was real, that the Lord had been so gracious and loving.

The Mother's Day following Sarabeth's birth, Gordon bought me a mother's ring, with a stone for each of our five children, all arranged in order of the colors of the rainbow—God had kept His promise. We had my Black Hills Gold ring attached to my mother's ring to make a family ring with a great amount of symbolism. Later, we added stones for Gordon and me.

Although fairly numb in our joy, I sensed from the beginning that something was not quite right with Sarabeth's stomach. Even when just breastfed, she struggled with her stomach. Once cereal was introduced, it became more evident. When we consulted our doctor, he suggested Karo syrup until she was older, when he recommended mineral oil short-term. Our predicament was that this problem was long-term. By the time she was eighteen months old, her growth chart revealed that she had gone from the ninetieth percentile for height and weight to under the fifth percentile. On one hand, we found people, including those at the doctor's, insinuating we were too concerned. Their easy answers did not work for us. On the other hand were those pushing us, insinuating we were not doing enough. The days were wearisome, trying foods that were supposed to help and avoiding the bad, still with no change.

Something was definitely wrong, and as there were no answers through the medical field, we were thankful to hear of a chiropractor who specialized in stomach problems. He gave us enzyme capsules to sprinkle on her food, which made a dramatic difference, proven two different times, the first when we ran out of capsules and had to wait for an order and the second when new enzymes were introduced with no results. That time, we ended up at the hospital emergency room.

During this especially stressful time, there were positives also, ever needed and appreciated. The summer following Sarabeth's birth, Gordon and his dad closed in our carport, making a new room for Eric and providing his old room for Sarabeth, who had been sleeping in our bedroom. Her birth was truly the fulfillment of these scriptures: "Though you were ruined and made desolate and your land laid waste, now you will be too small for your people, and those who devoured you will be far away. The children born during your bereavement will yet say in your hearing, 'This place is too small for us; give us more space to live in.' Then you will say in your hear, 'Who bore me these? I was exiled and rejected. Who brought these up? I was left all alone, but these—where have they come from?'" (Isaiah 49:19–21). Sarabeth grew and changed much that first year. She was slow in walking, not learning until almost eighteen months, which was understandable considering her stomach problems. Instead, she preferred to sit on my lap and listen to stories.

Church was a trial. When I tried to leave her in the nursery, it was a fruitless attempt. As she became older, I succeeded in leaving her in the toddler room, only to have someone come to get me during the service because she was crying. Finally, when Sarabeth was about two and a half (January 1995), we decided to have our church time at home.

Sarabeth's stomach problems lasted for five years. Finally, in 1997, knowing she would soon begin prekindergarten, eventually attending school for longer periods, we insisted on a referral to a specialist. Thankfully we found a group of pediatric gastroenterologists from Denver who came to our hospital once a month. At our first appointment, the doctor performed a physical exam and ordered x-rays, from which he determined there was nothing mechanically wrong. He had us get her system totally cleared and regulated with medicine. Within a few months, she was fine.

In sharing these years, 1990–1997, it seemed best to tell of our hopes and the promises of 1990 and 1991 and their fulfillment in 1992, with the birth of Sarabeth and subsequent struggles first. But I also feel the need to recap what else was happening with both Eric and Sarabeth. During the first five years, Eric's time at elementary school (kindergarten through fifth grade) was good. He liked all his teachers and his favorite subjects were physical education, math, and reading. The last two years were his first two years of middle school. A typical boy, his loves involved airplanes, football, basketball, Legos, fishing, fly-tying, and catching bugs, bees, butterflies, and crawdads.

The first five years of Sarabeth's life were also the last five of our spring years (1990–1997). Much besides stomach problems occurred. The first year was one of great growth, with a deep love for Gordon and Eric developing. As I said, she was slow to learn to walk and rolled for a long time before even crawling. By the second year, she became more active and was growing mentally, loving books and increasing her vocabulary daily. By her third year, she continued to enjoy books, especially nursery rhymes. As time passed, she found it fun to roughhouse with her dad and brother. In 1996, she began preschool two mornings a week and enjoyed playing with other kids, something we did not have access to in our mostly older neighborhood. I was especially happy to find a school that was just preschool, with Sarabeth there the same amount of time as the others. Her favorite activities included playing with horses and dinosaurs, her dollhouse, and reading. She began prekindergarten the following year, learning much: printing, letters, cutting, tying her shoes, and zipping. Her favorite activities consistently were to playact and sing on the toy microphone.

The spring years held much for us, both good and bad. The first five years of Sarabeth's life were especially trying, with not only her daily suffering and my feelings of helplessness, but also with painful thoughts of my mom, whose health was continuing to decline. It was especially sad when she was moved to the nursing home in the spring of 1996, moving from Salida to Pueblo, back to Salida, and then finally to Canon City, an hour from Salida. I prayed the medical personnel were correct when they shared that she was unaware and, therefore, not really suffering. The time she spent in the nursing home often haunted me, and I have had to remember that it was only for a season. When she seemed to be failing fast that fall, all of us siblings spent a couple weeks in Salida, traveling to Canon City many times to be with her. She rallied after that. When Dad broke his hip socket that winter and was unable to make his weekly trip to see her, she quickly deteriorated. A year after her initial entry into the nursing home, she died. Gordon and I were thankful to see her a couple of weeks before this and take Dad for the first time since his accident, as he had been released to travel again. It provided one last time to tell her how much she meant to me and what a good mom she had always been, important last words we never had a chance to say to our kids who left us too early. Every memory of the nursing home is painful still. Maybe that is why the Lord has continually sent me dreams of her returning home. The locations change, but the theme is always the same: our family is all together, and she is with us and is fine, her old self. I always tell her, "Oh, Mom, I am so glad you are okay now and that they let you come home." And it is true. She is home now, in a better home, one with no more suffering. We were all thankful when her time of suffering ended, knowing she now has joy instead of the heartache she endured so many years, that she is with her parents, sisters, our three kids, and now, Dad, waiting for us to come too one day.

The year of 1997 ended our springtime years and also initiated our summertime. That year held both joy and sadness for us. Mom's death in the spring was followed in the fall by the death of Roberta, our previous neighbor. Joy came with the births of babies for Mark and Debbie and Judy and Tim in the summer and fall. The end of spring came, with both the end of the blooming of some beautiful flowers, but also the promise of the blossom, new life and hope. Our God, the Maker of the seasons, is also the Wise and Compassionate Controller of the seasons. We are thankful to Him!

CHAPTER 7

The Return

Then the nations around you that remain will know that I
the Lord have rebuilt what was destroyed and have replanted
what was desolate. I the Lord have spoken, and I will do it.
—Ezekiel 36:36

U pon returning from my journey, my heart was filled with
joy and hope. I had seen what the Lord had done, both
physically and mentally, healing me after many years of
pain. And He also brought my heart's desires for a family and home.
The promises of 1990 and 1991 produced our completed earthly
family—my husband, Gordon; son, Eric; and daughter, Sarabeth—
within our beloved home and our precious family in heaven also. I
felt blessed.

Much time had passed since my first visit to my heavenly home,
so the day the Lord asked if I would like to see what He had accomplished while I was away, a thrill of anticipation welled within me.
Because He had forewarned me about His working from the inside
out, I did not expect to see much difference on the outside. From the
minute we emerged from the trees in the woods, however, I could
see that Someone had been caring for the landscaping. It looked as
though there may be a Gardener, as much had been done with plants
and shrubs, which previously looked unkempt. What a peaceful and
serene scene, an inviting place even if there had been no house!

As we approached, desire to see my house was welling within. Often on the journey, I had wondered about it. As it turned out, this glimpse was to be only the first of many. On this day, it was revealed that even the outside, though not complete, was near done, with new glass on the north end and new windows throughout the house. Only the siding and shutters showed signs of needed repair.

Unlike our earthly homes, whose repairs last but a short time, as time erodes the materials, the repairs made by my Lord are eternal, because all His materials come from within His kingdom. Even at that, He often makes changes and/or brings additions, as I have come to see through the years. As we have traveled through the kingdom together, He has made more revelations, and new additions have come to my house. I have learned that it will always be experiencing new changes that keep it (and me) fresh.

But for now, I want you to experience, at least in part, that first wonder unveiled after my long absence. At least, that is my intent and desire. Have you ever tried to explain to someone the beauty of a place recently visited, the wonder of it fresh in your mind, yet somehow the words seem inadequate to convey its majesty to others? Sometimes even pictures do not do justice. That is how this attempt is for me. So bear with me. My beautiful home has come from the loving hands of my Lord and is precious, but I fear my descriptions may fall infinitely short of what my heart has seen and now treasures. I will try.

You will notice that some of my descriptions are short, while others are lengthy, the reason being that some of the rooms, naturally, have required more work than others have. Come with me to see the completed work and amazing revelations my Lord has given. "'The glory of this present house will be greater than the glory of the former house,' says the Lord Almighty. 'And in this place I will grant peace,' declares the Lord Almighty" (Haggai 2:9).

CHAPTER 8

The Great Room Or Self-Esteem

When my Lord opened the east door, it no longer creaked, and the sight before us took my breath away. All the wood used on the floor, benches, shelves, table, stairs, and banisters glowed with a golden sheen, and the scent of lemon filled the air. The windows invited all nature inside. They were crystal clear, but the most amazing part of the windows was the rainbows they and the sun cast upon the floor. As I lifted my eyes to the massive north wall, tears welled, seeing the original rock wall now completed with a mosaic of colored stones at the top, depicting a rainbow.

I was drawn to the wooden shelves protruding various places below the rainbow. Each shelf held special mementoes saved from my journey. Now the tears came. My Lord knew the whole of my painful journey. He cared more than I had ever known. It touched me deeply.

As my hand caressed the wood of the leather-padded benches underneath the windows and surrounding the room, I noticed all the wood was engraved with roses and small hearts, each with subtle chalk enhancements. Then it was that I smelled the flowers on the table in front of the fireplace. They were roses of all colors. Their smell and the lemon oil permeated the air and brought a feeling of both peace and joy to my heart. My Lord must have known how overwhelming this was for me as He was mostly silent, leaving me to observe without interrupting my thoughts. But He seemed to read the pleasure in my eyes.

After descending the steps to smell the flowers, my eyes were attracted to the beautiful south wall, with the gorgeous rock fireplace (and cubby for wood) rising high to the second floor. The stairs still rose from both sides of the room, near the doors to the outside, but the two rooms above were no longer closed up by doors and walls, instead opening to look through intricate wooden rails at the large room below. It gave a cozy loft affect to the great room.

Next, my eyes were drawn to the east door, where a special cubby hole beckoned beyond the stairs, a type of bay window, with a desk, looking out to the sparkling stream and sunken garden. Above the lower window was a stained glass window with roses and a rainbow. How precious of my Friend not only to know but also to care enough to show me His tenderness and love.

****

...for as he thinketh in his heart, so *is* he.
—Proverbs 23:7a, KJV

As far back as I can remember I have been shy and quiet, terms I have come to know quite well. And for just as long, those terms have had a negative meaning. Teachers in grade school assured my parents I would grow out of it. I remember the embarrassment I felt when my grandma scolded me for not responding assertively to someone who spoke to me. In junior high, at the end of the school awards assembly, I received two ribbons, one for Quietest Girl and the other for Most Well-Behaved Girl, neither exactly complimentary at that age. Even in high school, as I shared with my most understanding mom, I understood *shyness* to be negative, as she related that she also had been shy and that it would get better as I grew older. I did feel some reassurance at that since my mom loved to talk and seemed to have no problem conversing with anyone. Still, not one person ever told me that it was my personality, that the Lord had made me this way, that it was okay, and that I did not need to strive to change. So there has always been a drive within me to change even though deep in my heart I always felt best and most comfortable and at peace, alone and quiet. My desire has always been to be behind the scenes, and I feel self-conscious in public. When with friends, I always seem to do best one-on-one instead of in groups.

As I struggled with this through the years, I cannot even guess how many times I asked the Lord, "Why am I such a mess? I am just a misfit." I could so identify with both Rudolph and his elf friend, Hermey.[1] God seems to have consistently given me the position of "always the last, always the least," in the minority in each experience of life, never fitting in anywhere. Yet I desperately wanted and tried to do just that. In high school, the party scene attracted me, as drinking magically removed the constant shyness. Not being part of that scene in college made for lonely times for me. Working after college brought the same feelings, as my goal was to start a family, while many I worked with were single and into the partying scene. Church also was a real test for me, as most people there were outgoing, where my shyness stood out horribly. In fact, becoming a Christian intensified those feelings, and I found much comfort in the following scriptures: "I am a stranger on earth" (Psalms 119:19 a) and "Your beauty should not come from outward adornment, such as braided hair and the wearing of gold jewelry and fine clothes. Instead, it should be that of your inner self, the unfading beauty of a gentle and quiet spirit, which of great worth in God's sight" (1 Peter 3:3–4). Compassionate Friends was also difficult as it involved sharing in a group setting, which became even more demanding once we took on the leadership role. There, I could so identify with the thought of being a misfit among other misfits. In the story of Rudolph, both he and his friend, Hermey, found their niche, their place, where they belonged. How comforting! Of course, this was always a favorite story of mine. But could it ever happen, would it ever happen to me? "Yet, O Lord, you are our Father. We are the clay, you are the potter; we are all the work of your hand" (Isaiah 64:8).

Although the Lord does indeed seem to work from the inside out, He did provide an encouragement for my outside early on. Many years ago, when Eric was young, a woman from Bible study introduced us to the book *Color Me Beautiful* by Carole Jackson. She also helped determine the season of colors that look best on each of us. In the book, the author shares ideas concerning individual clothing personality, including accessories and makeup.[2] This was fun, a real boost, seeing how the Lord made me physically and trying to be my best in that area.

Many years later, a neighbor told me of the book *Eat Right for Your Type* by Peter J. D'Adamo. In this book, the author presents descriptions of the four blood types and indicates both the most beneficial foods and those foods each type should avoid for health. This book also was reassuring, as it explains that people with my blood type are prone to ulcers because of our acidy stomachs.[3] Having experienced numerous health problems during and following grief, this book has been most welcome. Both books were helpful in revealing how the Lord made me physically inside and out. Still, the biggest challenge for me was not the physical or my outside but my inside.

Finally, in the fall of 2000, at the age of forty-four, my good friend Mary Lou lent me a book, called *Self-Esteem, Gift from God* by Ruth McRoberts Ward. The author presents different types of personalities and criteria so the reader can determine his own personality type. Her premise is that if we understand how God made us, we can accept ourselves and more easily realize both our worth and purpose, which is self-esteem. Through this book, I came to see that I am an introvert, with these characteristics: (1) tend to think before speaking; (2) tend to be more of a listener, except with familiar people; (3) have a strong need for much privacy (alone time); (4) find people, especially groups, to be draining; (5) feel best in one-on-one situations; (6) feel better writing than speech-making; (7) do not like public recognition; (8) tend toward pessimism and depression; (9) appear self-reserved; (10) am more of an observer than a participant; and (11) hate being pushed or rushed. The real catcher is that introverts comprise only one quarter of the population![4] No wonder I have always felt out of place. No wonder many introverts feel this way.

There have been times I have seen articles in the newspaper concerning a person, usually a man, who committed some crime, and the comments of neighbors and coworkers follow this line: "Oh, he was a loner, kept to himself, had few friends, but he was always polite." My heart always goes out to this type of person. For all our culture has promoted universal acceptance and tolerance for others, the introvert is still often rejected. Still, in junior high and high school, he is expected to give oral reports and to participate in class. And if he does not, the teacher may assume he is stupid. At church, he is considered spiritually immature. In both instances, the introvert is expected to fill the same mold as the extrovert, even though God made us all different, even as He made varieties in all His other creation: the animals, trees and flowers, food, all of nature. This attitude is understandable for unbelievers as they expect us all to fit into the same mold, with God removed from the picture. If we do indeed come from monkeys, we should all be the same. Sadly, even in church, the most outgoing often seems to be the most accepted. And from leaders' points of view, it makes sense. People who are articulate and have no problem voicing their thoughts and opinions are much more easily understood than us shy and quiet ones, whom others cannot figure out. Who would not desire the extrovert over the introvert?

So what is the Lord's perspective on all of this? Do we introverts also have worth? Or did He create us as the junk pots, not meant for anything good but the trash heap (Jeremiah 18:1–10)? If I believed that were true, I would not have endeavored to write this book to encourage others. The Lord has shown me that He has a place for every one of us in this sad and, many times, cruel world, and each place is one of worth and value.

Paul said that as believers, we are all parts of one body (1 Corinthians 12:12 and especially 22–25; Romans 12:4–8). We all have different functions but belong to the same body and are, therefore, needed. He even said that some of the parts that seem less important are treated with special honor and that hidden parts are treated with special modesty. As introverts, we fit into this category. We are the behind-the-scenes people, not showy or noticed. As such, we often feel worthless, yet we all realize, in the physical illustration, at least, that all parts are needed. When I broke my tendon in my ring finger and had to have a splint for six weeks, I realized how useful that finger is, not just as a holder for my ring! Others share similar stories of body parts being injured and how difficult it is on the rest of the body. As each individual part is essential to the whole body, so is each person in the body of Christ. We are all valuable!

So as introverts, where do we fit into the church, into the world? We do not need many people, and we crave much alone time and do best one-on-one with others. I believe the Lord's place for us is an important one. I believe He has called us to a closer walk with Him, that He can equip us to go to the hurting people one-on-one and minister to them. It is also an honorable place. Finally, the least is valued. I believe we are as the priests in the Old Testament, meant to walk closely with the Lord so that He can speak to us for both ourselves and others. The Lord desires to speak to all of us in the body, and He says He has no favorites. We are all called into relationship with Him, but we each choose how close we will become. As in any relationship, the more time we spend together, the closer we become. Many crave much time with others, and they need it. That is how the Lord made them. But for those of us who desire more alone time, God is calling us to draw nearer to Him, to walk beside Him constantly and hear His voice, so we might reach others in a quiet and behind-the-scenes way. "'I will bring him near and he will come close to me, for who is he who will devote himself to be close to me?' declares the Lord" (Jeremiah 30:21b).

This illustration is most obvious to me in the personalities of Peter and John. Peter seems more of an extrovert, whereas John's personality seems to typify that of an introvert. Peter was a leader, while John was more of a helper to him. Both were close to the Lord, but the Lord ended up using them in different ways. Peter's main purpose seemed to be in public, evangelizing. John also helped him, but he eventually was imprisoned on an island and alone with the Lord, resulting in the writing of the book of Revelation.

Acceptance at church is fundamental to many people's lives. It is essential that we be kind to one another, accepting our differences in the body and not judging. Many times, however, we seem more intent on competing, as is true of many families, which is what the Lord says we are. There was an excellent illustration of this in the newspaper one day, a picture of a two-headed snake. The article said the two heads would fight with each other for food not realizing they shared the same body. It is often like that in the church. Knowing the truth that we are in a battle, we often forget who the enemy is, aiming our weapons at each other and the world instead of at our true enemy, who is, meanwhile, laughing at our stupidity.

When we consider the physical illustration of our body, we can see how detrimental it is to attack any other part of our body, only because it is different. If we see the analogy, we are to be as our physical body is, each part nurturing the other, helping in weakness, injury, and sickness, with no judgment, so that we may all be made whole. We need to learn to accept those parts that seem not to fit in, knowing the Lord has a place for them also.

It is a sad but true fact that churches sometimes seem to have lost the most important message of Jesus dying for our sins and our acceptance of Him so that He can live in us and perform His work through us. Instead, the devil often uses his age-old trick of bringing legalism into the church, leading to many different denominations, who have each taken a part of the law and focused on it, coming up with their own church doctrines, which only cause divisions and a great rejoicing on the part of our enemy.

A good example of this could be seen when we stopped going to church in 1995 and started having church at home every Sunday. The main reason we left was because I was continually unable to stay in the church services as someone always came to get me for Sarabeth. That was discouraging as I felt a need for a break from the constant daily care with her stomach problem and desperately needed some time to be refilled. Finally, the time came to stop attending. Our church time at home was not exciting and did not have the special singing and sermons, but I pray that the Lord honored our attempts at worship and used it for good. There are Christians who would condemn us, quoting these scriptures: "Remember the Sabbath Day by keeping it holy" (Exodus 20:8) and "Let us not give up meeting together, as some are in the habit of doing, but let us encourage one another—and all the more as you see the Day approaching" (Hebrews 10:25). Yet there are examples of how today's church attendance differs from the past: (1) the Sabbath day was actually on Saturday and (2) the early church often met in homes, not in the temple (1 Corinthians 16:19c). In speaking to the Samaritan woman, Jesus answered her question about where worship should take place by answering: "Believe me, woman, a time is coming when you will worship the Father neither on this mountain nor in Jerusalem ... Yet a time is coming and has now come when the true worshipers will worship the Father in Spirit and truth, for they are the kind of worshipers the Father seeks. God is spirit, and his worshipers must worship in spirit and in truth" (John 4:21, 23–24). In other words, the time or place we worship the Lord is not the most important factor but instead how we worship Him. The church is people, people who have Jesus living inside of them, not necessarily a building or congregation. Before He came and died for us, people sought the Spirit of God in the temple, a building. "The Lord said to Moses, ... 'Then have them make a sanctuary for me, and I will dwell among them'" (Exodus 25:1, 8). Now the Lord lives inside each of us Christians. We are His temple. "Don't you know that you yourselves are God's temple and that God's Spirit lives in you?" (1 Corinthians 3:16).

That is why He also said, "For where two or three come together in my name, there am I with them" (Matthew 18:20).

Our family celebrated God's day of rest also, remembering the Lord in a loving way once a week and being determined not to relegate it to only once a week. I also see that I have never had to worry about forsaking fellowship with other Christians. From the moment I became a Christian (and even before), the Lord has brought Christians all along my path, even though I often had no church home. He brought them in the place I felt best: my aloneness and speaking one-on-one to people. My first year of college here, my roommate was a Christian. I also made friends with another Christian woman I met through the orientation program that year. When Gordon and I were first married and living in an apartment, another Christian woman came to me, selling door-to-door, sharing her faith, and inviting me to church. After that, the Lord led me to the church I was to attend for eleven years, 1984–1995. Through the years, I made friends with other Christians in Compassionate Friends and others who have lost children. Then the Lord brought me another Christian friend, Mary Lou, with whom I walked for many years, and times of sharing with my sister Judy, another Christian. Through those many friends, I have come to realize not only that the Lord provides Christian fellowship but sadly that there are many different opinions, most of which are menial and not foundational to our faith but instead simply cause divisions. Through the years, with these friends, however, I have shared more thoughts and more deeply than at church on Sunday, or at cell groups, which were difficult, as I was either unable to speak or revealed too much. Also, Christian radio has provided much encouragement with praise songs and teaching. So my life has been filled with fellowship, brought in the place I can best accept it. (Later on, Gordon and I did return to church.)

I am not advocating that all people leave churches, but in my case, I have come to realize that the Lord had a plan for us leaving. Because of my tendency to be a people-pleaser, the Lord had to help me to hear what He was saying. Also, because of my past, which included many beliefs that were untrue, and because I was listening more to people at church than to the Lord, He chose to pull me away so He could teach me Himself, showing me what was untrue from my past and helping me to hear His voice and to learn to please Him instead of people. "This is what the Lord says—your Redeemer, the Holy One of Israel: 'I am the Lord your God, who teaches you what is best for you, who directs you in the way you should go'" (Isaiah 48:17). "Therefore I am now going to allure her; I will lead her into the desert and speak tenderly to her. There I will give her back her vineyards, and will make the Valley of Achor a door of hope. There she will sing as in the days of her youth, as in the day she came up out of Egypt" (Hosea 2:14, 15). This is the same way He worked in Moses's and Paul's lives, with the knowledge that much in their pasts had to be relearned as it was not the truth.

In people-pleasing, I was giving glory to man and not to God. The Lord impressed two scriptures upon me: "Am I now trying to win the approval of men, or of God? Or am I trying to please men? If I were still trying to please men, I would not be a servant of Christ" (Galatians 1:10). "See, I have refined you though not as silver; I have tested you in the furnace of affliction. For my own sake, for my own sake, I do this. How can I let myself be defamed? I will not yield my glory to another" (Isaiah 48:10–11). I was essentially pouring my heart out to others and listening to them before God. He desired for me to save that deep intimacy for Him alone.

As I have found out, it is essential and actually the Lord's desire that each of us find out who we are, how He made us individually, our personalities, and the gifts He has given to us to bless others. This knowledge is foundational (a much-needed prerequisite) in dealing with other people. It helps us to see and accept ourselves through God's eyes and to let go of the judgment of others.

The trigger that brought about our final decision to start having church at home came with two events, both demonstrating how legalism can creep into church, causing pain and disunity. At the beginning of 1995, within a few months' time, I had three different people from church, all of whom I barely knew, inform me that I had to do what they said. In January, while at an open house, a couple asked if I went to their church. I explained that, "Yes, I do," but they might not have seen me as I spent most of my time in the nursery with my daughter. As they asked more questions, I told them that she did not stay well and that often the staff came to get me. They became adamant, repeating many times that I had to leave Sarabeth. Once I finally escaped from them, I retreated into the bathroom in tears. Gordon and I spent the rest of the evening in the basement watching movies with the kids, who had no condemning words for us.

Later, I encountered the same attitude once again when Gordon, Eric, and I went to a Rollerblading class. An acquaintance from church was there with her son. She obviously already knew how to Rollerblade and was, in fact, quite good at it. I, unfortunately, did not and was not having a good time with it. In trying to increase my speed, I fell many times and finally hurt my arm. When the class began practicing ascending ramps, I knew it was beyond my skill level and felt the need to sit out and watch. At that point, the woman came to tell me I had to do that part of the class. Seeing that she was not one of the instructors and she had not paid for my participation in the class, I responded kindly, but convincingly, that I did not intend to try. Both incidents highlighted many times certain Christians felt the need to tell me what to do and what I was doing wrong. Both incidents only served to increase my desire to leave.

Now the hand of the Lord is most obvious. In the past, I have heard pastors speak about church attendance, using the analogy that we are sheep, with the church being the flock and the Lord the Shepherd, the point being that if we stray from the flock, we will be a prime target for the wolves. For a long time, that frightened me into staying at church, even as I struggled with not belonging. Finally, I came to realize that in my walk with the Lord, there were many years when I was *not* in any one denomination. In fact, during the years we were attending church, we experienced the most tragedies, not due to going to church, however, but to the Lord's timing. By their logic, something did not connect. I have come to realize that all along I have been in the flock. How can I be sure? Because I have been following the Shepherd daily. I would much rather follow the Shepherd than to follow the sheep knowing how stupid we as sheep can be. If we follow the flock, we may go off the cliff. My job is to keep my eyes on the Shepherd, not on His flock. If we follow the Shepherd daily, we will be in His flock. He says that His sheep know Him, hear Him, and follow Him. We need our eyes to be focused first on Him.

Does that mean that we do not listen to any other Christians? No. The Lord has brought us leaders and other Christians to help us. We need to heed their words but always take them to the Lord for verification. That is why I say throughout this book, do not take my words and accept them. First, always ask God what He is saying to you. That is our responsibility as Christians: to learn to hear God's voice and to seek His counsel first. I believe that the purpose of the church is to encourage and build up because life can be overwhelming. Always, our first response to pain in ourselves and others should be to seek the Lord. If a person feels judged and condemned, even if it only comes from part of the church, he will not find encouragement. God has brought me to a place of encouragement and hopefully to a point of sharing that reassurance with others in the same way.

Having both a husband and a son who are avid fishermen, I was not surprised that the Lord used that analogy to teach me. One day on a walk, I commented to Gordon about Jesus calling us to be fishers of men and how I could not quite see how the analogy fit because I do not believe that we are called to clean the fish. That was when a true fisherman helped me to understand. He said, "That is because God is the fisherman. We are just the lures, the bait, the net." That made it all come clear. As the fisherman, it is God's job to clean the fish, not ours.

Too often we take our knives to the lake or river, determined to clean the fish before they are even caught. This results in flaying our knives through the water, with three sad consequences: fish fleeing unhurt, fish killed, and/or most tragically, wounded fish, vowing to never come near us again! Sadly, we have all been guilty of this, including me. But from personal experience, being pummeled by others never helped me, whereas the gentle working of God's Spirit has had a dramatic effect in my life. There may be times for leadership to intervene, but God's Spirit does the best work.

Just as the Lord has taught me about self-esteem, He has also shown me that He has been with me, guiding me all along the path, and that my Christian life has followed the same kind of growth as my physical life. This has consoled me. The church has been compared to a hospital. If it is indeed a place for healing, we all need to remember that healing the sick and wounded often takes time. They, most likely, will not be ready to reach out to help others until they find some healing themselves. In the same way, the growth analogy applies. As newborns and young children in a family, they will not be ready to give much to others until they have grown some. Then, as in a family, appropriate chores are given. That is a good time for trying many jobs, both to see where their interests may lie and also to see what talents and gifts the Lord has bestowed upon them. We need to remember that these are growing-up chores, not necessarily something that will be enjoyed as a ministry or career in the church later on. For me, working in the nursery was difficult because of my introverted nature. The toddler and preschool were somewhat easier, as Gordon and I enjoyed working together to teach the young ones Sunday school. None of those jobs, however, felt as good as when I volunteered for Love Care. It suited my nature, my personality, much better, in that it was a behind-the-scenes job, with little interaction with many people. Also, as I shared before, working in Compassionate Friends in the leadership role was not at all my niche. I am not an administrative person, nor do I enjoy working in groups.

Our Christian life is a process of growing, so we need never condemn ourselves. We also should not compare ourselves to others at church. There are many reasons others seem farther along.

1. There are those who are older in the Lord and are, in fact, usually an encouragement, as they are not condemning and have a great deal to teach us.
2. There are those that have not needed as many repairs on their houses and, therefore, have seen quicker progress.
3. There are those who are extroverts, feeling comfortable in sharing and participating in many activities.
4. There are those who know the right responses and actions, though not close to the Lord at all.
5. And sadly, there are also deceivers. They are mentioned in the parable Jesus gave of the enemy sowing weeds in with the wheat (Matthew 13:24–30).

Unfortunately, the last two are a reality. There may be other reasons also. We cannot know. Only the Lord knows each of our hearts. It is our responsibility to come to understand ourselves through the Lord's eyes, both inside and outside. As He reveals our personalities and gifts, we are better able to accept how He made us and discover His purposes for our lives. The others we leave to Him, for we are not to judge, either ourselves or them. "I care very little if I am judged by you or by any human court; indeed, I do not even judge myself. My conscience is clear, but that does not make me innocent. It is the Lord who judges me. Therefore, judge nothing before the appointed time; wait till the Lord comes. He will bring to light what is hidden in darkness and will expose the motive of men's hearts. At that time each will receive his praise from God" (1 Corinthians 4:3–5).

I have come to be thankful for my position as "always the last, always the least," for I am never alone. It is there that the Lord loves to walk.

CHAPTER 9

The Upper East Room Or Self-Respect

I turned and touched the banister as my Lord beckoned me to ascend the steps. At the top, I could now see the whole room, a restful room. It was good to see its floor now replaced and of the same wood used below. The east wall had a bay window similar to the one on the first floor but with a padded bench. The open window let in a cool breeze, which rustled the leaves on the tree outside. Next to the window was a big bed facing a fireplace. On its other side was a comfy chair of soft brown leather. The south wall was a bookcase filled with books of all names, some I could see that were dear to me. Interspersed on these shelves were also more tokens of my trip. What was most touching to me about this room was the design of the walls. Impressed into the plaster were hearts, each containing a tiny jewel, all different, so that the effect of rainbows was here also, with rubies, emeralds, sapphires, and other precious stones, beautiful not only to behold, but also of great value.

****

Do not give dogs what is sacred; do not throw your pearls to pigs.
If you do, they may trample them under their
feet, and then turn and tear you to pieces.
—Matthew 7:6

This room in my house had been severely lacking, really an empty room. Until 2001, I had little understanding about self-respect and am sincerely still in the process of learning. Growing up, all I ever knew was that I did not have it. It was difficult to watch Rodney Dangerfield on television. He consistently made jokes about receiving no respect. What others found to be funny gave me an uncomfortable feeling and brought embarrassment because what he shared was a profile of me!

In 1989, the Lord brought the scripture, "Am I now trying to win the approval of men, or of God? Or am I trying to please men?" (Galatians 1:10a–b). That seed sat germinating in my mind as the truth became more obvious. Yes, I was trying to please man, to earn his approval and acceptance.

Another link in the same chain was connected in the fall of 1999, as I reread a book, *The Birth Order Book* by Dr. Kevin Leman. It helped me understand the characteristics of the middle child, which I am.[1] It was important to see how I had been consistently led by others, allowing firstborns in my life to influence most of my decisions. There had also been a tendency to be a negotiator between firstborns in my life, especially within our immediate family, where I have lived with three firstborns, Gordon, Eric, and Sarabeth, who all loved to make plans, but often conflicting plans. For me, the goal was always one of trying to keep the peace. Meanwhile, frustration and anger were often building inside as my own needs, thoughts, desires, and feelings were not considered. That seems to be the tendency of most middle children, who have grown accustomed to being told what to do. In our compliancy, we rarely speak up to voice our own opinions or thoughts, eventually rebelling.

In the past, a friend of mine who had numerous trials shared she could not understand the source of the constant anger in her life. Honestly, her anger was understandable, considering all that she had suffered. In sympathy with her, I shared my struggles with my temper through the years. During that time, I had read numerous books dealing with anger, two of which were *When You Feel Like Screaming!*

Help for Frustrated Mothers by Pat Holt and Grace Ketterman, MD,[2] and *When Anger Hits Home Taking Care of Your Anger Without Taking It Out on Your Family* by Gary Jackson Oliver and H. Norman Wright. The second one spoke of keeping an anger log, which I did for a long time, charting date, time, intensity, primary emotion triggering the anger, and the issue.[3] It helped me identify the underlying emotion of most of my outbursts: pure frustration, dealing with little ones full-time, with few breaks. I also noticed that hurt, fear, and embarrassment were often triggers for the anger. The ultimate source eluded me, however, until 2001. What has been the biggest source of anger for me? Lack of self-respect.

What is *self-respect?* In consulting the dictionary, it means to treat ourselves with honor and esteem, showing consideration and even appreciation.[4] To me, self-respect means to honor myself enough that I take care of myself, but it does not mean being selfish. It means considering my own feelings, thoughts, and opinions as worthwhile as others and being able to stand up for myself.

At the beginning of 2001, our family began making plans to travel to California to visit my older sister, Mary Kay, and her family during spring break. She had been asking us to come for a long time, and we hoped we could finally manage it. We also invited my dad, the one stipulation involving the arrival of our income tax refund. It was my way of determining if it was the Lord's desire for us to go. That was especially important since I had been struggling for a year with a recurrent ulcer. It was at its worst point right after the New Year. Because of that, I diligently sought the Lord for the wisdom to know if we should go. Memories of Eric's hospitalization in San Diego years earlier had resurfaced. Finally, we informed everyone we would go if the check came. Meanwhile, I prayed daily that the Lord would guide us in this way. Since then, I have berated myself, thinking I should have sought His guidance through different means, as this kept us waiting until the bitter end, still planning, all of us fairly certain it would happen. From the beginning, however, planning was a frustration, as Mary Kay and Gordon, understandably, each began making plans, only different plans. That left me in the middle, trying to please both of them, trying to be a negotiator while wondering if I would feel well and have enough energy to sit at the beach, my ultimate desire, peaceful nature.

As it turned out, our check did *not* arrive in time, and that left me having to inform both my sister and my dad. Of course, they both volunteered to lend us money. And Gordon too received suggestions at work, such as using our credit card. It took much courage for me to stand up to all three of them. Ultimately, they all missed the point, that the Lord was saying no, for which I was grateful. At that point, the only foods that I was able to digest were pasta and milk. That would have made a miserable trip for all of us.

Later, during the summer, the Lord revealed these thoughts: (1) my main purpose in planning the trip was to please others—if my health had been better, the desire to go would have been there too, and (2) my kind Lord had seen it would have been too much for me, so He stood up for me since I could not. He also helped me to see that it was part of the testing time, a time of seeing if I would choose to follow Him, pleasing Him alone, or if my people-pleasing would ultimately win over.

In this situation, He was also teaching me about loving myself, which is akin to self-respect. I have heard it said that we are not to love ourselves but instead to deny ourselves. I think we are to do both. As we focus on the Lord, and love and obey Him, that leads to our doing those things that are loving to both others and ourselves so that we are balanced.

Loving and Serving God
(Balanced)

		People–
Selfish	Learning to do	Pleasing
(Off Balance)	What Jesus desires	(Off Balance)
	Caring for ourselves and others	

99

Loving and respecting ourselves and others

Self-Serving	Self-Serving
Always caring for ourselves before others	Always caring for others before ourselves
Not respecting others	Not respecting ourselves
Often leads to controlling others	Often leads to being controlled

When we learn how *not* to be selfish or to be people-pleasers but instead to listen to the Lord and be guided by Him daily, we *will* be denying self, going a different way than our natural tendency. "Jesus replied, 'Love the Lord your God with all your heart and with all your soul and with all your mind. This is the first and greatest commandment. And the second is like it: Love your neighbor as yourself. All the law and the Prophets hang on these two commandments'" (Matthew 22:37–40). "After all, no one ever hates his own body, but he feeds and cares for it, just as Christ does the church" (Ephesians 5:29).

Perhaps one of the hardest areas with which I have had to deal is various controlling people. Since we have been married, Gordon and I have traveled back to our hometown numerous times, usually for the holidays. There have been difficult moments there occasionally when a normally passive me has lost my temper and reacted negatively to what seemed inconsiderate remarks. Once home again, anger and guilt would always surface. Finally, the Lord began to teach me about my anger. He first showed me that He too had suffered with part of his family (John 7:1–5) and those from His hometown (Mark 6:1–4), as well as with the Pharisees. He knew and understood what I was feeling. We are told to do all we can to get along with others. "If it is possible, as far as it depends on you, live at peace with everyone" (Romans 12:18). But He also understands firsthand that it often does not work. "Do not suppose that I have come to bring peace to the earth. I did not come to bring peace, but a sword. For I have come to turn a man against his father, a daughter against her mother, a daughter-in-law against her mother-in-law—a man's enemies will be the members of his own household" (Matthew 10:34–36).

For most of my life, I have felt on the defensive, always reacting to hurtful situations. The Lord helped me see that my initial way of reacting to these situations was to say nothing. Although hurt, I would not reveal it, but instead kept it inside until I was alone, where anger and tears would consume me. It always seemed as if I were supposed to minimize the problem, but I have come to realize that most little fights usually have underlying big issues, such as pride, competition, and inconsiderateness. It is important to recognize and deal with the underlying issues. After Matthew's death, my reaction to hurtful situations did a dramatic about-face, as my response to those who were rude and/or inconsiderate was one of intense anger. It is like a pendulum, with no response on one side and overreaction on the other. The Lord began to show me the middle ground, the balance, where He wanted me, responding without an angry outburst, the pattern He Himself gave for us.

Reaction to Painful Remarks

Younger Years (Off Balance)	Later Years (Off Balance)
No response on my part	Responding with much anger
Going home hurt and angry	Going home feeling guilty
No self-respect	No respect for others

Correct Response

(Balanced)
Jesus's response
Answering with no anger
Showing self-respect and respect for others
Taking His emotions to His Father later
Forgiving, with the Father's forgiveness, those who hurt Him

Often, people have suggested that we need to respond as Jesus did. "Answering not a word" is what they say. The only time He did *not* respond, however, was before His death, knowing it was the whole reason He had come to earth. In reading the gospels, it does not take long to see that Jesus usually did answer, even showing intense anger when it was appropriate, when His Father's house was treated with disrespect. Our anger may be kindled as well when our loved ones are mistreated.

Jesus is our example, and He demonstrated how to react to those who are essentially bullies, trying to push and control others. His response to them was with the truth from His heart, and He spent hours alone with His Father later, probably diffusing, pouring out His heart, filled with hurt and frustration, to His kind, understanding, and loving Father. Jesus is the perfect example of self-respect and respecting others. He came to help the sick and sinners and did not push anyone. He only reached out to the misfits of the day, not seeking those who were consistently unkind to Him. He had to be around them, both family and Pharisees, but He was not seeking them. He said He was seeking the sick and the lost sheep. "It is not the healthy who need a doctor, but the sick" (Matthew 9:12b). "For the Son of Man came to seek and to save what was lost" (Luke 19:10). They were the ones who needed a doctor and a shepherd. Unfortunately, those who were really sick and lost did not see their own need and turn to Him so that He could heal them.

When Eric was small, we encouraged him to be good, when Christmas was approaching, so that Santa would bring him something. One Christmas morning, we heard him exclaim, "I must have been good enough!" The Pharisees were under the same notion that they were good enough, either not seeing their sin or dismissing it because "it isn't that bad," certainly not as bad as others. They also believed that they were good enough, simply because they were descendants of Abraham, but the Bible says, "For all have sinned and fall short of the glory of God" (Romans 3:23).

Still, Jesus's heart was hurting for them as He cried, "O, Jerusalem, Jerusalem, you who kill the prophets ..." (Matthew 23:37). He felt a heart of compassion regarding them, but unfortunately, He was unable to help them until they turned to Him, exactly like today. Neither can we be friends with those who are controlling and manipulative. We may have to be around them at times and must respond accordingly, but the Lord's example is the best for us to follow, not seeking those who are bent on hurting us. He wants us to do all we can to get along with others, understanding that with some people, it will never be enough. It is a hopeless proposition. So we need not berate ourselves over it! If Jesus cannot help them, neither can we, and the Lord does not want us to be controlled by them. Jesus also said that within a family, there would be discord. We cannot expect to live in a peaceful world. Often people in our own lives treat us similarly, especially if we have allowed it. The Lord helped me see how I have consistently allowed others to treat me disrespectfully.

****

Another area involving self-respect applies to men and women. For ever so long, women stayed home to care for their families, while their husbands were the breadwinners. With the sixties came huge changes, with more liberal thinking and the advent of the women's movement. I recall heated arguments around our dinner table in the seventies as my liberal aunt, who had recently left the convent as a nun, promoted the Women's Lib philosophy. Meanwhile, my mother defended her role as a housewife. Both were passionate about their ideas.

What was it all about? What is it all about? Having been home many years, raising our family, the source of women's frustrations and anger has become a little clearer to me. Staying home is a full-time job with many menial and monotonous tasks, for which there appear to be few, if any, rewards. Definitely none money-wise or emotional-wise. In fact, money is often tight, and husbands and kids are not prone to giving compliments on clean clothes or a nice-smelling bathroom! It seems to be a job where women are consistently expected to meet others' needs and none of their own.

There is, indeed, a legitimate, understandable reason for the Women's Lib Movement. We want to be appreciated, viewed as important and deserving of respect. A prime example comes when Gordon and the kids are on vacation. Because my evenings and weekends have been mostly theirs through the years, it is often hard for them to realize that I am not on vacation, even though they are. Most of my work—laundry, shopping, cooking—cannot be put off unless we go out of town.

Another example of the disrespect homemakers can encounter is depicted in the following story. When one of the newer employees at Gordon's office heard that I was a stay-at-home mom, he commented that he wished he were married to Gordon. Of course, when shared with me, it was not especially well-received, as it was also at the time Sarabeth was struggling with her stomach. It was also before this employee had children himself. He may hold a different opinion now, having had his own children and seeing how demanding, self-sacrificing, and time-consuming child-rearing can be.

There seems to be a feeling that if a woman decides to stay at home, she has no real worth. (It was interesting to hear of a study a few years ago that estimated the monetary worth of a stay-at-home mom's work to be over $130,000!) Those at home know that it is a full-time job. It is easy for us to resent people who try to solicit our help for many things. Yet I have found little time to devote outside of my work at home. I do take time alone with the Lord daily and time for walking, plus talking to my sister Judy. Those can be guilt-producing, but I have come to know they are essential for me to be able to function. The Lord, in fact, has brought those times for that very reason. This area of working can cause much contention. The difference I find between myself and those who work both at home and outside the home is this. My days are spent getting the following done: cooking, laundry, shopping, cleaning, errands, notes, cards, gifts, paperwork, and seasonal jobs for numerous hours so that my evenings and weekends belong to my family—that time is for them. For women who work both inside and outside the house, their days are spent at a job, with the nights and weekends devoted to doing the work I do during the week. That leaves little time for family.

For this reason and others, I sincerely question whether the Women's Lib Movement has indeed brought respect and freedom to women. There may be women in positions, which pay enough for frequent meals out, cleaning people, and even nannies. Yet the majority of women I know who work outside the home do not have these benefits. They have to work in order to make ends meet.

Not only do few women who work outside the home have outside help, but most have minimal help from their husbands, with either the kids or the house. This is a great benefit for husbands, who not only have help financially, but also have no increased responsibilities. I have often wondered, has that improved life for women and children? What has been the gain? The only area that seems to have become less demanding is the child-rearing. The demands of both career and home together take tremendous amounts of time, leaving little for the kids. We were often sad to observe the few parents involved in their kids' school and activities. At parent-teacher conferences, teachers commented that they generally see only the parents that do not need to go.

I personally do not believe that the Lord wants us women doing so much. He knew that the job of family and home was more than enough. To me, it is unfair that women should take on more, when most are already doing more than our part. By taking on half of the man's job, more pressure has been applied not only to women but also children, at the same time making the man's job easier! I believe it was God's plan for the man to be the breadwinner and also to help at home with the children, because I believe women have more than a full-time job at home, from morning until night. Children are the responsibility of both the husband and the wife, and for men who have the *privilege* of their wives working outside of the home, they should also provide help with the household chores.

As I write all this, I need to clarify that it is indeed my own conviction, not something that I feel the Lord has shown me. It is my own deep belief that I feel I need to share. My past has greatly influenced my beliefs concerning this, and my heart hurts for the Lord, whose gifts are not valued much anymore. I speak out as I have observed His pain for our kids, for our families.

Many are caught in this trap with no way out. Our society has made it especially difficult for a man alone to support his family. I have been blessed and am grateful to have been able to stay at home, and I do not condemn those women who have to work. To those of you who desire to be home but are unable, God knows your heart and your desire to be at home. He is not condemning you, and neither do I. It is also understandable that there are those who want and choose to work. Most people are extroverts and need people around them to function. Staying at home may seem a very restrictive life to them.

The question still needs addressed, "What about our families?" With most of our energies focused elsewhere, "Who is minding the kids?" Even staying home, I did not give the amount of time to my kids that they probably needed, and we played together most evenings and weekends. Still, my kids watched too much television, which our enemy loves, his avenue for retraining them.

When Sarabeth was in elementary school, we would have lunch together once a week at school. It always amazed me the number of kids that wanted to talk to me and wanted me to watch them. This, of course, was upsetting to Sarabeth, who also wanted my attention. Kids desperately crave our adult attention. The truth is we can never overdo in this area. They need us. At sporting events, we have observed kids searching the stands to find someone there to watch them! Our kids need us.

I had a good illustration of this the summer of 2002. In the process of writing this book, I wanted to know what I had done wrong (and hopefully right) with my kids. So I asked Sarabeth and Eric to please take a minute and make a list. Well, Eric, a teenager at the time, has still to deliver his, but Sarabeth had her list to me in a matter of a minutes. I do not remember if there were any good remarks, only the bad one. She said that I never spent time with her. Well, I had asked, yet my defenses came up at that. How could that be? If she had said yelling or being cranky, it would have been easy to accept. Once we talked about it, I realized what had happened. At the beginning of the summer, we had planned to spend one hour every afternoon playing together. But what ended up happening is that we scheduled so many summertime activities (two basketball camps, two swimming lessons, tennis, bowling, and horseback riding, all events we attended together) that the extra hour we had envisioned was gobbled up, with no time left over. Then in evenings, during the summer, we all usually played outside. So what she said was true: there never was any time to play the things that she wanted with me *alone*. The following summer, we halved our agenda, making it more manageable, and we even had time to play most days.

All the above does not answer the ultimate question: if women receive little or no respect from family and/or others when staying at home or by going out to work, how do they find the respect they desire and need while giving that same respect to everyone else that also desires and needs it? What is the answer? Where is the balance? I am definitely no authority, as the Lord has only begun to teach me about respect, but He has shown me the following.

Finding Respect
through a
Close-Knit Family
Maximizing Time and Money

(Off Balance)	(Balanced)	(Off Balance)
Daily	Daily	Daily
Mom works at home/	Mom and Dad	Mom and Dad
Dad works outside home	Work outside the home	Work outside the home
and	and	and
Evenings/weekends	Evenings/weekends	Evenings/weekends

107

Mom works inside the home and with the kids/ Dad takes time for himself	Both work in the house and take time with the family	Mom works inside home and with the kids / Dad takes time for himself

or

Mom works at home /
Dad works outside the home
and
Evenings/weekends
Both take time for extra housework
and with family

From this, we can see that men have an integral part to play in making a close-knit family. Their participation is crucial. Without it, all is off balance. As men and women share the workload, it does provide more time for family, the most important treasure we have. (Good resources: *Fireproof*[5] and *Courageous*[6] movies.)

The Lord also has shown me the following with regard to self-respect and women:

(1) Women are generally talkers. Many different sources have said that man's greatest need in marriage is sex, whereas a woman's greatest need is communication. Women are also emotional, whereas men do not seem to be (Adam's missing rib). Combining these two characteristics, the need for communication and our emotional makeup, makes us vulnerable, especially us women who are at home. We seldom have meaningful talk throughout the day. So when our husbands return home in the evenings, we bombard them with exactly what they do not want: conversation. If they found us at the door every evening in lingerie, they would be thrilled, but talking? That is frustrating for most of them, especially when they were probably looking for some time for peace and quiet.

It is also tiresome listening to someone who talks nonstop, which is probably the reason for our frequent remark, "My husband never listens to me." Most of us have probably said that at some point in our marriages. We do not feel respected when our needs are not met. We need to talk and share our emotions, which can be intense—to have someone listen and understand. Another side to this is that in our neediness, our husbands seldom get to talk. Plus, our society discourages men from sharing emotions. I believe this is the reason they are so needy in the area of sex. Whatever the reason, men are less apt to open up to us as much as we are to them, making us vulnerable.

Early in the spring of 2001, as Gordon and I were experiencing some of the same problems we had consistently encountered in our marriage (and just as consistently swept under the rug), I prayed to the Lord to finally bring an answer. After many fights, I wanted to understand at last. What was the source or part of it? His answer seemed to be lack of self-respect on my part. I was essentially giving all of myself (my inside being) to my husband and for nothing—for free. Just as giving our bodies to someone without expecting something valuable and of equal worth, a commitment, in return is disrespectful to our very selves, so in any relationship, especially marriage, if we give our all, expecting nothing in return, we are not showing respect to ourselves. As the truth of this came clearer, I wrote a letter to Gordon explaining that until he was able to open up to me, allowing himself to be more vulnerable, I was no longer able to be unguarded with him.

The analogy of life in everyday marriage to the sexual union of a man and wife is obvious. We are to be totally naked with each other not only in lovemaking but also mentally and emotionally, sharing not only our bodies but also our inside beings. In both instances, there is communication with each other at a deep level, with honesty and acceptance. If only one person in a relationship is sharing honestly, the other begins to feel superior.

Gordon has since been trying to open up more to me, recounting his day at work and even some frustrations with it. This has produced two positive results: (a) Through it, I feel needed and valuable, and (b) it has also removed the tendency on his part to devalue my feelings in my weaknesses and frustrations. There are other benefits as well. In refraining from talking as much, (c) it has allowed the whole family to speak up, and (d) it keeps some of the mystery alive in our marriage, something that we tend to lose with time.

You may wonder, however, how I obtain my own bit of communication. The Lord has shown me that He is more than willing to spend any amount of time with me—actually, the more, the better. He wants us to bring everything to Him throughout the day, and He is always there to listen, care, and understand, providing needed support daily. He also brought two wonderful outlets: my sister Judy, whose calls have been such an encouragement, as we both come from the same family, understanding the joys and frustrations from that, and walks with my friend Mary Lou, which provided a needful outlet for fears and frustrations with our older kids. The biggest source of reassurance with both of them, however, has been our shared faith. It is healing to have that bond. I believe this provides a much-needed outlet for us women, and it sure beats the cost of counseling! This time was especially hard to obtain when the kids were younger but became more of a reality once Sarabeth started school, for which I was thankful.

(2) If self-respect means each of us honoring and caring for ourselves, an area that is especially needful for women is time for ourselves. The old saying "A woman's work is never done" is true. We go from early morning to late night with few breaks. And for homemakers, there is added pressure of not allowing anyone to see us doing anything but working. We often feel guilty to be at home (the domestic goddess) and especially for taking time for ourselves, thinking of our hard-working husbands or other women out slaving in the workplace. But all of us require this time. It is, in fact, what the Lord is calling all of us to do, to stop—stop all the activity and take time to sit! He wants us to be as Mary, not Martha, taking time for Him.

As women, we need to ask ourselves, do most men not have some time to read the paper and/or watch television every day? And for those of us who have chosen to stay at home? As far as comparing ourselves to women who work outside the home, I would say that we do indeed work as hard, only with a different contingent. In fact, women who have little ones at home work harder than any of us. Children at home are more than a full-time project, involving self-sacrifice, in time, interruptions and energy, a monumental job. Yet few moms in that position receive any respect!

All women who are moms realize how busy life is, and we do need time for ourselves. The Lord has shown me that time for myself daily is essential: in the morning, time to pray and read my devotionals and Bible; in the late afternoon, time to read; and time alone with Him in the evening, before bed. I also take time for walks and talking to Judy. The total time this takes is the same time Gordon spends during the week in the evenings watching television. In looking at this, it is easy to see the Lord's timing is perfect. He wants me to start the day in a positive way, take a break before the hectic time of everyone returning home and suppertime, and finish the day with Him.

The Lord provided both of these important lessons, showing that, in meeting my needs for communication and time alone, I am honoring myself, caring for myself, which ultimately helps me provide the same care for others. We are not superwomen, contrary to what we have been taught. Trying to balance too much will only bring greater frustration and unhappiness. This is the most content I have ever felt. I also have to add that knowing what the Lord desires has relieved the pressure of trying to be what church and/or society may pressure or what friends and/or family may expect. We are always at our best when doing what God desires. A huge load of condemnation falls off as we realize, "if God is for us, who can be against us?" (Romans 8:31b). If God is for me, who even cares who is against me! There is no one on earth whose opinion matters as much!

****

Another area in marriage needing respect is the area of sex. As said above, the biggest need in marriage for a man is sex, whereas we women most need communication. Since I am a woman, my perspective relates most with our needs. We desire to share our most intimate thoughts and feelings and have our husbands listen and understand, or at least pretend to. In dating and early marriage, this is usually much more alive. With the arrival of children, however, our lives become more stressful, with little time or energy for one another. By the time our children are teenagers, it is easy to understand how a marriage can have lost its first love many years previous.

A good illustration of this is depicted in the movie *Bridges of Madison County.*[7] The story begins with the introduction of a typical 1960s family—Mom, Dad, and two teenagers, a daughter and a son— who live out of town on a farm. One of the first scenes shows them at supper, as Mom relates something humorous she has heard. However, no one responds, probably because most teenagers are preoccupied with their own lives, their thoughts and needs, and most husbands are not only weary from the monotony of work but also have no idea how deal with us women's emotions. This woman, obviously a homemaker, was also weary, but she felt something else, a loneliness, which her children could not fill and her husband was too tired and preoccupied to notice.

As it turns out, the husband and kids have plans out of town for a short time. The woman remains home, caring for the farm. Shortly after they leave, a reporter comes to research the area, namely the covered bridges of the county. Little by little, they share their stories, and she begins to fall in love, eventually sleeping with him. Why? Why did it happen so quickly, with no forewarning? You might say because she was lonely, which is part. But I feel it was mainly because a deep need to be listened to, appreciated, and understood was finally met. She found someone who was sincerely interested in her thoughts and feelings and not bored with her, who in fact found her to be extremely fascinating. Although I do not approve of her choice to sleep with him, it sure is understandable in her situation. Her need to be cared for was met, and she responded in the way that God made us women to respond. When we feel loved and listened to and understood by a man, we women respond in a sexual way.

Although this woman was tempted to leave, she chose to do the right thing and stayed, only revealing her story after her death.

There is a good book called *Sex Begins in the Kitchen* by Dr. Kevin Leman. It addresses the need for a husband to be considerate of his wife, helping around the house, which not only lessens her load, providing her more energy, but also tenderizes her so she will respond more willingly to times of physical love.[8] I feel this is true when the work is done in a considerate way, as he suggests.

In my opinion, however, the one most needful area of change for men is in the area of listening and being understanding. I believe that what we women most desire is to be cared for tenderly when we have had a bad day, to be tended to with respect, not trying to fix the problem, but mostly being attentive and caring and drying our tears. To me, that is the key, what primes the pump. But few men have understood. Often they cannot understand why their wives may not desire sex or why it is not as much fun when they do consent. This is my answer to any man who is pondering: husbands who desire sex, and good sex, need to listen and be understanding and accepting of their wives. We women were created in such a way that we respond. If our husbands are kind and gentle, we respond to them sexually.

If you were to ask us women what we would say a romantic evening entailed, it probably would begin with some peaceful setting: a quiet walk in the snow, a picnic in the park, sitting by the fire, or a quiet, candlelit dinner. We find those times romantic, setting the mood for intimacy. What does *intimate* mean? In consulting the dictionary, its general meaning is a close association or something private or secret.[9] Most often in our culture, it has come to mean only sexual union, yet we can see that is not its truest meaning. If we truly understand the meaning, we see that loosely giving ourselves, physically or mentally, to someone is devastating. We are valuable and have much inside to guard and not throw away.

At times, in our culture, there has been talk of being unable to find satisfaction. Many men seem to experience this in the area of sex. Even with sexual magazines and many sexual partners, they are still searching for fulfillment, always craving more. Why? (1) When the boundaries are removed from the blessings of God, it will never be as wonderful as God intended it. (2) Men in our society have been raised to be macho, not realizing that true intimacy requires honesty daily: (a) being vulnerable to their wives and (b) trying to understand and accept their wives' vulnerability. The sexual part of marriage is to mirror everyday life. If there is no closeness daily in marriage, sharing frustrations, needs, thoughts, feelings, and dreams, but only surface information, the physical act becomes only that, an act, a sport, which will never be fulfilling, because its purpose is for so much more. There is also another reason.

The sexual union, physical and mental, mirrors our relationship with the Lord. The Bible says it is an illustration of that. Many more women than men seem to understand and to have experienced this relationship with the Lord, which may explain why spiritual leadership in our homes often is lacking. Being intimate with God is being naked before Him, totally honest and open. If men do not comprehend this in their relationship with God, how will they understand the scripture, "Husbands, love your wives, just as Christ loved the church and gave himself up for her" (Ephesians 5:25).

When we come to know the Lord and His love, we see it is all compassion, understanding, and patience. I believe that many men, even Christian men, are hooked on pornography for this exact reason. Just as husbands are not to fulfill all of their wives' needs for communication, we wives are not to fulfill all our husbands' needs. A very real need for intimacy with God fills the biggest part. If that is lacking, even sexual encounters with a wife (and hundreds of others) will not be enough.

The physical act of revealing your hidden body to your spouse is the same as revealing your hidden self to that person. If you are not open with your mate daily, your sexual union will not be close either. When men do not understand this, they are missing much of the blessing the Lord intends for them to experience. I know, from personal experience in my own marriage, the most beautiful and fulfilling times of physical intimacy have come when both Gordon and I have been most open and unguarded mentally and emotionally to each other.

True intimacy involves sharing our hearts before we share our bodies. When one feels loved, the result is very beautiful lovemaking. Anything else is much less than what the Lord intended and certainly not fulfilling. Maybe that is why many people switch partners regularly, having known only disappointment in what is supposed to be fun and exciting! Without true love, lovemaking will never be as it was meant to be from the beginning. It is still a good idea to follow the owner's manual when we want the machinery to work properly, much less well. For any men who want to know, try priming the pump if you want water! But be forewarned, it may take your wives a while to trust your sincerity, especially if you seldom have shown understanding.

Again, all this is about finding the balance.

Intimacy in Marriage

Man desiring sex only	(Balanced)	Woman desiring sharing only
(Off Balance)	Blend between sex	(Off Balance)
Little or no other communication	and other communication	Little or no sex
Woman feels hurt and used	Both have needs met	Man feels angry and resentful

In the meantime, how are our needs for true intimacy met, women? We need to realize that even if our husbands become better in this area, they can never give us all that we need. Only the Lord can. Once again, the Bible says, "And my God will meet all your needs according to his glorious riches in Christ Jesus" (Philippians 4:19). He is longing for us to go on walks on the beach or through flower-covered fields with Him, to have candlelit dinners, any quiet moments we crave and need. The following scriptures have given me a special sense of comfort and worth.

It says in Hosea 2:14–15, "Therefore I am now going to allure her, I will lead her into the desert and speak tenderly to her. There I will give her back her vineyards, and will make the Valley of Achor a door of hope. There she will sing as in the days of her youth, as in the day she came up out of Egypt. 'In that day,' declares the Lord, 'you will call me "my husband;" you will no longer call me "my master."'"

In Psalms 45:10-11, it says, "Listen, O daughter, consider and give ear: Forget your people and your father's house. The king is enthralled by your beauty; honor him, for he is your lord."

It is interesting to see the deep compassion Jesus had for the prostitute. He saw inside to the longing of her heart. All the sexual unions she had did not touch the pain and loneliness inside, the yearning for care and appreciation. The only need previously met was one of making a living. She saw, therefore, in Jesus, a true friend and her inmost desire, to be loved and valued, met. Most of all, she finally felt accepted as she was. Women, we have a Husband waiting, who is calling to each of us to come apart with Him and know true love, not a physical union, which can be disappointing, but a union of heart and soul with Someone always near who truly cares.

Lately there has been talk of men desiring respect from their wives, and women love from their husbands. The following scripture is quoted, "However, each one of you must love his wife as he loves himself, and the wife must respect her husband" (Ephesians 5:33). This book, however, was written by Paul, who was not married. Married Peter seems to have hit the target: "Husbands, in the same way be considerate as you live with your wives, and treat them with respect as the weaker partner and as heirs with you of the gracious gift of life, so that nothing will hinder your prayers" (1 Peter 3:7). The word *weaker* may anger women, but due to our emotions, men seem to view us as such. It would seem the Women's Lib Movement was more about seeking respect than love. The sixties involved both sexes seeking love. Women seem to have not only a need for love but also a deep need for respect, both for what we do and who we are, not merely devalued as sexual toys.

We see signs all around of this disrespect. Men call romantic movies chick flicks. A commercial shows a woman looking for the perfect valentine for her boyfriend, after which we see him buying a six-pack and, as an afterthought, flipping a card he did not even read onto the counter. Later, the girlfriend opens the card, touched by its words, believing her boyfriend cares.

We women want to be valued and cared about. That is the ultimate and underlying issue of the women's movement, but please, women, let us think of the results of trying to obtain that. (1) We have made it harder on ourselves by accepting more responsibility than the Lord intended. (2) We are hurting our most priceless blessings, our children, either through abortion or unintentional neglect. In essence, many men still show little respect to women. In fact, it has removed more responsibility from their shoulders of solely providing for their wives and children, both monetarily and time-wise. Women, in our anger, we have been shooting fiery darts that have boomeranged on us and our children.

As I finish this part concerning men and women, I will review the main point. Although I do not endorse the actions of the women's movement, I certainly do understand women's frustrations with men. Our society has created many insensitive and uncaring men, who view sex as sport and us women as conquests. No wonder there has been rebellion. We women know in our hearts that we are worth more than that, with a much higher purpose than to be used for men's gratification.

What do I believe is the Lord's answer to all this?

1. Men need to
   A. become more vulnerable, first to God and then to their wives, and
   B. become more sensitive to their wives, allowing them to share and listening with understanding and tenderness.

2. Women need to
   A. share less verbally with their husbands, as we have too much for one man alone, and

      B. allow the Lord to be our husband constantly, filling our unmet needs, and also to seek women friends with whom we can share.

It is only then, as our needs are met, that we will feel a closeness and tenderness to each other daily. There seems little hope for our society, as men seem reluctant to do their part. But various men's groups provide some encouragement. Although I know little about them, it is my prayer that they are teaching these foundational truths to men. It is essential if we want marriages to begin and last. More people are opting out, knowing the dissatisfaction in families they came from themselves.

In closing, the words one woman spoke when I was still out working are appropriate as an example of women's needs. It was Valentine's Day, and flowers were delivered to many in our office. When she did not receive any, she told me, "You know, my husband has never sent me flowers, but do you know, whenever I have been sick, he sits with me and waits on me, and you know, I would rather have that!" How profound are her words! All of us ladies like the candy, the flowers, and the perfume. But what do we really want? Tenderness when we are sick, tired, cranky, sad, and/or frustrated, to be sincerely loved and cared for. It is as Jesus said to the Pharisees, "But go and learn what this means. 'I desire mercy, not sacrifice'" (Matthew 9:13 a) and "You give a tenth of your spices—mint, dill, and cumin. But you have neglected the more important matters of the law—justice, mercy, and faithfulness. You should have practiced the latter without neglecting the former" (Matthew 23:23 b-d). "He who has ears, let him hear" (Matthew 11:15).

We all need to learn respect for ourselves and others once again. If all women respected themselves, seeing their worth in God's eyes, there would be no more pornography or prostitution. If men learned to find true love from God, they would not have those desires.

****

One last note. I need to add a final section that pertains to this: Although science is not inherently evil and has indeed brought much good to our world, it also has done a great injustice to us in some areas, promoting disrespect for all human life. Modern-day science has had a major effect upon our society. Theories, which are ages old, have now become accepted and taught as truth, even though they are labeled as theories, such as the big bang theory and Darwin's theory. These two ideas alone have had a profound influence upon our culture with three primary results:

1. Our values have become skewed with
    A. the riddance of the true God,
    B. the elevation of science to a level replacing God (they alone decide the value of life),
    C. the devaluation of human life, resulting in abortion and the desire to clone human life and the extreme animal rights movements.
    All three of the above have led to a major lack of respect to ourselves.

2. Death and grief have become minimized and even ignored. With the teachings of the absence of a Creator, the universe creating itself, the evolution of animals from fish (ever wonder how these originated?), the evolution of man from monkeys, there is little to look forward to in death. Science has no answers because they need evidence and proof, so they tend to ignore death. You will never find a dying person calling for a scientist; they can give no hope or comfort. That is why people who have ascribed to their teachings struggle even more when they lose a loved one.

3. Ours has become a society of instant gratification, no waiting.

If we base our beliefs on the scientific premises that there is no God and nothing after death, then we might as well get all we can now. "'Let us eat and drink,' you say, 'for tomorrow we die!'" (Isaiah 22:13b). "Take life easy; eat, drink and be merry" (Luke 12:19b, a favorite lie of the enemy from the beginning of time). So we find teenagers being taught that we are merely animals and that sex is natural. ("If it feels good, do it.") Even adults tend to believe this, amassing great material wealth (no matter how far into debt we become)—all to have it now.

Oh, that we could return to seeing our value from God's perspective, our worth in His eyes! We are worth much. "No man can redeem the life of another or give to God a ransom for him—the ransom for a life is costly, not payment is ever enough—that he should live on forever and not see decay" (Psalms 49:7–9). Although science has made positive and valuable contributions and has had a powerful role in our world, it has also brought a lack of respect to human life in some areas. I am reminded of the story of the Tower of Babel. The people then felt that they were in control, but God was truly in control. Likewise, today in some areas, science is playing with fire. They seem to be winning, but I am comforted, knowing our God is still in control—He has not left His throne. He wants each of us to know that we are special, unique creations, resulting from His deep love.

CHAPTER 10

The Upper West Room Or Freedom from Legalism

We stepped to the back of the room and, in the space between the two upstairs rooms, found another larger bay area, with a door to a small balcony, looking to the south and the amazing cliffs. It was wonderful having so many windows in my house, drawing all of nature nearer. We headed into the west room, an exact replica of the previous one, at least in its layout. The south wall was a bookcase, with the west wall containing a leather chair and a bed and bay window. Another fireplace was opposite the bed. Both rooms were cozy and inviting. This was the room that had previously been packed full of covered furniture. Now it was, like the other room, modestly decorated and so welcoming. Its walls were unique also, in that the plaster was embossed with butterflies that looked as if they were just emerging from the wall itself. They too had a rainbow effect, each enhanced with many different chalk colors. They seemed symbolic of freedom.

****

So if the Son sets you free, you will be free indeed.
John 8:36

This room in my house was in need of the Lord's extensive remodeling, much renovation. Having grown up in the Catholic Church, my beliefs were centered on God's acceptance being determined by my behavior and works. If I were only good enough and did good things, He would accept me—in other words, a tremendous compulsion for perfection. Because I never was, and never will be, perfect, I lived a good part of my life feeling distant from God, as if He would tolerate me as long as He did not have to see me or be around me, as He could not quite bear how much and how often I messed up. There seemed to be nothing I could do right, much less well.

One would have thought that becoming a born-again Christian would have brought a major upheaval of this viewpoint, and in some ways, it did. I came to accept that I had a place in heaven because of what Jesus did for me, His gift to me, but my daily living still reflected my old beliefs. Somehow, I realized Jesus's love for me, but the love of the Father was incomprehensible. He seemed distant and unconcerned except for when I failed. The sad part is that my day-to-day life manifested this, trying to become the best person I could, which meant trying to become like the Christians I saw at church, trying to change my personality to conform to theirs, a hopeless situation. I also berated myself for not doing the good they seemed so capable of doing with no real effort: praying aloud, being involved in social functions, and numerous other areas where I am definitely lacking, definitely inadequate. Although certain that Jesus loved me, I could never accept that the Father did. There was constant struggle as I attempted to live up to these high expectations.

It was not until the time of my spiritual college (fall of 1995–2003) that the truth began to come into focus. As I began to review my life with the Lord, I could see that my growth has most certainly been characterized by the Lord's amazing grace, which is to say that it has had nothing to do with what I am or do or what I have been or will be, have done or will do, but instead only what He has done for me. I have come to realize that all the Lord wants from me (us) is my (our) friendship. He does not want us trying to be good enough or striving to do great and wonderful things for Him. He is God—He can do all that Himself! What He *will not* do is make us love Him and desire to be with Him, which is His greatest desire! Is that not amazing? God's greatest desire, our friendship, is also our greatest need! Oh, but how Satan has tricked us! He wants us wasting our time and energy competing with one another in behavior and works, ultimately feuding because of it so that our eyes are on us and not on God. We are so busy in other areas, we often forget the Source; we do not spend time with our Lord, which breaks His tender heart.

In looking back on my Christian life, it is obvious that there has been little done on my part, but it is even more obvious that, through it all, Jesus has been my constant Friend and has somehow conveyed that so clearly that I have clung to Him and His friendship, even in my ignorance. I can also see amazing growth in my life from *His* doing, not mine.

Jeremiah 31:31–34 says, "'The time is coming,' declared the Lord, 'when I will make a new covenant with the house of Israel and with the house of Judah. It will not be like the covenant I made with their forefathers when I took them by the hand to lead them out of Egypt, because they broke my covenant, though I was a husband to them,' declares the Lord. 'This is the covenant I will make with the house of Israel after that time,' declares the Lord. 'I will put my law in their minds and write it on their hearts. I will be their God, and they will be my people. No longer will a man teach his neighbor, or a man his brother, saying, "Know the Lord," because they will all know me, from the least of them to the greatest,' declares the Lord. 'For I will forgive their wickedness and will remember their sins no more.'"

This is the new covenant He made with us. In the Old Testament, the people were living under the law, forever trying, by their own efforts, to be and do what the law demanded and forever fearful of punishment for their constant failures. But the Lord promised and did, indeed, bring this new covenant, in which He lives within us, so that His law is inside, enabling us to *want* to do His will. And when we fail, which we all (including us Christians) do and will continue to do, we feel sad, instead of fearful of His judgment. "There is no fear in love. But perfect love drives out fear, because fear has to do with punishment. The man who fears is not made perfect in love" (1 John 4:18). This sadness comes instead because we sincerely want to do what is right to please our Lord, our dearest Friend. I have come to realize that not only does the Lord not condemn us but He understands also, and not only does He understand but He expects us to fail. He knows that we are only human. "As a father has compassion on his children, so the Lord has compassion on those who fear him; for he knows how we are formed, he remembers that we are dust" (Psalms 103:13, 14).

Our trying to be perfect by our own efforts means that we are trying to be God, who alone is perfect. Surely, that is not His intent. Instead of focusing on that and condemning ourselves, He wants us focusing on our friendship with Him. Jesus's analogy was, "I am the vine; you are the branches. If a man remains in me and I in him, he will bear much fruit; apart from me you can do nothing" (John 15:5). If we stay close to Him, He produces the fruit. It is His work, not ours.

The only words of reproach that Jesus gave were to Pharisees, who were bound by legalism, not only to their man-made rituals, but also to the law itself, so much so that they condemned Jesus for healing on the Sabbath. They were so enamored with the letter of the law that they missed its purpose: to protect us from harm. Jesus called us to something different than their ways "and be found in him, not having a righteousness of my own that comes from the law, but that which is through faith in Christ—the righteousness that comes from God and is by faith" (Philippians 3:9).

The Pharisees felt proud of their works and position. They did not wish to lose any of it. But they missed the grandeur of the Son of God being among them, all because of that pride and fear and legalism! Pride enjoys telling others what to do and feeling more important than others and discounting them, at the same time boasting of its own accomplishments and expecting honor and praise. The Pharisees did not know humility, which is acknowledging our weaknesses, and our strengths, being honest about them. Only through humility do we see our need of God. Because of their high position, the Pharisees were also perfect judges, never understanding Jesus's words: "You hypocrite, first take the plank out of your own eye, and then you will see clearly to remove the speck from your brother's eye" (Matthew 7:5) and "I desire mercy, not sacrifice" (Matthew 9:13b).

An excerpt from *Streams in the Desert* has brought comfort to me. In my legalistic days, it probably would have made no sense, but it does now. In essence, it says it easier to obey all the rules than to endure suffering, to do many things than to totally give up, and to carry a heavy cross than to be nailed to it.[1] In the first cases—obeying, doing, and bearing the cross—self is glorified (pride). It is only when a person suffers and gives up, having to hang upon a painful and humiliating cross, that pride is destroyed. There is only humiliation, but with that come qualities our Lord has Himself and desires to see in us, those He commends: compassion, understanding, and lack of condemnation.

In the Bible, there are numerous examples of the difference between the legalistic person, who is working for His master, and the son, who is accepted and loved by His Father. The easiest to see, because we have been discussing it, is Jesus and the Pharisee. Jesus was working out of love for His Father and for the hurting people He encountered. The Pharisee, however, was motivated mostly out of pride and superiority to work for God, which was actually all for his own glory. Another closely related example, and actually an analogy of Jesus, involves Joseph and his brothers. Others include the prodigal son and his older brother and the story of Mary and Martha. In each of the cases, the second set of people was working to be accepted (the Pharisees, Joseph's brothers, the prodigal's brother, and

Martha). Because they were working hard, self and pride ended up being most evident, along with resentment, jealousy, and judgment toward the first set, who seemed to be doing nothing. They felt that they should be commended for all their hard work while the others did nothing. The difference is in the relationship. The first group had a relationship, so they were no longer working for their masters. They were instead accepted as sons, no longer slaves. "So you are no longer a slave, but a son; and since you are a son, God has made you also an heir" (Galatians 4:7). Looking from the point of view of the accepted son (Jesus, Joseph, the prodigal son, and Mary), he had nothing to brag about except what his father had done for him. Jesus constantly acknowledged His Father. His acceptance came from His close relationship with His Father. Therefore, He was not striving to be good enough or to do amazing things. That was His Father's job, which was accomplished through Him. Once again, the balance can clearly be seen below.

Good Works/Self-Improvement

Good results	Bad results
(Off Balance)	(Off Balance)
Self in forefront	Self in forefront
Self is glorified	Self is downcast

Living in the Vine
(Balanced)
Following Jesus daily
God is glorified

The above has been my experience also. I have been abiding in the vine, and He has been doing the work. I rest in Him and cultivate my friendship with Him. He does the rest, so it has become what the Lord has done for me, not what I have done for Him, so that "no one can boast" (Ephesians 2:9b). Most often He works by promises, providing His words to me. Then I wait, resting and spending time with Him, until the fulfillment of the promises has arrived.

The Old Testament was about the law, rules, and punishment. But God dealt differently with certain people who He had relationships with, like Noah, Abraham and Sarah, Jacob, Joseph, Moses, David and his family, Hannah, Mary, and the prophets. They all had a relationship with Him, in which He made promises to them and they believed Him and trusted Him to do what He said He would. In Galatians 3:6, it says, "Consider Abraham: 'He believed God, and it was credited to him as righteousness.'" That is how we are supposed to live now, in New Testament times, in relationship with Jesus, talking to Him, being in His Presence, listening to Him, and believing what He speaks. To all the people above who were His friends, He revealed what their future would be, and they believed Him and waited and trusted Him to do what He said knowing it was His work and not theirs. Their work was only to believe Him and wait for Him to do as He had said. That is what it means in John 6:29 when Jesus says, "The work of God is this: to believe in the one he has sent." We do not have to feel the burden of trying to do everything right. That is not what He wants or even expects from us. He does not say we should not sin but "if we confess our sins, he is faithful and just and will forgive us our sins and purify us from all unrighteousness" (1 John 1:9), and "therefore, there is now no condemnation for those who are in Christ Jesus" (Romans 8:1). Our righteousness and everything else come from Him alone and our being in relationship with Him.

The Lord provided a good example of this with Eric. When Eric was in fifth grade, I stood by his bedroom door one day while he was in school, and I was angry once again because his room was such a mess. But as I stood there, I felt like the Lord said, "Do you want a clean room or a relationship with Eric?" That spoke volumes, and after that, I stopped bugging Eric about his room and left it instead with the Lord, who brought teachers to tell him later about the messiness, which he seemed to take better from them. But the best part was the change I saw in Eric. We became closer to each other, and once I stopped pushing him, he became more willing to do what I wanted him to because it was what he wanted. It was out of love, not being forced. The people in the Old Testament knew they could not obey all the rules, and eventually they rebelled. That is what Eric was doing to me all the years before my change the day in his bedroom, rebelling because he felt pressured, knowing he could not please me. The way I first dealt with him was like the Old Testament, but the change was like the new, being in relationship, not having to be good enough or to work to be accepted. In the same way, Jesus living in us and having a relationship with us makes us want to obey because we love Him and He is inside making us what we should be. And He knows we are going to mess up out of our humanness, but He promises to forgive us.

Galatians reinforces this. It retells the story of Abraham and Sarah. God gave them a promise, but when it was not fulfilled in the time they thought it would be, they surmised it may come through Sarah's maidservant, Hagar. Satan tricked them like he did Adam and Eve when he asked Eve, "Did God really say?" (Genesis 3:1b). And he does that to us too. They thought they had misunderstood, but they really had not. The Lord's promise was to Abraham and Sarah. Paul explains all that in Galatians 4:21-31, saying that we are to be like Sarah, who was in covenant relationship with Abraham, not like Hagar, who was under the rules of the servant, a slave, not free, like Sarah. The promise came through the free wife.

In not understanding all the above, I have been like the servant in the story in Matthew 18:21-35, who was totally forgiven by his master, but then went and demanded that someone who owed him little pay him back and had him put in jail when he was unable. I think the servant felt obligated to his master, not realizing that his debt was totally paid, and so he was still working to repay him. Yet in truth, he did not owe his master anything, and neither do we. He only wants us to be His friend, which takes away all condemnation and makes it easier for us to treat others with the same grace.

The Lord wants us to realize this and not seek to be good enough. We simply need to be in relationship with Him, and He does the work as we trust Him. "But seek first his kingdom and his righteousness, and all these things will be given to you as well" (Matthew 6:33). It took me a long time to understand that all that saves me for eternal life is believing Jesus died for me—faith. It has taken me even longer to comprehend "walking by faith." It is being close to Him and letting Him take care of everything else. He merely wants our friendship, which brings freedom. I never understood the scripture, "Take my yoke upon you, and learn from me, for I am gentle and humble in heart, and you will find rest for your souls. For my yoke is easy and my burden is light" (Matthew 11:29–30). When we live in His Presence and talk to Him and listen to Him, there is no pressure. It is when we are living by the past and other rules we are bound up. All we need is Him, and the more time we spend with Him, He can work to change us and make us what we should be. It is His work, not ours. Also, the more time we spend in His Presence, the better we can hear His voice, because He does speak to all of us. John 10:27 says, "My sheep listen to my voice; I know them, and they follow me." He wants to show each of us, like Abraham and the others above, the plans He has for our future.

No wonder this is good news. We do not have to attempt to be good enough or to work to attain approval. Instead, we cultivate our friendship with Jesus. We are already good enough because of what He has done: His death for us. And He lives within us, "for it is God who works in you to will and to act according to his good purpose" (Philippians 2:13). He does the work, not us! "So if the Son sets you free, you will be free indeed" (John 8:36).

In conclusion, I want to add a note about the law. To better understand why it was given in the first place, Galatians 3:15–25 provides many answers. Ultimately, Paul says that the law was given to lead us to Christ (verse 24): "So the law was put in charge to lead us to Christ that we might be justified by faith." As we come to realize that we are unable to obey the law, we then begin to see our need of a Savior. In Old Testament days, the prophets spoke of a Messiah coming to save the people. In fact, even now, devout Jews are waiting for this Messiah, not realizing that Jesus was the fulfillment of the prophecies, the promises. They were and are looking forward to that. So the law basically was given to show us our need of a Savior.

Are there any other reasons that the law was given? After Adam and Eve sinned, the Lord eventually sent the Ten Commandments because He wanted to reveal to us the traps Satan had set so we could avoid them. But He knew that we, like the Israelites, would continue to fall for the ultimate trap, believing the lie that God is trying to keep something good from us. Even if we do not fall for that trap, we will still sin because we are all impatient and unloving at times.

At this point, I want to add that as a parent, I can understand this other purpose for the law. The rules we parents have for our children are to protect them. They are not to deny them access to something fun, as Satan, from the beginning of time, has made us believe. Which parent is more loving? The one who allows all, even at the expense of the child's welfare, only to look good to the child? Or the one who sets limits to protect his child, even at the expense of looking bad in the eyes of the child? God's heart in giving the laws at the beginning was to guard His children from the traps Satan set to bind us. I did not tell my young kids not to play in the street because I was mean or wanted to keep them from having fun. My ultimate reason was to protect them from the dangers there. God's heart of love wants to protect us from getting hurt. I have sinned enough in my own life to know exactly how the trap works. At first, sins are appealing and fun, but eventually they hook us, and somehow the good times disappear, being replaced by increasing pain. All sin is like this. "Jesus replied, 'I tell you the truth, everyone who sins is a slave to sin'" (John 8:34). That is why the Lord hates sin: because sin harms us, His creation. Seeing it in this light takes away any condemnation we might feel toward others caught in traps: drugs, alcohol, pornography, and homosexuality, whatever it may be. God's heart hurts for us when we are caught in traps. He has called us to something better. Jesus said that he came not to abolish the law but to fulfill it (Matthew 5:17) through the new way of the Spirit, not the old way of written code. This is only accomplished by His living within us, helping us to be and do what He desires, His will. Rebelling against the Lord makes no sense when we understand that He died for us. He is on our side.

At this point, some may ask, "Will some not take this knowledge and abuse it? Will this not give them license to sin and/or do nothing?" To this, I reply, "Of course, but we have to remember that those who would take license have already been driving without one." Jesus is much more concerned with the humble, who are hurting and honestly need this truth and its subsequent comfort.

Our enemy loves legalism because it binds up the individual and causes division in the church. It is a tactic he has used forever within the church. We begin in grace, but then we begin to feel the need to improve ourselves, both in behavior and performance. It is the story of Peter walking on the water. He began trusting the Lord, but then felt he had to somehow keep himself up. That is when he sank. We need to learn to live with the Lord, allowing Him to change us and guide us in what He wants us to do, trusting Him to do that very work through us. And always remember, the Lord is not working on us to make us perfect but, instead, loving.

I have come to realize that my name, which sounds flowery, is not a coincidence. The Lord has been teaching me to "consider the lilies ..." "And why do you worry about clothes? See how the lilies of the field grow. They do not labor or spin. Yet I tell you that not even Solomon in all his splendor was dressed like one of these" (Matthew 6:28-29). My life is His example of living by grace, undeserved favor, resulting in blessing. I am forever thankful to Him, our loving Gardener.

****

Understanding the Word of God

Now we see but a poor reflection; then we shall see face-to-face.
Now I know in part; then I shall know
fully, even as I am fully known.

—1 Corinthians 13:12

When we first become Christians, we are often encouraged to begin reading the Bible. It was eye-opening, with the revelation of many truths new to me. But there were also scriptures and stories that did not make sense to me, and honestly, some still do not. But I have found that, with the removal of the blinders of legalism from my eyes, many are no longer confusing.

Also, as the years have passed, I have grown in the Lord and had many experiences, through which I have come to understand the difference between head knowledge and heart knowledge. We can read and even memorize many scriptures and yet never have them bring life to us. We are only gaining head knowledge or intellect, which does not stay with us. But when the Holy Spirit speaks through the scriptures and our experiences, it becomes heart knowledge, something we comprehend deep within us, which has become part of us and is not easily forgotten. It has a profound and lasting effect. This has definitely been my experience. At certain times in my Christian life, I determinedly tried to memorize many scriptures. Most of them are long forgotten. In contrast, those I learned during trying experiences are deeply engraved upon my heart, never to be forgotten. I may not know the exact location, but Jesus, our example, did not give that information when He was refuting Satan (Luke 4), but only the quote itself. The enemy already knows it is truth. A good analogy is book learning in school. It is helpful but never makes total sense until a person gets to lab. Also, with head knowledge alone, we never learn compassion.

It seems that often the greatest times of experiencing true insight come as we experience hardship in our lives. Our weakness and total dependence upon God bring revelation of many misunderstood scriptures. I have found that when I sincerely bring my questions to the Lord, He always answers, although it may not be right away. Sometimes, the truth cannot come until we have gone through certain experiences, and the Lord does not explain because we are not yet ready. We need the lab time first. Another thing to remember is that we should never anticipate His answers, as they are often very different than we have imagined, and never condemning, as we often fear. I have recorded some scriptures and stories that have caused me the most confusion and guilt below.

1. The story of the woman caught in adultery (John 8:1–11). The Pharisees brought her to be stoned. Jesus's reply was, "If any one of you is without sin, let him be the first to throw a stone at her" (verse 7). Of course, they all had to leave. The part that brought confusion to me was when Jesus told the woman, "Go now and leave your life of sin" (verse 11).

2. The story of the man Jesus healed in John 5:1–15. After his healing, Jesus also told him something similar: "Stop sinning or something worse may happen to you" (verse 14).

3. The story of the rich man asking Jesus what he needed to do in order to get to heaven (Mark 10:17–21). Jesus was pleased with him for doing the things He mentioned. But He gave him one more requirement: to go and sell all his belongings (verse 21).

4. When Jesus admonished us to "be perfect, therefore, even as your heavenly Father is perfect" (Matthew 5:48).

All the above produced tremendous guilt and fear inside me as I realized I still sin even as a Christian (if you can imagine). And I have felt guilty over material possessions after reading the story of the rich man. As the Lord began breaking legalism from my mind, a new, different meaning began to emerge. In all these instances, Jesus was desiring and prompting each person to see his/her need of

Him. His intention was to illicit their honesty: "Oh, Lord, I want to change, to do what You say, but I am unable." The law was set up to bring us to Jesus, to help us to see that we cannot live this life by ourselves. We all need Jesus. He wanted the woman, who I have always assumed to be a prostitute, to be able to confess to Him privately, "Honestly, this is how I make my living. How will I survive?" I believe He was also waiting for the healed man and the rich man to say, "I want to do what You say, but I am unable." He wanted them to see their need of Him.

Another source of fear and confusion for many involves the unpardonable sin. After struggling with that many years ago, I read a book *The Holy Spirit* by Billy Graham. His explanation was that this sin is actually rejecting Jesus, which is blaspheming the Holy Spirit. He pointed out that if someone is troubled with fears regarding a sin he has committed, that in itself shows he has not committed the unpardonable sin. If he had, he would know no remorse.[2] That is good to understand, as it seems to be one of the enemy's recurrent tactics in our lives.

Often alcohol has been a source of controversy in the church. The fact that Jesus turned the water into wine (not grape juice) at the wedding (John 2:1–11) would seem to show His approval. For me, it has never been a problem when others have a glass of beer or wine occasionally. Personally, I do not drink at all, because my last time, I became so sick that there has been no further desire for any alcohol. "Doing all in moderation" seems to be the key. For some, alcohol, gambling, etc., can quickly become an addiction, a trap that can have devastating results for both the addicted and their families also. Having recently toured a beer manufacturing plant and hearing the amount of beer that company alone produces in a year, it surely seems there may be a genuine problem with addiction. Having heard of the trials this can bring, it seems an area for which caution is necessary. Perhaps that is why the Lord took away my desires for it.

Water baptism is another area of contention and division. Yet few baptisms are biblical. In the New Testament, adults were baptized in rivers and lakes, the intent being that it was a public display of a changed heart. It benefited both believers and nonbelievers. The Lord says that, if we are going to follow the law, we must follow the whole law. "For whoever keeps the whole law and yet stumbles at just one point is guilty of breaking all of it" (James 2:10).

One of many areas in which I have struggled with guilt is concerning tithing. Being a homemaker and never having been able to give the 10 percent mentioned in the Old Testament, I have taken my concern to the Lord many times. Finally, He began to show me I should instead tithe my time with Him each day. It made sense, as the old saying goes, "Time is money." I now feel that the Lord did this to squelch my feelings of guilt. I know that He is not worried so much about the tithe of money or time as much as our surrendered lives for Him to use each day, our willingness to be vessels for His use. But I also realize that many churches and nonprofit organizations are dependent upon help from all of us, especially with the economy as it is now. We have tried through the years to give what little we were able, trusting the Lord to multiply it.

The following scripture too can bring similar feelings of guilt and unworthiness: "If anyone loves me, he will obey my teaching" (John 14:23a). I have come to see the true meaning of this. It does not mean if we really love Him, we will make ourselves obey Him. Nor does it mean if we obey Him, then it proves that we love Him. I believe it means if we truly love Him, we will be obeying Him as the natural consequence of the loving.

The Lord took much condemnation away from me regarding Halloween. Because our kids attended public schools throughout their education, this holiday has provoked a great deal of stress within me as it seems to embody much evil, of which I do not agree. Yet it is the only time of year that kids can dress up, and they always enjoy the treats. The Lord helped me see what my response should be through a different situation that happened one winter. Sarabeth had bought me a special necklace for Christmas. It happens to be a red cross, of which I had been reading. Although its meaning to some may be evil, God showed me that He brought it to me for good. Not only is it treasured because it is from Sarabeth, but it also has our family embodied within it. Lengthwise, there are three dots at the top and three at the bottom, denoting the Father, Son, and Holy Spirit in heaven and our three children. The crossbar has two dots on either side, denoting Gordon and me and Eric and Sarabeth. In the center of the cross is a flower, exactly like the one on my Black Hills Gold family ring, our family, six outside dot petals and one inside—seven of us! The Lord showed me that what the devil intended to be used for evil, for his glory, was instead turned to something the Lord used for good. I also picked out a black fleece jacket at Christmas as a gift from Gordon. Once home, I noticed it had a red dragon on the inside of it, another symbol of evil. Once again, the Lord showed me that He brought it to me for good, not evil. In the same way, the Lord delights when we substitute good instead of evil at Halloween time, not just fleeing from the evil, but standing up to it with good. He wants to take things the devil has used for his own glory and turn them around for His glory and praise. Once again, there is a balance. "And we know that in all things God works for the good of those who love him, who have been called according to his purpose" (Romans 8:28).

Response to Evil

Accepting evil, being part of it	Fleeing evil, fearful of it
(Off Balance)	(Off Balance)
Results in glorifying Satan	Results in glorifying Satan

Challenging evil
(Balanced)
Participating in a godly way
Results in taking the land of the enemy
For our own to the glory of God

This brings up another point. As Christians, we are often encouraged to give glory to God in our lives. I think what it means is often misunderstood. Although God is high above us and deserving of our love and praise, He is not an egotistical dictator demanding it. Instead, the act of giving Him glory and honor is really us passing on the good news to others, inviting them to know His great love also, a blessing for all of us.

Another parable that has brought fear into my heart is the story of the virgins, which is supposed to be consoling (Matthew 25:1–13). Jesus told the parable of ten virgins with their lamps of oil waiting for the bridegroom to come. Five of them were prepared, with oil in their lamps, and five were not. When the latter ran out of oil, they asked the first five to share but were told instead to go to buy more. In the meantime, the bridegroom came, taking the remaining virgins inside and shutting the door. When the others returned, they were not admitted; it was too late. This story always brought fear to me, wondering if I would not be ready and, consequently, left out. But I now find it encouraging as I view it without the lens of legalism.

What Jesus was saying is that we need to be as the first virgins, with perpetual oil in our lamps. How do we attain this oil? It is placed within us when Jesus's Holy Spirit comes to live within us. Like the woman in the Old Testament story (1 Kings 17:7–16) whose pot of oil never ran dry, we are the same. Once the Holy Spirit lives within us, we will never run dry. What were the virgins doing? The same as we are, holding their lamps filled with oil and waiting for the Bridegroom's return! Our job is to be holding the Spirit of the Lord within us and to be looking for Jesus's return. Those were the faithful virgins. Jesus did not say that they were out doing many great works for Him. Instead, they were holding their lamps, naturally giving out heat and light to themselves and others, because of the *oil* within their lamps, as they were faithfully anticipating the bridegroom's arrival. The others had to buy their oil and were not prepared when the bridegroom arrived. I have always wondered what would have happened if the last five had arrived in time. The answer is given in Matthew 22:11–13, another story of a wedding banquet. In this story, one guest was found to be without wedding clothes and put out. That person without wedding clothes is someone who snuck into the party, dishonestly or by his own works (oil that was bought). Paul says, "For all of you who were baptized into Christ have clothed yourselves with Christ" (Galatians 3:27). So He is our wedding garment. We have both oil and wedding garments when the Lord is living inside of us, and we need to wait in anticipation for His return.

The parable following the oil one was upsetting to me as well. In Matthew 25:14–30, Jesus tells the story of three servants, each given talents by their master before he left on a journey. When he returned, he sought each one to see what they had done with their talents. Two had doubled their talents and had profits to give to their master. The third came in ashamedly, saying he knew his master to be hard, so he hid his talent and was now returning it. The master then became angry, responding that the man should have at least put his money on deposit with the bank to earn interest. The master afterward had him thrown out of his house.

Well, if you are anything like me, that is a tough story. I always wanted to identify with the first two, the faithful men, who produced more for their master, but most always felt like the last man, who hid his talent, so I feared God's displeasure and punishment. That was while legalism's harsh dictates were binding me. Now with the Lord's help, I understand. We are all given talents at birth, work that the Lord puts within us to fulfill in our lives. But we can never accomplish it alone. Jesus said, "I am the vine; you are the branches. If a man remains in me and I in him, he will bear much fruit; apart from me, you can do nothing" (John 15:5). Our part is to put our talents on deposit at the bank, which means to give our lives back to God for His use, to ask Him to come within us and work through us. That is the first step: to deposit our money. Then the bank uses our money to make more money. That is how it works with the Lord also. We give our talents to Him, and He takes them and multiplies them to produce more, just like the bank. But of course, the Lord is not concerned about money. He owns everything; He has no need for money. He is concerned about lives. He wants to live within us to do the work to produce other believers.

I believe the first two not only deposited their money in the bank to multiply but also attained wisdom to multiply it as opportunities arose. With God living in us, the same thing happens. As time goes on, He leads us to invest our talents too. Once they are in His hands, they will multiply because He is the vine. "Now it is God who makes both us and you stand firm in Christ. He anointed us, set his seal of ownership on us, and put his Spirit in our hearts as a deposit, guaranteeing what is to come" (2 Corinthians 1:21–22). "Now it is God who has made us for this very purpose and has given us the Spirit as a deposit, guaranteeing what is to come" (2 Corinthians 5:5). "Having believed, you were marked in him with a seal, the promised Holy Spirit, who is a deposit guaranteeing our inheritance until the redemption of those who are God's possession—to the praise of his glory" (Ephesians 1:13b–14).

J. R. R. Tolkien's series of books *The Lord of the Rings*[3] resurfaced to the forefront once again, with the release of the three movies.[4] To me, this story is a much longer version of the above parable. My first encounter with these books was during my freshman year of college. I fell in love with the story immediately and bought and read it many times afterward. But I have to admit that I never did see any kind of correlations in it until lately when my mind was once again refreshed with the story. After such a long time, I had forgotten many details. It was also before I became a Christian. The most impressive part, however, has been the significance of the story to each of our lives. Whether the author intended it, there seem to be many analogies to life. Knowing that he was also a Christian, I have to believe these were intended. I have recorded my observations below.

For those who know nothing of the story, I will give a brief account. There is a prelude book to the series entitled *The Hobbit*, which is the story of a creature called a hobbit living in the days of dwarves, elves, men, and wizards. He lives in a quiet and peaceful land with no excitement. Then he meets Gandalf, a wizard, and his life becomes much more exciting than he ever imagined or desired as he is chosen for an important mission: to help thirteen dwarves recover treasure stolen from them by a dragon. Bilbo, the hobbit, although reluctant, makes the journey and in fact proves quite brave and resourceful.[5] His journey is the introduction to the major story, *The Lord of the Rings*.

The key element in the story is that on his journey Bilbo finds a ring, a magic ring, that makes him invisible and helps him immensely in the quest for the dwarves' treasure. When his adventure is over, Bilbo treasures his keepsake at home in his little quiet hobbit hole. As we are to discover later, this ring is an evil ring. In the very beginning of time, rings of power were forged: three for the elves, seven for dwarves, and nine for men. But another ring was forged by Sauron, a powerful and evil being, to control all the other rings. The truth is finally discovered by Gandalf that this ring Bilbo found is actually the one ring. On Bilbo's 111th birthday, before a big celebration, he voices his intentions of going away. Before leaving, however, he reluctantly (with the urging of Gandalf) leaves the ring behind to his nephew Frodo. Later as Gandalf researches the one ring and finds out the truth about Bilbo's ring, he returns, urging Frodo to leave the Shire, his homeland, as news of the ring's whereabouts has reached Sauron, who has been searching for it for a long while. He has sent out his nine evil ring wraiths, the original nine men who had been given rings of power, now being totally controlled by their master, Sauron.

From the beginning of the journey, Frodo encounters danger but finally arrives with three hobbit friends and a newly made friend, Strider, at the house of Elrond, an important and wise elf. Here an urgent council is held to decide the fate of the ring, which cannot return to its master without fatal consequences: the loss of all their lands and freedom and the conquering of their home of Middle Earth. The fate of the ring is decided then as two men, a dwarf, an elf, four hobbits, and Gandalf unite on a quest to destroy the ring, the only way of which is to take it to Mount Doom, in the land of Mordor, Sauron's home, and cast it into the fire where it was originally forged.

As they begin their journey, with Frodo as the ring bearer, the power of the ring is strong. He is often tempted to put it on, which is unwise, as it pulls its evil master and his servants to him. Also on the quest, it becomes obvious that many others desire to obtain the ring, believing that they themselves can use it for good instead of evil. But because it has been forged by Sauron, it cannot be used by any without the eventual result being evil. At the end of the first book (movie), the fellowship is broken, with Frodo and his best friend, Sam, alone on the journey to destroy the ring.

For me, there is a striking analogy to life and our Christian lives in this story. I believe that we are all Frodos, each with a plan for our lives, given to us at birth by God. And we are the only ones who will be able to perform that particular purpose. Frodo does not understand his purpose until he meets with Gandalf. Eventually he comes to understand that he is to destroy the ring of power that has come to him, an arduous task as it turns out. In his travels, not only is he often tempted to use the ring himself, which can lead to his destruction, but he also has to deal with others who desire the ring and are drawn to it. We, who have come to the Lord and have Him living in us, also eventually become aware of the plan He has for us, which is essentially the same as Frodo, to destroy the ring of power in our own lives and follow the Lord instead. On our journey to do what the Lord has shown us, what He originally put into our hearts, we are essentially on the quest to destroy the ring of power each of us possesses. It was passed to us after the fall of Adam and Eve, an unwelcome gift from Satan: the desire to have power and control, both our own lives and others.

With Adam's and Eve's disobedience to God and their subsequent eating from the tree of knowledge of good and evil came this desire to be in control, the notion that we know what is best for our own lives and others' as well. That is the ultimate battle raging around us. And like Frodo, those of us who are following the Lord are sometimes tempted to wear the ring ourselves, which means going our own way instead of the Lord's way. As we follow the Lord, as Frodo followed Gandalf's advice, we are in the process of destroying the ring, not yielding to its power to control. And we continue on, facing all the hardships on the way and trusting the Lord to bring us eventually to the Mount of Doom, where the ring of power will be destroyed. "For our struggle is not against flesh and blood, but against rulers, against the authorities, against the powers of this dark world and against the spiritual forces of evil in the heavenly realms" (Ephesians 6:12).

Those who do not desire the Lord in their lives use their rings constantly, pushing to control their own lives and those of others, never realizing that they are essentially giving their power and glory to Satan. We cannot be neutral in this battle on earth. We either choose to go our own way, using the ring and letting Satan control our lives or we choose to give our lives to Jesus, which begins the journey to destroy the ring that desires to be back with its master and to trap and bind us.

It is sad to see those who reject the Lord, who fail to realize the best course for them is to follow Him. He created us and knows each of us individually and the purposes He has for our lives. He alone knows the best way to take each one of us to attain our hearts' desires, some of which we do not even realize are there.

In planning for high school graduation, Eric's and Sara's classes were asked to pick favorite teachers to participate in both baccalaureate and graduation. It was interesting to listen to each of them as they shared. Most related that it is important to find your passion and put your heart into doing that. They are proof it works! To me, this means finding what the Lord implanted in us at birth. Some seem to know right away; for others, it takes a while. Once we know, however, we will be most fulfilled as we allow the Lord to work through us in that particular area to help others. (Good resource: *The Dream Giver* by Bruce Wilkinson.)[6]

The Lord is on our side! Satan has always been a deceiver, trying to blind us to that truth and encouraging us instead to choose our own way, his trap. We need to follow Frodo's example, going the way Gandalf revealed and eventually destroying the ring, though the way was difficult. "A righteous man may have many troubles, but the Lord delivers him from them all" (Psalms 34:19). We do that when we ask Jesus to forgive our sins and come to live within us, following Him daily, this instead of following our own whims, which are only ruses of the enemy. Following the Lord will ultimately bring His very best and comfort on the journey as He never leaves us. He alone can show us the desires of our hearts and fulfill those: "Delight thyself in the Lord, and He will give thee the desires of your heart" (Psalms 37:4). "For we are God's workmanship, created in Christ Jesus to do good works, which God prepared in advance for us to do" (Ephesians 2:10).

I am thankful to the Lord for the insights He has given. It is always best to ask Him as He is faithful to respond at the right time, His words full of understanding and compassion!

CHAPTER 11

The Shower Room Or Emotions—Mental Output

U nderneath each stairwell were short halls leading to the rest of the house. On the left (or east) side, the hall opened to small rooms on either side, now hidden behind closed doors. Never having seen these before they were remodeled, I was curious to see them now. Opening the east door exposed a big walk-in shower, with benches around it, three sides of frosted glass, while the fourth, looking outside, was clear (the outside glass resembling the stone on the house) so that the lovely view of the stream, bench, and sunken garden were evident. Since these windows faced east, the morning sun filled the room with light. What a refreshing place!

****

Trust in him at all times, O people; pour out
your hearts to him, for God is our refuge.
—Psalms 62:8

For a long time after Sarabeth began experiencing stomach problems, I condemned myself, convinced the cause was weak faith at the beginning of my pregnancy. Since then, the Lord has brought a clearer understanding. He reminded me that we need only have faith as big as a tiny mustard seed; so, although my faith was weak, I did believe the promise, even if trying to help some myself.

I have since come to realize that the Lord had a lesson in mind, a lesson regarding emotions. He helped me to understand the analogy between our physical digestive system and our mental system, which He made to be very similar. Just as we eat and drink and our stomachs and bowels digest the food and liquid, in the same way, our minds take in food daily through our senses: seeing, hearing, tasting, feeling, and smelling. All the input to our senses is digested by our brains. As with food digestion, there is then an output. The output from mental digestion is what we call emotions. Whatever we see, hear, taste, feel, or smell is input into our brains and produces an emotion: anger, guilt, happiness, sadness, fear, hurt, embarrassment, and many others. As with physical digestion, we can also experience problems with mental digestion. Perhaps that is why Paul encouraged us to "take every thought captive to make it obedient to Christ" (2 Corinthians 10:5b). In other words, he is saying to watch what you eat mentally. Two of the most obvious problems in physical digestion are constipation and diarrhea. Neither are normal long-term, and both can be debilitating and may even be indications of more serious health problems.

The Lord began to show me, through this, that if we try to ignore our emotions and hide them (or stuff them), as I did as a child, we will eventually become extremely constipated. Anyone familiar with chronic physical constipation knows how it affects every area of a person's life. It becomes extremely limiting, with much pain and struggling every day, a helpless situation.

In the same way, we cannot ignore the output from our minds, our emotions. We have to express them in some way. Otherwise, we become constipated not only in pain ourselves but also a source of great concern to others. Men especially seem prone to this. In our society, they have been taught to be tough, to be able to take anything, to be macho. They have forgotten gentleness and think crying is for women only, but Jesus cried, showing compassion. It does not show lack of strength but instead great strength. This macho attitude can eventually lead men to hurt others and/or themselves, after holding in years of emotions, finally erupting like a volcano.

It is also true that once a person has been constipated for a long while, the process to clean him out is long and painful, definitely difficult for the person and those surrounding him. In the same way, after an extended time of suppressing emotions, it can be a long and not easy process for a counselor to help a person become cleaned out.

What is the answer? Physically, to become regular and to remain so with diet and/or medication, so as to never be in a position where bowel movements occur any longer than two days apart. That also is the answer regarding mental output problems. The emotions need to come out regularly, to be expressed in a positive way. Like physical output, it is a private and personal part of our lives. I believe the Lord is the best one to pour out our hearts to because He sympathizes and does not condemn. Plus, we can put those emotions and our problems and/or worries into His hands, knowing He will deal with them in the best way. That is most likely the reason Jesus often went off alone, to pray, pouring out His heart, His emotions, to His kind and loving Father. That was His example, one we should try to follow every day.

The opposite end of this same spectrum is another digestive problem, diarrhea. This is an equally distressing experience. Another illustration comes to mind regarding this area also. When something drastic happens in our lives, there is much unacceptable input into our brains and, therefore, much output. Often, especially during the first year or so, we have little control over that output, those emotions. It is the mental equivalent to physical diarrhea. When a person has this problem, he has no desire to be in public and should not be. It is not only an uncomfortable situation for him but also for those he encounters, who often do not know how to respond. Their question "How are you doing?" may be only a greeting and not a sincere desire to know. As I look back upon my grief years, I now know that one of my biggest mistakes was continuing to attend cell group and even weekly church. When a person has diarrhea, the *best* thing for him to do is to stay close to home, which is usually his desire also, a desire that is best heeded. He needs to be home. Others will not understand his lack of control in public, especially those who have never experienced the problem themselves. If anything, he needs one or two close friends to be with him to help, especially when he has accidents. The other possibility is a group of people who are experiencing or have experienced this problem themselves. They can be a source of understanding and encouragement, like the leper colony. Being out in other groups at that time seems unwise as a wounded person is extremely vulnerable to hurtful comments, misunderstanding, and judgment. This person also needs to turn away from those who come to help but have ulterior motives. As a wounded person, he does not need further pain.

Job is a great example. His friends came with words of "comfort and wisdom." Unfortunately, they were not good comforters and, in fact, ended up hurting him more. We need to protect ourselves, being in an unsafe place already. The Lord can provide comforters, and He will. He did for me. And lest we forget, He is the best Comforter of all and will stay through all our bouts of diarrhea. "When my heart was grieved and my spirit embittered, I was senseless and ignorant; I was a brute beast before you" (Psalms 73:21-22). "Then Job replied: 'If only my anguish could be weighed and all my misery be placed on the scales! It would surely outweigh the sand of the seas—no wonder my words have been impetuous'" (Job 6:1–3).

Many grieving people have shared reluctance about attending church at first and on significant days, feeling the need to be alone. I too have known that feeling and should have heeded it more. At that time, however, I was so bound by legalism I could not miss. It was difficult to be in public at those times, however, especially for an already introverted me. Even going to the store can be trying for the grieving as certain foods, songs on the intercom, or people may engender painful memories. We need to heed the voice inside beckoning us to be alone, away from crowds. In her book *To Help You Through the Hurting*, Marjorie Holmes prays for the Lord to help her not to wear her feelings on her sleeve.[1] Although not comprehending her meaning at the time I read the book, in the middle of grief, I have since come to understand. Because it is difficult *not* to have our feelings come out for a long time, I believe it is best to avoid the public, instead confiding in close friends and especially the Lord.

Another analogy from this regards shock. When something drastic happens, either physically or mentally, we feel no desire for food (physical input) and/or any mental input. In fact, our bodies and minds cannot take in anymore and will reject it. When Matthew died, Gordon and I, normally big eaters, had no desire for food for twenty-four hours. In the same way, for many months, our minds could not accept the input that kept coming, "Our child is dead." With both miscarriages, there was no feeling of shock, probably because pregnancy had always frightened me, and after the first miscarriage, every subsequent pregnancy, up to and including the last, was a challenge. However, once Eric and Matthew had arrived, I had no further fears of them leaving us. So Matthew's death was an extreme shock. My mind continually returned to finding him in his crib. I wondered why until our Compassionate Friends' leader shared that it was a reality check. My mind could not accept the input. "It cannot be. It must be a dream." In fact, it seems that dreams must be the invention of a kind Lord, providing a cushion when something terrible does happen. We can always hope for a while that we are going to wake up. Finally, however, after the horrible memory continues to bombard our minds, we reluctantly begin to accept its truth and to hurt terribly. Without the initial cushion, we would probably literally die on the spot from the intensity of the pain.

When the unbelievable terrorist attacks occurred in September of 2001, the television news repeatedly showed the scenes they had captured on film. It was difficult watching the footage, knowing that many people had died. Since then I have come to realize that it was a reality check for all of us. We could not believe it was real. Our minds needed to be convinced. Our minds consider certain events okay, and they are easily processed, but something contrary is immediately rejected. "It cannot be." "It must not be real."

God invented emotions. They can often be strong and should not be ignored. We need to understand that they are the natural output of the input into our brains and not deny them. We also need to realize the need for proper expression of them so that we do not become "constipated" and also know the appropriate way to handle the problem of "diarrhea" when it occurs.

Jesus used the analogy of marriage in his teaching about our relationship with Him. Marriage is an intimate relationship that we share with only one person, revealing our nakedness to them and trusting them with it. In the same way, Jesus wants us to be totally naked before Him in our spirits, which means to be totally honest with Him. When we are naked before our spouses, if we truly feel accepted, we do not worry about our imperfections, knowing we are loved as we are. In the same way, Jesus desires for us to share everything with Him—good, bad, and even the worst—knowing that He accepts us as we are and loves us unconditionally. Nothing is too shocking to reveal to Him, and we do not need to sugarcoat it for Him to accept it. The Psalms provide great insight into being honest and consequently close to the Lord. David (a man after God's own heart) and others, whose work is included, were totally open before God, even asking Him to punish their enemies. How many of us would pray that way today? Even though we may feel that way, probably few would admit it, even to God, or maybe especially to God. The funny part is that we cannot hide anything from Him, as Adam, Eve, and Jonah all found out. "'Am I only a God nearby,' declares the Lord, 'and not a God far away? Can anyone hide is secret places so that I cannot see him?' declares the Lord. 'Do not I fill heaven and earth?' declares the Lord" (Jeremiah 23:23, 24). He only wants our honesty. "In my integrity you uphold me and set me in your presence forever" (Psalms 41:12).

What we have to remember is that the Lord is the perfect judge and ultimately in control. By now we should know that He does not always answer all our prayers. Instead, pouring our hearts out to God provides a good, appropriate release of frustration, anger, pain, and so many other emotions. He desires for us to live in this way for two reasons. One, so that we will be healthy mentally, properly digesting and ridding our brains of waste. But He also desires this so that we can become closer to Him. He wants our friendship most of all! And is that not what a good friend is? Someone we can share good and bad with, who continues to accept us and does not correct or condemn us for our thoughts and feelings? I have come to know Jesus as my dearest and best Friend in the world. I can tell Him anything and everything, knowing He always understands, in fact better than I do. I have shared my anger at Him and others, things concerning my sex life, my fears, my most intimate secrets, and have found that He loves me just the same no matter what I think or feel. The only people on earth who do not feel emotion are those in the grave. Instead of ignoring those emotions, playing dead, we need to learn to express them daily.

Jesus was treated unfairly on earth and much since then. He knows firsthand what it feels like to be condemned (Psalms 69:1–21). He sympathizes with us and is on our side rooting for us. "Therefore, he is able to save completely those who come to God through him, because he always lives to intercede for them" (Hebrews 7:25, one of my favorite verses). Tell Him everything. He wants to know and truly cares. It is the foundation of our friendship, being ourselves, totally naked.

CHAPTER 12

The Tub Room Or Healing Hurts

Directly opposite the shower room was the tub room. Oh, how relaxing and peaceful it proved to be. The fireplace of the great room also opened into this room. Facing the fireplace sat a big hot tub, complete with bubbles and steam. This room opened also to the west side and the hallway under the other stairwell. The west room across from this housed towels and linens.

****

Nevertheless, I will bring health and healing to it;
I will heal my people and let them enjoy
abundant peace and security.
—Jeremiah 33:6

It is appropriate that this lesson follows the lesson of emotions because it also is an analogy pertaining to the body. As our mental digestion mirrors our physical one, just so, our mental reflects the physical regarding wounds. When we are hurt physically, depending upon the severity, the wound often takes a while to heal, and even once it has healed, it leaves a permanent scar. As with emotions, once again, the mental wound mirrors the physical one. When we have experienced a hard trial, the blow or wound is to the mental. This may come through a physical problem, but a wound is still inflicted upon our mental being. This also requires healing and can take as long, if not longer, as physical healing does. When wounded mentally, we have to work through the healing, drawing out the poison and ridding ourselves of it, through our emotional outlet. However, as with a physical wound, even after it is healed, a scar remains. Therefore, subsequent injuries in the same area will cause it to hurt once again, where it normally does not bother us. Having had three C-sections and three ulcers, I can assure you of four truths: (1) it takes a while each time for healing to occur; (2) it leaves a permanent scar; (3) most of the time, I am unaware of the scar; and (4) it still hurts occasionally when something unexpected aggravates the scar.

To understand this, an example is helpful. If someone says something hurtful, it may bother us for days or longer. Then if we take it to the Lord, healing will begin. After a while, the initial pain is gone, but forever, if the wound was deep, a scar will remain. Normally, because healing has occurred, it no longer bothers us, rarely coming to mind. However, if that same person is hurtful once again, the same area becomes rewounded with the scar from the previous offense hurt again.

It is imperative to understand this illustration, especially regarding forgiveness. Often we feel that our wound is healed and that we have forgiven because the initial feelings and memory are gone, only to have them resurface with another injury. What we fail to understand is that, when we forgive, we are not going to completely forget. Contrary to the saying "Forgive and forget," the scar is still there. It does not mean that we have not forgiven, because we have not forgotten. We tend to beat ourselves up because the memory and bad feelings return with the new pain.

I believe the Lord has provided our memories of these events for a couple reasons: (1) to help us avoid danger in the future and (2) that we be able to help others with the recounting of those events and the Lord's help. A hot stove should elicit caution inside, especially if we been burned many times before. There are those that quote the scripture Jeremiah 31:34c, "For I will forgive their wickedness and will remember their sins no more." Also, Hebrews 10:17 and 18 say, "Then he adds: 'Their sins and lawless acts I will remember no more! And where these have been forgiven, there is no longer any sacrifice for sin.'" As the Bible recounts many sins, I have come to believe that the Lord does not forget those events but forgets the punishment for those sins. He chooses not to remember from the point of view of punishment and He will never pay us back.

One of the most profound of these examples concerns Peter and his denial of Jesus. The Bible shows that Jesus forgave him. If He forgave and forgot, why is it recorded for us to read? I believe it is to teach us, those who have come since, about our human-ness and tendency toward sin and to help us know more about the Lord and His loving character, demonstrated in such forgiveness provided by His own death. It should already be apparent to most of us that we are sinners and in need of His mercy. How reassur-ing to see Peter, who was one of the disciples closest to Jesus, also still a human, capable of failing and, even more comforting, to see the Lord's tenderness and compassion toward Peter. "For everything that was written in the past was written to teach us, so that through endurance and the encouragement of the Scriptures we might have hope" (Romans 15:4).

Our pastor shared that love is an action, not simply a feeling. I believe forgiveness is the same. It was heartening after my first mis-carriage to read that forgiving someone does not mean he did not commit the offense against us, only that we choose not to get even. That is how the Lord deals with us. Our sin is offensive, yet He chooses to forget our punishment. Not only does He not hold our sin against us, but He Himself has already paid for all punishment we deserve. In fact, as shared earlier, He lives to intercede for us (Hebrews 7:25). For us Christians, our sins are covered with Jesus's blood. We are washed white as snow, but only because of Jesus. Our names are written in the Book of Life, and we are free from judgment. Though our sins may be many and horrific, we go free. "He does not treat us as our sins deserve or repay us according to our iniquities" (Psalms

103:10). "Blessed is the man whose sin the Lord will never count against him" (Romans 4:8).

Regarding ourselves and the act of forgiveness, if we have dealt with our wounds, taking all the pain, and our responses to it, to the Lord, the Master Physician, the wound will eventually heal and not resurface, until we encounter similar wounding in the future. Normally, we will not even be aware we have a scar. We are not conniving or planning our revenge. We have forgotten any punishment we may have felt was deserved. If wounded again, with the same pain and emotions resurfacing, we need not beat ourselves up. Instead, we need to do as we did originally, taking it all back to the Lord, pouring out our hearts to our kind Friend, who is ultimately the only One who can place His forgiveness for the offender into our hearts. That is true forgiveness.

For years, I wrestled with thoughts regarding forgiveness and finally asked the Lord about our personal responsibility when others hurt us but never seek our forgiveness. It seems much easier to forgive when asked by a repentant offender. Eventually Jesus brought the answer, showing me His response in His crucifixion, extending forgiveness even as His enemies were in the very act of killing Him. Obviously, He was saying we are to forgive every time, releasing our offenders from prison to run free, not denying their guilt, but choosing not to retaliate. My next thought was that Jesus extended forgiveness to them, but that does not mean they went to heaven. He reminded me that repentance is necessary for that to occur. What it means for us is that we need to forgive every time, even if not asked, but that does not mean our offenders can live with us, a key point in dealing with abusers. We can forgive them from a distance, releasing them, but also protecting ourselves. Joseph also needed to see his brothers' repentant hearts before they were allowed to live with him. Jesus invites us all to Himself and His Kingdom, but He also shared, "Many are called but few are chosen." That is because only His friends can enter, a reasonable requisite. Even in our lives, we would only invite friends to live with us, not our enemies.

We need to let the Lord live through us, providing His love and forgiveness to others. We cannot do it ourselves. God eventually brings merciful feelings as we bring Him our sad, angry ones. (Good resources: *The Way of Agape*[1] and *Be Ye Transformed*,[2] both by Chuck and Nancy Missler.) For me, He has also implanted *feelings* of compassion and understanding through the following:

1. *Joseph's example.* He saw that ultimately his brothers' actions, though cruel, were God's will for him and for his life, both for his good and the good of others.
2. *Jesus's example.* He prayed for His Father to forgive those who killed him because they did not know what they were doing. Ignorance is often the reason people do and/or say hurtful things. They are unable to comprehend.
3. *Examinations of hurtful peoples' pasts.* These often provide great insight into the reason for the cruelty. They themselves may have experienced pain in their lives that has never had the Lord's healing touch.

This same analogy also applies to grief, which takes a tremendous amount of time and work to rid ourselves of the poison that enters through our deep wound. Eventually we heal. However, that does not mean that we forget what happened or the person we lost. The scar is there and always will be. After much healing, we may be able to go for longer periods without experiencing much pain, but we will never forget that person because love never dies. That is why with time and healing, you may hear people speak of their loved one without crying, but they will never totally stop thinking of that loved one. The fact that they can speak without emotion shows the incredible amount of healing that has occurred. Once healed, does that mean that we never will cry or hurt again? No, certain days, situations, smells, sounds bring tears again. We are healed, but the scar remains, and certain events aggravate it, which triggers the pain once again.

Mental scars are as physical ones. We need not berate ourselves, feeling we have not forgiven or not been healed because pain and other emotions sometimes return. The Lord is there to accept it all, and us in our humanness, with comfort and love galore. We only need to turn to Him, who alone is the Healer and the source of all true forgiveness.

CHAPTER 13

The Basement Or Grief

The day we once again descended into this room, I was having many doubts as to how it could ever be anything but a dismal basement. How surprised and delighted I was to see the changes my Lord had managed to bring to it! On this first visit, the sun was shining through the high east window, which happened to also be open, letting in a cool and gentle breeze. Before I had even noticed that, however, what caught my eye were the carpeted stairs and walls! How glorious! It was as a beautiful rain forest with growths of green all around, all unusually realistic, but what made it even more so was the fact that this carpet was three-dimensional, with some parts indented and others embossed on top. It felt as if birds could be nesting nearby. What had been not only dismal but also frightening was now inviting. The staircase curved to the north, halfway to the landing.

What a precious view was now before me. Various places, high and low, on both the north and south walls were recessed niches, just the right size to cuddle and read, as nests perched high in a tree. Those down low were easily entered from the floor. The others had mini ladders. All had lights mounted into the walls. Very cozy! Directly in front of us, on the west wall, was a semi flat rock face with soothing water trickling down. On either side were bookcases with many books I had read previously. Once again, there were memorable tokens of the journey.

On the south wall was a narrow door. When I asked about it, my Lord assured me He would show me later. More hidden places! It was only as we were leaving that I spied the most delightful nest, just opposite the open window, looking out to the fruitful garden below. What peace!

****

I will give you the treasures of darkness,
riches stored in secret places,
so that you may know that I am the Lord, the
God of Israel, who calls you by name.
—Isaiah 45:3

It is better to go to a house of mourning
than to go to a house of feasting,
for death is the destiny of every man; the
living should take this to heart.
Sorrow is better than laughter, because a
sad face is good for the heart.
The heart of the wise is in the house of mourning,
but the heart of fools is in the house of pleasure.
—Ecclesiastes 7:2–4

One of the best characterizations of grief is shown in the movie *Cast Away*.[1] It is one of my favorites because it depicts grief so well and is indeed an example of it. The story begins with a supervisor for FedEx working in Russia. Chuck returns home for Christmas to be with his girlfriend. When unexpectedly called away for work, he promises to return for New Year's, and he gives her an engagement ring. As it turns out, the plane he is on encounters a terrible storm over the ocean and crashes. He alone washes up onto the shore of an uninhabited island.

With the loss of civilization, his former life, girlfriend, and job, Chuck is grieving many losses. His reactions are typical of grief. At first he is in shock as he drags himself from the ocean, trying to get his bearings and evaluate what has happened. As he begins to assess his situation, he is feeling hopeful and somewhat in control. He only needs to write *help* in the sand and someone will rescue him. Unfortunately, it is not long before the water washes away his words and plans. Then he tries using logs, still with the feeling that someone will come to the rescue, that everything is going to be okay. Hope is still alive. As the day passes, he begins to see this is not the case, that rescue may be prolonged. He begins to feel hungry and thirsty and must learn how to survive in this new and totally different world, and he finds it is not easy. In fact, it is intolerable. Eventually he learns to open coconuts in such a way to drink their milk. Later he finds small amounts of fresh water on the tiny island. From the start packages begin washing ashore from the plane, a reminder of his previous life. He stacks them to the side, unopened. They become his hope. He will return and deliver them one day. Our family went to see this movie at the theater two different times. Both times, the audience laughed when he began to sort the boxes. But to those who have experienced grief firsthand, his response is understandable. When something major and disruptive happens, we desire so much for the mundane again—to have no challenges, to return to the normal, uneventful, boring routine of life. But it cannot be the same as much as we desire it! Instead, every minute becomes a challenge.

From the beginning, Chuck holds on to his most priceless possession, a pocket watch from his girlfriend with a picture of her inside. He had almost lost it before the crash and unbuckled his seat belt to grab it, which in truth probably saved his life as he was free to use the life raft. Like him, we all have things we hold onto, in order to keep hope alive. Then the awful day comes when the body of a fellow FedEx employee washes ashore. Once again, the horror of the crash hits him, with the realization of how traumatic it was and how difficult his new life has become. Shortly after this, he sees the light of a ship one night but is of course unable to get its attention. This prompts him to use the raft, on which he reached the island. But he is disappointed and discouraged when he is unable to get past the breakers and cuts himself badly in the effort. This is followed by a great storm.

Time goes on, with no rescue. Finally, he resorts to opening many of the packages in hope of finding something useful, leaving one still to be delivered, one remaining hope. In the boxes, he does find interesting and useful items: skates, videotapes, a soccer ball (which becomes his best friend, Wilson, someone to talk to). Chuck has to learn how to make a fire and catch fish, lessons for daily survival. In between these events, he experiences all the different emotions of grief: anger, fear, sadness, loneliness, frustration, and finally, despair, the point where all hope is gone.

At this point, after three long and merciless years, he determines to hang himself. Not wanting to prolong his suffering, he performs a practice run with a dummy to make sure his plan will work. His attempt is thwarted when the tree breaks, shattering his plan to be free of pain.

A year later, a porta potty washes ashore. With hope renewed, he begins building a raft, using the skates to skin logs, with those strips and videotape holding it together. The porta potty works as a sail, the final addition to his raft, on which he and Wilson make their escape past the breakers into the ocean. When a storm comes, the raft is hit, and Wilson is lost. Chuck almost loses his life trying to save his "friend." In despair, he collapses, finally rescued by a huge cargo ship.

Once back, Chuck finds life again to be uncertain. Forever his has been changed because of his ordeal. He finds he cannot easily return to his previous life. Few understand what he has been through, as he realizes in the seafood served at his welcoming banquet and the many conveniences he has not had for so many years: a bed, a lighter, electricity. His biggest heartbreak, however, occurs when he learns that his former girlfriend is married and has a toddler. Everyone had assumed that he was dead and determined to go on with life. Once again, Chuck's hopes are dashed. The movie ends with him returning his one package with the realization that there is somehow a bigger plan for him: his life was not preserved for nothing.

Until someone has experienced a great loss in his life, he cannot possibly understand the intensity of grief. Unfortunately, the comforters in our lives are often people who have not experienced deep pain, so their answers are often of a simple and shallow nature. Some are innocent and, in fact, trying to be comforting. Their remarks did not hurt as much as those who seemed to be on a higher level and had answers that were condemning and painful.

I too have made remarks I regret, so I understand how it can innocently occur. Most of us want so much to bring consolation that we often simplify or rush those who are suffering. I remember at one of our first meetings as Compassionate Friends leaders, in hopes of providing encouragement, I shared what I had been learning in the midst of grief. Afterward, one of the previous leaders told me that she would rather have her son back than anything she had ever learned. In my attempt to provide solace and reassurance, somehow my words did not convey that. "When words are many, sin is not absent, but he who holds his tongue is wise" (Proverbs 10:19). All of us would rather have our children back, but there does come a point when we realize that nothing can bring them back. As David said, "I will go to him, but he will not return to me" (2 Samuel 12:23c). At that point, we try to see what can come from the awful devastation: some purpose, some meaning, some good out of the worst that has happened. What is important is to place no burden on those who may not be at that point yet. We all need to be extremely tender in our approach. Wounded people are suffering enough already and do not need any more pain inflicted upon them. I personally recommend to a grieving person, especially those who have experienced the loss of a child, to attend a support group. People who have been through similar circumstances have more understanding of sorrow. Therefore, they are not so apt to judge.

Through the years, the Lord has taught us much. Because of our involvement in Compassionate Friends for eight years (1987–1995), I have heard many share hard words others have spoken, inconsiderate actions shown, and/or thoughtless expectations made of them. This portion is provided as a comfort and a voice for those people who have experienced the loss of a child and in an effort to educate others so that they may have a newer depth of understanding and compassion for those who grieve. I have included misconceptions that have been most painful for us and for others who have shared with us. Unfortunately, it does not touch every sensitive area. The following are *some* major misconceptions about grief.

Misconception no. 1: Men are strong and do not need to grieve. They do not hurt as much as women do. They can support their families and go on with life with little help.

Gordon felt especially hurt and angry when people would ask him how I was doing, never how he was doing. He too felt great pain but was unable to express it at work or at church. Thankfully he consented to going to Compassionate Friends, where he could safely express his feelings. In our culture, few men do feel comfortable sharing. Somehow, our society has portrayed them as invulnerable to pain, which is wrong and often has devastating results.

Misconception no. 2: With the loss of a person, age is the determining factor in the depth of pain experienced.

The loss of a baby is considered a small loss and a miscarriage no loss at all. Shortly after Matthew died, my mother-in-law shared with me, "It can't hurt as bad to lose a baby as an older child." My response was one of anger, and I have since thought much about it, praying that I will never have to find out, as the pain I experienced was honestly more than I could bear. Since then I have come to conclude that she only spoke what most people believe. Years later, she shared more thoughts over Thanksgiving dinner. "Why would it matter if you lost a baby before it was born? You never knew that child." Once again, my response was in anger, and once again, I have come to realize that her thoughts are common.

In thinking this through, I resort to logic. Let us consider her premise. Many people die daily, and unless their circumstances are close to ours, we usually feel no pain. Why? Some are very old. If we use the criteria above, should we not feel great pain when the oldest people die? One response may be that it is not age but if you know a person. To which I could reply that many of my parents' friends have died, and I have felt sadness, but not intense grief. Why? The reason we feel no pain is not due to age or knowing them but because we did not love them. Love determines the depth of pain we feel when someone dies. If you love someone, you will hurt terribly when he or she dies. We can always judge another situation, but unless we have walked that path, our logic will be faulty.

There are other considerations. One is this: There has been no other time in my life when I have been as close to my children as I was while they were residing inside of me or during the first year following their births. At that point, babies are most needy, and we are at their constant beck and call. At least that is how it was with our children, whom I worried about and cared for even while in my womb. Once born, all three were up many times at night and did not sleep all that much during the day either! Perhaps God allows that so the bond will be especially close. In considering this, we need to realize that because of their dependence upon us, their family, they are naturally not as close to others, unless they have been in the care of others while the parents work. In our case, our babies were closest to us during that time, and few others had formed a bond.

It is said that grandparents suffer a unique grief when a grandchild dies because they grieve for not only the grandchild but also their own child. When a baby dies, however, unless the grandparents live close by or have felt a special excitement from the beginning, the loss felt by them may be minimal because no bond of love has formed. So they may judge the loss as inconsequential since they felt no great pain. This is not true of all grandparents, as we witnessed through Compassionate Friends. In most cases, however, I feel the loss of a baby will be felt deepest by the parents and siblings, who have developed a strong bond of love.

If few see the value of a baby outside the womb, even fewer know its worth while inside. Miscarriage is considered no loss by many, and I have even encountered this same attitude in the church. Two different women, both of whom lost babies younger than Matthew, and after Matthew's death, each informed me that my miscarriages were losses but not the same as the loss of their babies or Matthew. In considering their comments, I have come to believe that they have observed the lack of respect for the unborn and do not wish for their babies to be in that category.

I have met many women who have experienced miscarriage. Some of them felt emotional pain while others did not. Those who did not were unaware they were pregnant and had just found out and/or they did not want the baby. One woman even shared that she would have aborted the baby had she known. The ones who experienced grief in their miscarriages dearly wanted their children; in fact, many were thrilled after having waited a long time in order to conceive. For those of us who have longed for children and struggled trying to have them, the grief is intense and the lack of understanding from others is both hurtful and anger provoking.

Another point many fail to consider is that once a life is conceived, time is evoked, and from that time on, that person is indeed alive and still growing in our minds and hearts for eternity. For those of us who wanted our children, they did not stop existing simply because they are no longer here. For the rest of my life, I will remember our kids and their ages. All the milestones and important days are there, never forgotten—kindergarten, middle school, high school, graduation, college, and marriage. Forever I will wonder what they look like and what their interests are. It is not a coincidence the Lord has brought many kids in their various grades along our path. He is the great Comforter, and we have been comforted to know these others.

To any of you who have lost babies at any point, from conception on up, please take heart. The Lord has shown me the value of our children. "For you created my inmost being; you knit me together in my mother's womb. I praise you because I am fearfully and wonderfully made; your works are wonderful, I know that full well. My frame was not hidden from you when I was made in the secret place. When I was woven together in the depths of the earth, your eyes saw my unformed body" (Psalms 139:13–16a). God shares your pain not only because He is loving and compassionate but also because He is hurting Himself that what He has created in His image has been so devalued! Go to Him with your pain, for He is the Creator of your child and is sad for you. He cries with you. Know your child is valuable and loved not only by you but also by the Lord Himself. Know too that you have a special someone waiting in heaven.

Another area many people who have not experienced grief fail to understand is the following: the extreme and intense pain of missing the loved one is only one part of grieving. Grief also involves two other major struggles: (1) Trying to understand why this awful tragedy happened is overwhelming and involves much soul-searching. All our previous beliefs are reexamined in light of this new and shocking development in our lives. "What do I believe?" becomes the focus of our thoughts daily. (2) There are intense and immediate fears for our present and future. The fears of parents before losing a child are minimal compared to those whose child has died. Feelings of terror, which are both justified and understandable, overwhelm us at times. "What I feared has come upon me; what I dreaded has happened to me. I have no peace, no quietness; I have no rest, but only turmoil" (Job 3:25, 26). "God has made my heart faint; the Almighty has terrified me" (Job 23:16). Before our loss, our fears were unrealized and easier to dismiss. One woman at a Compassionate Friends meeting shared it this way. "Until you have seen your child in a coffin being lowered into the earth, you cannot tell me what to feel." Fear takes on a whole new meaning. Life is never so simple again. Some who are naive may say that if you only have faith, you will not have to deal with that fear, and I answer that both fear and faith take on a new meaning once your child has died. The only way to understand is to follow our footsteps. More on fear is shared in another misconception.

When life begins, it does not end—our children are still alive. Those who did not love them have forgotten, but we will never forget because we love them and know they are waiting.

Misconception no. 3: Couples who have lost babies need to hear of new babies.

Many women have shared their hurt about this. For most, those comments are unwelcome, and being around babies is extremely difficult. It is especially upsetting to hear of pregnant women who wish they were not and of women having abortions. Often I have wondered if people may only be trying to bring encouragement that the prospect of having another baby is still alive, but it usually takes a long while for that renewed hope to come. Mostly my inspiration came when a fellow sufferer, someone who had also lost a baby, was able to have another baby.

Misconception no. 4: When a couple loses a baby, they can "always have another."

This remark is fairly arrogant, as who knows that it will come true. Hopefully it will, but it is only in God's hands. None of us knows what will happen. Even if the remark proves true, the child is not a replacement toy for the one that was broken. Both children, all people, are unique. When someone dies, we have lost a one-of-a-kind person, not simply one of hundreds of replicas.

Misconception no. 5: If a person who has lost a baby later has another, there are no more struggles with grief issues.

This can be especially complicated. With the loss of our first child through miscarriage, I dealt with fears that the Lord was saying I would not be a good parent, and therefore, He was not going to bring other children into my life. When the Lord brought the blessing of Eric, I was determined to be the best mom, my chance to prove to myself (and God) that I could do fine. Right away, however, I found parenting to be much more challenging than I ever imagined, with me extremely impatient in the process. I have found that with the loss of a child and subsequent blessing of another, there is often the desire and intention to be the best parent, but we all fail. All of us get tired, frustrated, and impatient at times. This can be especially difficult as guilt can be overwhelming, even convincing ourselves God will probably take our remaining children. This is natural, but we need to realize we are human, and God understands our weaknesses and will eventually help us overcome those especially trying areas. He is not condemning but is as a parent of a child learning to walk, encouraging us to try again when we fall and giving us His unconditional Love and patience. He will (and does) help, as I can attest with Eric. It has been miraculous how the Lord mended our relationship. When he asked me to wear his jersey to the senior night football game (at the coach's suggestion), I cried knowing he did not have to and that the Lord brought a deep love to us after a bumpy start. I have also had to realize, however, that like a person who quits smoking after many years, some damage (natural consequences) cannot be reversed.

Another difficult area for us was reconciling the fact that if Matthew had lived, we probably would not have had another child in heaven and Sarabeth here with us. For years, that was a source of conflict in our minds, because we love them all and could not accept any of them not being part of our lives. Finally, years ago, the Lord helped me realize the He could have brought any or all our children here to live. That was totally in His hands. Now we have a big family (something I loved as I grew up) that will someday all live together in heaven. God's plans are always the best plans! I do not have to wonder or care whom He chose to live here and who is in heaven. I am eternally thankful for our family that can grow up together for all the years of eternity!

Misconception no. 6: When a person experiences a great loss, he/she can grieve but should soon get on with life. Eventually he/she should get over it, not needing to speak of the loss anymore, especially if it has been a year or more.

Losing a loved one is like a physical amputation. It takes a long time to recover, and we are *never* the same, always aware of our loss. Every day for a grieving person, just getting up requires great strength and courage, especially at first. Our lives forever changed the day our children died. Our lives abruptly stopped, but unfortunately the rest of the world did not, but few understand.

The reason is that society has great fear about death, and therefore, talking about it is to be avoided at all costs. The thought can be terrifying, and it is definitely easier to ignore than to admit it is a daily reality. Naturally then, when the loss of someone close occurs, we are even more devastated. For those of us who have lost a loved one, we cannot forget them that easily—not in two weeks, not in two years, not in a lifetime—if we genuinely loved them. Forgetting would lead to our insanity. Our minds know that our child has died eventually, although it does take time for the shock to wear off, for us to believe the unbelievable. Once our minds are convinced, our hearts ache as we go through grief, a long process. If we try to live as if nothing has happened, we will short-circuit.

Few people realize how interminable grief is, and few give grieving people time to recover from what is often the deepest wound of their lives. An example of this is that many workplaces seem to give little time off work to those who have had a loved one die. Although work can be helpful, it takes a while to be able to function once again.

Our society has been in great denial concerning death. With 9/11, we have had to face issues long avoided. In losing a person we have loved, it is only right and appropriate that we grieve long and hard. It shows that our loved one had value and that we do, indeed, cherish them. Grief is a respectful response to those we love. Also, though it has been many years, I have not and will not ever forget our kids or my mom or dad or others whom I loved that have died. Neither will anyone else that has experienced that amputation. My great-aunt Teresa lost her only daughter, who was a teen at the time. She also lost her only grandchild, Lani, who was also a teen. She talked of those losses until the day she died. She obviously went through tremendous pain and looked forward to being reunited.

I have had the experience and have heard others share the same: that as they told someone about the death of their loved one years previous, the person will abruptly interrupt with, "Shouldn't you go to counseling?" What they do not understand is that often those who are most healed are the ones who can speak of their children and not cry. Others cannot even begin to speak because the pain is still too intense. Healing helps us to be able to talk of our loved ones but not forget them. We will always remember them and sometimes even cry at certain times and with certain memories.

What we need to remember, as bereaved people, are two things:

A. The people who make hurtful comments most often do not understand. They have not had to face death head-on and do not realize the intensity of it. They will one day, however, as none of us is immune to death taking those we love. With that loss, hopefully, they will also learn compassion. Then you can be there to help them.

B. Only people who have experienced tremendous suffering and worked through the agony, finding God's healing, can be comforters. We would never dream of intentionally saying hurtful words and are especially careful because we do not want to inflict more pain. God comforts us that we may pass it on. Second Corinthians 1:3–5 says, "Praise be to the God and Father of our Lord Jesus Christ, the Father of compassion and the God of all comfort, who comforts us in all our troubles, so that we can comfort those in any trouble with the comfort we ourselves have received from God. For just as the sufferings of Christ flow over into our lives, so also through Christ our comfort overflows."

I feel the Lord has shown me that not only does He not condemn us in our grief but He actually commends us, desiring for us to remember our loved ones and to have our eyes constantly focused on our real home. "But store up for yourselves treasures in heaven, where moth and rust do not destroy, and where thieves do not break in and steal" (Matthew 6:20). With two busy and active kids, the days slipped by quickly, and although our kids in heaven are always in my mind, there were times the closeness of an anniversary eluded me. The Lord was always faithful to remind me. Something triggered the memory—one of their names somewhere, a seasonal item, a song, or a scripture, something from the time. The Lord wants our focus to be on our real home. Those of us who think often of our kids in heaven are not offending the Lord! We are actually pleasing Him! He wants our thoughts there with Him and them. That is our true home. We are here temporarily, even if eighty or ninety years! That is nothing compared to eternity! "The length of our days is seventy years—or eighty, if we have the strength; yet their span is but trouble and sorrow, for they quickly pass, and we fly away" (Psalms 90:10). "For he knows how we are formed, he remembers that we are dust. As for man, his days are like grass, he flourishes like a flower of the field; the wind blows over it and it is gone, and its place remembers it no more" (Psalms 103:14–16).

Misconception no. 7: Christians should not grieve, but if they do, it will be less intense.

As I shared before, earlier on the day when Matthew died, I sat down to read my Bible, thankful for a half hour of quiet. My particular reading that day was 1 Thessalonians 4. Verse 13, says, "Brothers, we do not want you to be ignorant about those who fall asleep or to grieve like the rest of men, who have no hope." Often Christians use this scripture to defend the position that we should not grieve, but that is not what it says. It says not to grieve like those who have no hope. It does not say that we are not to grieve. Even with the hope of heaven, we have still lost a valued person who cannot be replaced, and there is a void in our lives, a place that only one filled. In this area, there are many subcategories of misunderstanding in the church.

A. You should never be angry with God and definitely not show it if you are.

From personal experience, I can refute this, as I have been extremely angry with God and told Him so, not just once, but many times. I have come to see that He understands and knows our frustrations and questioning anyway. When we are sincere before Him, He is not going to retaliate as we share our feelings. He wants us to be honest. It is when we try to hide our feelings and sins (like Adam and Eve) that we are in danger, because the anger will not go away on its own, continuing to burn and eventually causing us to leave the Lord. We need to tell Him what we are feeling. Job was honest. David was honest, and God called him "a man after his own heart" (1 Samuel 13:14b).

B. Depression is sin and should never be experienced in the life of a Christian.

Not long after my second depression began, a speaker at church shared that depression is sin, a misconception dear to my heart to refute. There are many hurting people in the church, suffering great pain and loneliness yet unable to obtain help because of this lie! I know. I have been there. There is a very real stigma about depression. In the world, a person who is depressed and being treated is labeled crazy. In the church, that same person is sinning. Oh, that all those judges could go through *one day* of intense depression, just one day! How eye-opening! How much more compassion might come to the world and the church! I know. I have gone through two deep depressions, the first (1983) lasting probably six months and the second (1989) a good year. Maybe the intensity of that will hit you if you remember that one day alone would change the hearts of most. We need to wake up and realize this is the time to address the subjects of depression and of death, the great unmentionables, and soon. People are dying around us because it is hush-hush.

If you know anyone who is depressed, he/she needs immediate help. Do not ignore it. Not only is it a most frightening place, it is also especially lonely. Most leave—most, but not all. The Lord does not leave, but often, with condemnation, we begin to believe He feels the same. That leads to fear we cannot even approach Him, sure of his disapproval. "Do not hide your face from me" (Psalms 143:7b). "Listen to my prayer, O God, do not ignore my plea; hear me and answer me. My thoughts trouble me and I am distraught at the voice of the enemy, at the stares of the wicked; for they bring down suffering upon me and revile me in their anger. My heart is in anguish within me; the terrors of death assail me. Fear and trembling have beset me; horror has overwhelmed me" (Psalms 55:1–5).

So what does depression feel like? One of the best illustrations is depicted in the movie *Honey, I Shrunk the Kids*, where an eccentric scientist discovers a way to shrink matter, both objects and people.[2] Unfortunately, by accident, his kids and the neighbor kids end up shrinking themselves. Not realizing what has happened, the scientist sweeps them up and puts them out in the trash at the back of the yard, an extremely long way from the house, especially since they are under an inch tall. They encounter many unexpected obstacles and trials—sprinklers, ants, and a mower—as they attempt to return to the house for help. Though fictitious, the similarity is especially close to the reality of depression. Like those kids, someone who is depressed is immediately zapped, although the descent may have been going on for a long time, into a terrifying world, full of unwelcome and frightening perils, as he/she tries to return home, back to a "normal" life. Other analogies include (1) being in a deep fog, which no sun can penetrate, or (2) falling into a sandpit, with towering walls and no way out. The symptoms of depression include lack of energy, concentration, and sleep, lack of desire for previously enjoyed things, memory problems, inability to make decisions, fears, feelings of going crazy, susceptibility to Satan's voice and suggestions, and eventually, total despair.

What causes depression? There are many roots, which seem to come from one source ultimately. One root is the result of grief, a natural part of the process as we work to a place of healing. Unfortunately, in this life, a person must experience pain and live in it, if there is to be healing. If stuffed, it is not gone but still growing. The only way to deal with it is to expose it, to bring all the emotions into the open and allow the Lord to touch us.

The deepest root of depression, I believe, is exhaustion. The story of Elijah is a good illustration of this (1 Kings 19). He had run ahead of Ahab's chariot. Then he was physically drained and became mentally worn. When grief hits us, we are on overload in our lives. There are monumental questions, spiritual and otherwise, much to understand. Our mind is working full-time, trying to understand, plus we are thrust back into the busyness of life, wondering desperately, "My life has stopped. Why hasn't the world?" We still have to live, to get up every day and try to keep pace. How monumental to do our regular work and have all the mental and spiritual issues to contend with, so much input into our weary brains: our own thoughts, what others say, and the unrelenting emotions associated with it all. Plus, due to grief, our bodies are often neglected, causing exhaustion, from not eating and sleeping right. In the past, it was a nervous breakdown. Nowadays, many psychologists and psychiatrists attribute it to a chemical imbalance.

Small wonder this occurs! How many people in our country are not already stressed with the pressures of everyday life. Adding the death of a loved one (or other horrific problems people must deal with) is monumental. The energy involved in living after a major tragedy is overwhelming compared to the stress of everyday life most live with. It makes no sense to condemn the depressed.

After answering the questions of what depression feels like and what causes it, we next need to ask the most important question of all: what does *the Lord* think about depression in a Christian? Surely He too disapproves of our feelings, for not being strong or a good example. This is what the Lord showed to me: "Blessed are those who mourn, for they will be comforted" (Matthew 5:4). "The Lord is close to the brokenhearted and saves those who are crushed in spirit" (Psalms 34:18). "He heals the brokenhearted and binds up their wounds" (Psalms 147:3). "Mourn with those who mourn" (Romans 12:15b). "In their distress, he too was distressed" (Isaiah 63:9a).

It does not take much research to see other characters in the Bible who went through depression, David and Job, in addition to Elijah. David provided those suffering with a source of tremendous compassion and reassurance through his heartbreaking and beautiful psalms. Job also poured out his heart of discouragement and pain to the Lord. Elijah was depressed and sat under a tree, wanting to die (1 Kings 19:3, 4). In this example, we can see exactly how the Lord viewed his depression and how He dealt with it. From the beginning, we see His comfort. "The angel of the Lord came back a second time and touched him and said, 'Get up and eat, for the journey is too much for you'" (1 Kings 19:7). Later, at Elijah's lowest point, the Lord came and showed him the wind, an earthquake, and fire. So was God angry with him because he was despondent? No, the wind, the earthquake, and the fire were not God's words to him. God's words had come earlier as a gentle whisper of encouragement: "The journey is too great for you." He then showed Elijah that He was not in the wind, the earthquake, or the fire but, instead, was a still, small voice of sympathy and refreshment. Afterward, He brought him a helper, Elisha.

When a person is exhausted—physically, mentally, emotionally, or spiritually—the need is rest. What he is apt to see, however, is the wind, the earthquake, and the fire, the hard circumstances and the harsh words of others and the enemy. The Lord's answer is rest, what He provided for Elijah, and then He speaks in His small, still voice with soothing and strengthening words. That is what He did for me, provided rest and food, His very words giving sustenance for the journey.

To those in the throes of deep depression, be encouraged. The Lord is close to you, even though you may not feel Him and may even think He has abandoned you, as I did in 1989. He cares deeply for you. Do not give up. For me, both times, the process was slow, but the Lord had beautiful promises and fulfillments after my times of suffering. Depression is often the darkest hour before dawn. The following practices were of great assistance to me.

1. Most of all, I rested often in the Lord's Presence. "Come near to God and he will come near to you" (James 4:8a). This was my biggest comfort. During the first depression, I learned to picture myself on His lap or sitting by Him on the couch as I rested my head on His shoulder. It was difficult to get my muddled brain to concentrate, but became easier the more I practiced. During the second depression, once again, I found resting in His Presence to bring the most relief and also His revelation of our Secret Place.

2. Psalms became my daily reading. David wrote consoling words, expressing exactly what I have been unable to myself. I also found reassurance later in the words of Isaiah, Elijah, and Job—promises of better days.

3. Reading the paper and watching the news were avoided. These prompted more fear and despair, contributing to more depression.

4. Being in nature or looking out at the peaceful scenery on sunlit days brought comfort.

5. Listening to praise music throughout the day lifted my spirits.

6. Doing a half hour aerobics daily provided physical exercise and helped mentally also.

7. Writing my pain in a journal—totally honest about thoughts and feelings—was healing.

8. Taking a good multivitamin boosted my immune system and my spirits.

9. Counseling provided a good outlet both times.

10. The second depression, when I believed the Lord had left, my suffering was especially intense. That time, I took antidepressants for nearly a year. They have often taken a bad rap because some people who have been taking them have committed terrible crimes. What I feel may be misunderstood in all this, however, is that antidepressants, unlike antibiotics, which usually bring immediate results, are much slower working, and most require counseling at the same time. Coming out of depression is a long process. I have often wondered if *that* is not the reason for the crimes and not necessarily the antidepressants themselves. For me, they provided a slow help in recovering from the second depression. At this point, however, I do need to add that recent reports show the side effects of some antidepressants cause suicidal tendencies, especially in teens. Therefore, it seems essential to check and weigh side effects of *all* drugs before taking them.

11. Later, reading books specific to grief, helped me. Ten years later, too late for me, I read a book by Jan Dravecky, *A Joy I'd Never Known*.[3] It is especially helpful for those in the church with strong opposition to antidepressants.

12. Rebuking the enemy lessened fear and depression. "Submit yourselves, then, to God. Resist the devil, and he will flee from you" (James 4:7).

13. Repeating certain scriptures in times of agonizing fear brought relief.

14. Having a nonjudgmental friend to share intense emotions with was a great help.

15. Working on crafts or other creative ventures relieved the intense pressure, as those activities require the use of the other side of our brains, helping to lessen the depression.

16. Last of all, but not least, many people were praying. Those not in the middle of constant pain could offer prayer often, and their prayers were more involved than my intense plea, "Help!" But I also know the Lord hears our hearts, even when our minds cannot form a coherent prayer. "In the same way, the Spirit helps us in our weakness. We do not know what we ought to pray, but the Spirit himself intercedes for us with groans that words cannot express. And he who searches our hearts knows the mind of the Spirit, because the Spirit intercedes for the saints in accordance with God's will" (Romans 8:26–27).

This list is not in any order of importance to me, except for the first one, which was my lifesaver. Also, to someone in the midst of depression, this list will be overwhelming. Finding one suggestion that gives comfort and being faithful to it each day brings hope, encouragement, and eventually energy to try others. Also, these are simply ones that helped me. There certainly must be others that have sustained people in the past, recorded in other books specific to depression.

To those wanting to help others through depression, encourage them with the above suggestions, knowing that at first especially it is hard as it is so difficult to concentrate. Most of all, be there for them and listen with no judging or condemnation! They are in a different world now and need someone to give hope they will make it back. The kids in *Honey I Shrunk the Kids* wanted desperately to return home. Eventually they did, but it was a long and arduous journey. Please remember, the Lord is not condemning them, and neither should we!

We sometimes read of horrible tragedies of murder and/or suicide in the paper, not understanding how such devastation could occur. I do understand. When we are depressed, we are also extremely weak and vulnerable, which provides Satan an opportune time for attack. With no energy and all our reserves down, we have little ammunition to defend ourselves. During my first depression, I was afraid to sleep at night because of tormenting thoughts that I may get up and kill Gordon or myself during the night, both thoughts planted by the enemy.

Depression is nothing to ignore. It is a dangerous position to be in and to be around. We owe it to one another to be supportive in times of weakness and certainly not judgmental. That needs to become the greatest focus of the church—encouraging one another—with no room for condemnation.

C. Fear should have no part in the lives of Christians.

I believe that the greatest Christian who ever lived experienced fear at certain times in his life. In fact, Jesus, our ultimate example, went through tremendous agony before his death. Paul, Job, and David speak of fear, even terror. In our humanness, none of us wants to suffer.

Fear, like other emotions, is output from what we see or experience through our senses. When a person has had a major tragedy in his life, he will experience turmoil. It is a normal response to intense pain. The sad part is that often one tragedy will hit us, and many will follow. Job is a prime example. Although our circumstances were not as extensive as Job's, the years between 1983 and 1990 were filled with difficult situations for our family. It is impossible to have many trials and not be fearful to continue on the path of life. "But we were harassed at every turn, conflicts on the outside, fears within. But God, who comforts the downcast, comforted us by the coming of Titus, and not only his coming but also by the comfort you had given him" (2 Corinthians 7:5b–7a). "God has made my heart faint; the Almighty has terrified me" (Job 23:16).

At cell group one evening in 1989, after expressing my battle with ongoing fear, a man shared, "Fear knocks at the door and faith answers and says, 'There is no one there.'" This is easy to accept until faith is tried. At that time, with my faith at an all-time low, it provided little help.

Not long after, our pastor's mother, who had a stillborn child years before, listened to my fears and prayed. She also said to put on my armor daily. Although unsure how, she was kind and sympathetic when asked. She had no catchy verses or condemnation, only the practical answer. I have since learned to rebuke the enemy and picture the Lord placing armor on me every day.

Fear and depression often dwell together, depression feeding much upon fear. The practices above and those mentioned in the depression section helped me immensely, especially as I became more aware of the Lord's Presence and practiced spending time with Him.

Today, doubts still overwhelm me at times, especially concerning health issues. When three children die unexpectedly, with no explanations, the fears for the family are tremendous. A panic sometimes hits, and I have learned to rebuke the enemy and remind myself of the promises the Lord gave in 1990 and 1991. I have also found relief in repeating comforting scriptures.

Misconception no. 8: Your emotions are separate from your body and do not affect it.

Often medical personnel do not understand the stress grief can take on our bodies. Two immediate symptoms of grief are digestive problems and a feeling of pain or heaviness in the chest area. Long-term health problems can lead to major illnesses. We have had numerous medical problems through the years. Like Job, sickness came to us following grief. It seems a natural consequence. As shared above, when they come, fear and panic often follow. After expressing overwhelming distress at our doctor's office, I wrote a letter explaining our past to the new nurses. Whether it helped them, I do not know. It did help me to express my emotions.

Others at Compassionate Friends meetings have shared similar problems not only with medical people but also with police or emergency room personnel at the time of the death. That is another objective of Compassionate Friends: to educate medical personnel, police, and emergency technicians to show compassion and understanding. Many have not personally experienced the loss of a loved one and do not realize the depth of grief involved.

We had a clear illustration of how effective a person can be in his job when he has had personal experience. Eric had been having trouble with his shoulders sliding in the sockets. After years of football and basketball, he started going to physical therapy and was recommended for surgery. Gordon and I were impressed with the doctor as he listened to Eric. When Gordon asked if the problem is hereditary since he too had it in high school and college, resulting in surgery, the surgeon shared his same experience. He was concerned as he contemplated his recommendation. Since he himself had been through it, he had an understanding that others without that background could not give. As the Lord has shown me, experience brings empathy when knowledge may not. "Knowledge puffs up, but love builds up" (1 Corinthians 8:1c).

Misconception no. 9: Trials in life bring us closer together.

Although this statement sounds right, it is not always accurate. The divorce rate among couples who have had children die is incredibly high. When two people are grieving, their same emotions seldom coincide. When one is up, the other may be down. Men are less apt to share their feelings, while women generally want to talk. With energy levels low, the intimate times may be fewer. Trials in life put great stress on marriages and families, with remaining siblings often receiving little support. Mom and Dad have enough trouble functioning daily and coping with their own pain, with little left over for their grieving children, who are often more lost than the parents are. Compassionate Friends is for not only parents but also for siblings, who can meet with others to express their feelings. Without understanding, healing cannot begin. All of us need this support, but few more than those who have experienced great losses.

Misconception no. 10: Time heals all wounds.

This is a nice cliché but not necessarily true. Unless a person works through grief, not just ignoring it, healing cannot begin. True healing comes from the Lord, but He has brought us to help each other. Those who have gone through similar trials are best suited to give comfort, understanding, and encouragement, all necessary ingredients on the road to recovery. The total cure, however, will only come once we are reunited with our loved ones!

Misconception no. 11: The greatest loss a person can experience is the loss of a child.

There were people who shared this thought after we lost Matthew, and I pondered it many times, sincerely hoping they were right. I have since come to believe the statement is not necessarily accurate. It may have been in the past, but not now for most people in our country. Whatever is most important to a person constitutes a devastating loss. It seems most couples today take for granted that they will have a family. It is simply an expected part of life. Once again, as with depression, if each couple experienced what we have, the value of children would rise significantly. Nowadays we value our positions, houses, and cars over our families. We spend our time and energy building something that will one day resemble the original World Trade Center. For all its immensity, it became rubble. And though a devastating loss, most of us would agree that the greatest loss was not the buildings but the people inside who died. Our positions, houses, and cars will not last, and oh, the price we pay, the time and energy given to attain them! Meanwhile, our children, the true treasures, the precious blessings from the Lord, are sacrificed. How the Lord must grieve our skewed priorities.

I remember much from the sixties. Although I was only in junior high at their end, I felt the significance of those days, with their main emphasis: "We do not need moral rules or fancy things, we need love" ("Make love, not war!"). There was great rebellion. My older sister made a poster for my locker in junior high that read,

"People are more important than things," the thought, which seemed to epitomize the feel of that day. How, how have we come this far and back to believing exactly the opposite? Was it because the solution to the problem, more freedom—no rules, "free love," and drugs—was found to be a faulty one that we threw out the whole idea, both the premise and the hope for answers? We are much worse than we portrayed our parents, much more materialistic, valuing things, which do not last, much more than one another. How sad! Oh, that we could all value our families and one another—to see our true worth and the return of respect. "Do not wear yourself out to get rich; have the wisdom to show restraint. Cast but a glance at riches, and they are gone, for they will surely sprout wings and fly off to the sky like an eagle" (Proverbs 23:4, 5).

Misconception no. 12: "It will never happen to me" or "God will not give you more than you can bear" or numerous faulty premises.

All of us grow up with certain premises we accept as truth, and these premises provide a protection until they are proven faulty by an experience in our lives. Premises are needful so we can cope with daily tragedies—terminal illness, catastrophic injuries, accidents, death. I do not need to go on. There is much pain on earth. Except we have a coping mechanism, we could not continue to live, because of fear of what may happen to us. This coping mechanism is really our foundation, and it can either be faulty and weak or solid and strong. It is Jesus's story of the houses, one built on the sand and one built on the rock (Matthew 7:24–27). There is a home here that is a prime example of Jesus's illustration. It was built on a hill overlooking the Colorado River. After a few years, the owners discovered the foundation cracking and moved out. This was followed by a court battle with everyone pointing fingers at one another, the truth being that the foundation was not a good one for building a home. Every time I pass that house, I am reminded of the Lord's words to build on a solid foundation. The above two premises are faulty foundations.

For unbelievers and even some believers, the first notion, "It will never happen to me," is prevalent. Job 12:5 says, "Men at ease have contempt for misfortune as the fate of those whose feet are slipping." This is what I call the teenage premise because teenagers often ascribe to it: Nothing bad is going to happen to them. Parents need not worry; they are invincible. Most have also been protected within their parents' home, often not realizing how difficult life can be. Although in this evil age, they are not as shielded as in the past. It is hard to reason with someone who believes this, and unfortunately, this belief stays with them and is only broken when something bad actually does happen. Once it does, they are forever changed and unable to live that carefree life ever again.

The second premise is a Christian one, which I have heard many times and seen framed also, which says, "God will never give you more than you can bear." It is tempting to believe this and even feel a sense of pride: "God must think I am strong, since He gave me this difficult trial." But this is what Paul said in 2 Corinthians 1:8b–9: "We were under great pressure, far beyond our ability to endure, so that we despaired even of life. Indeed, in our hearts we felt the sentence of death. But this happened that we might not rely on ourselves but on God, who raises the dead." I also know from personal experience that He has given me more trials and pain than I could bear. Because of that, I have questioned if the above phrase was indeed a scripture or simply a coined phrase. In looking it up, the only scripture that I have found is 1 Corinthians 10:13, which says, "No temptation has seized you except what is common to man. And God is faithful; he will not let you be tempted beyond what you can bear. But when you are tempted, he will also provide a way out so that you can stand up under it." What this is speaking of is temptation. God will provide an escape from temptation. I have, as yet, been unable to find any scripture that says that He will not give us more trials or pain than we can bear. I think He does indeed allow unbearable trials and pain because we are not to bear them. We cannot. He carries us. "In all their distress he too was distressed, and the angel of his presence saved them. In his love and mercy he redeemed them; he lifted them up and carried them all the days of old" (Isaiah 63:9).

The above two premises are only two of many. I have recorded them because they are most common. Others include "I'm basically a good person," "I pray enough," "I fight the enemy daily," "I often help others," "I am doing my best." All these involve our own self-efforts and relate to the beliefs of those who ministered to Job. Unfortunately, they are all faulty premises.

In looking up *premise* in the dictionary, it is described as a foundational belief on which to base arguments, resulting in a conclusion.[4] *Premises* are land and buildings on it.[5] What we need to remember about premises is that they are propositions, not necessarily truth. So when we base our life upon a faulty one, we are in for a major, life-changing shock when it is proven false. That is why the shock of grief can be so profound—our premise has been shattered, and it is not easy to replace something believed for so long. This time it has to be proven solid, not faulty. The searching for a new foundation can take a long time. Meantime, incredible fears are present. Premises are meant to be tested. Jesus said all would be salted, tested, to see what foundation we built on.

The faith I had before 1983 is different from the faith since 1990. The first was based upon my belief that because I was sincere, trying to be good and do good things, He would protect me from especially hard trials. I expected the normal difficulties of life, but nothing major. The faith that came after 1990 is based upon God's Word, the only solid foundation, upon His promises to me, with the knowledge that I may sometimes misunderstand, believing that God loves and cares about me, only allowing those things that He knows will be for my ultimate good. The Lord wants all of us to have that foundation in Him, certain of His love despite anything that happens, knowing we can count on His constant Presence and eventual deliverance.

Misconception no. 13: The way in which a person dies, suddenly or after prolonged suffering, determines how intense the grief for those left behind.

As stated earlier, I believe it is our love of a person that determines how great the pain when he dies. If you have genuinely loved someone, it will hurt you terribly when he dies. I have experienced the deaths of our three children and my mom and dad. All our children died suddenly with no real warning, whereas Mom's death was a slow process, lasting more than ten years, and Dad's a year. All I know is that all five deaths hurt tremendously, and I went through the same stages of grief with each of them, although not in any particular order: shock, denial, confusion, anger, fear, depression, guilt. I believe the difference was that most of my grieving for Mom and Dad occurred before their deaths, whereas none of my grieving for the kids could have occurred beforehand. When Mom and Dad actually died, I felt great relief because I did not want them to suffer anymore. That does not mean I do not miss them, but after seeing Mom get progressively worse for ten years and trying to communicate and both of them struggling their final year in the nursing home, I was thankful they were finished with their anguish.

With Mom, there was shock and disbelief also, because she was so young (60) when her first symptoms appeared. But my mind had time to prepare, even before the beginning of her illness, for the fact that my parents would one day die. As a person grows up, there is a day when he realizes this, and his mind begins to accept the fact that it will indeed happen one day. When a child dies, our minds are never prepared because children are not supposed to die before their parents. The shock of that is unsettling, once again a faulty premise. The shock of the miscarriages was less intense than Matthew's death because I never took for granted any of my pregnancies after our first baby died. With both Eric and Matthew, however, once they were here, I never thought about them dying. The shock of Matthew dying was especially intense.

With all five deaths, however, there was grief, with all the stages. It hurts to lose those that we love, whether suddenly or after prolonged suffering. And the desire to see them and be with them becomes stronger as we draw nearer to their Home.

Misconception no. 14: With Godly sorrow, you feel no sadness for yourself.

In our case, we were not sad for my mom or dad or even our kids in their deaths. We felt sorrow for ourselves. There are certainly times when a person may feel sad for the one who has died, but that was not the case for us. Ecclesiastes 4:2–3 says it best: "And I declared that the dead, who had already died, are happier than the living, who are still alive. But better than both is he who has not yet been, who has not seen the evil that is done under the sun."

The misconceptions stated above are ones most prominent in my mind. Of course, there are others. I would encourage anyone struggling with hurtful words from others to consult the Lord. In all areas I was striving, the Lord refuted condemnation and brought consolation. Often, our culture, and even the church, has fostered faulty thinking. We need God's heart and mind, which is never condemning to His children, whom He loves. "For we do not have a high priest who is unable to sympathize with our weaknesses, but we have one who has been tempted in every way, just as we are—yet was without sin. Let us then approach the throne of grace with confidence, so that we may receive mercy and find grace to help us in our time of need" (Hebrews 4:15–16).

CHAPTER 14

The Kitchen Or Needs and Desires

The left hall led to the kitchen, a warm area. On the east and south walls were soft blue/green countertops, above which were cupboards of the same beautiful wood used in the whole house. Below these were windows, looking out to the beloved sunken garden to the east and the porch and sloping green lawn to the south that met another bubbling stream below.

The cupboards were engraved with all my favorite kinds of fruits: cherries, melons, bananas, pears, berries, and apples. Each had the same slight hint of color I had seen previously. Behind us, on the north wall, was an old-fashioned hearth and kettle. Into the top was built a type of oven. On the south wall, where the cabinets ended, there stood a round table and chairs of the same precious wood design engraved with fruit likenesses. These looked out through full-length windows to the patio. Much care had been given to providing not only basic needs but also my most cherished desires!

****

And my God will meet all your needs according
to his glorious riches in Christ Jesus.
—Philippians 4:19

> The Lord will guide you always; he will satisfy
> your needs in a sun-scorched land
> and will strengthen your frame. You will
> be like a well-watered garden,
> like a spring whose waters never fail.
>
> —Isaiah 58:11

We each have legitimate needs the Lord made within us. The most apparent ones are the following:

Physical	Mental	Spiritual
Air/Shelter	To be loved and accepted	To be loved by God
Food/Water	To love others	To love God in return
Rest/Sleep	To have work to accomplish	To have a relationship
Health/Sex		with God
		To know God's
		desires for us

When any one of these needs is unmet in our lives, we suffer. And our lives will be off balance so that we often hurt both others and ourselves as we attempt to fulfill our basic needs. As was obvious in my life, I searched, trying to attain unmet needs from my past. Mostly my search was one for approval from men, which led to many wrong choices and subsequent pain. We all search. Some may judge my life as comparatively easy in contrast to theirs, while others may feel that they have had most of their needs met. Whichever you may be, with many unmet needs or few, you are not whole until all are fulfilled. Is it possible on earth? I believe so.

Our greatest need is a spiritual one: to have the empty space inside filled with the only One who can fill it—Jesus. Until we ask Him into our hearts to live, there is a hollow, empty spot, forever causing pain. Many search their whole lives not realizing Jesus alone can take away that emptiness. "What a man desires is unfailing love" (Proverbs 19:22a). (In the same way, the Lord has one special place in His huge heart for each of us, and until we fill it, He is missing His greatest desire.)

The amazing thing, and something that has become more obvious to me each passing day, is this: once He is living inside us, He not only fills our empty spot, our greatest need, but He also, like the sun's rays, infiltrates all the other areas of need for the past, the present, and the future. What we feel we have missed or lost, He can restore. "I will repay you for the years the locusts have eaten—the great locust and the young locust, the other locusts and the locust swarm—my great army that I sent among you" (Joel 2:25). We will always fail one another because we are human and faulty, but God can fill in those gaps. And when the Lord meets our needs, we no longer expect others to.

I have heard some say that the Lord is not Santa Claus, and we should not constantly be voicing our needs and/or desires to Him. But through my experiences, I believe He is much concerned with not only our needs but also our desires. Maybe we have missed or have lost certain relationships, a mother, father, brother, sister, grandparents, etc., and/or certain experiences, sports, school, travel, etc., and/or certain material needs. Whatever we need or desire, the Lord delights to give us as long as He knows it will not be harmful. "Delight yourself also in the Lord; and He will give you the desires of your heart" (Psalms 37:4). Many times it is even something He has put into our hearts. What we feel sad to have missed or once had and no longer do, He can restore, and it is often His heart to do so. Our God is loving, a kind Father. These scriptures are encouraging.

> He satisfies my desires with good things, so that
> my youth is renewed like the eagle's.
> —Psalms 103:5

> No eye has seen, no ear has heard, no mind has conceived
> what God had prepared for those who love him.
> —1 Corinthians 2:9

I have known people who shared their regrets of never attending college, and at the same time, I have been amazed at the irony of life. My wish was to be married and starting a family the whole time I was in college, the very thing others had. Why do we always wish for what we do not have? And why does the Lord not always bring our greatest desires? I believe it is because He knows our greatest need is a spiritual one and that the best for us is to seek Him first. "But seek first his kingdom and his righteousness, and all these things will be given to you as well" (Matthew 6:33). So ultimately, we will come to realize our need and desire for Him above all, even the gifts He may bestow. The older I have become, the more dependent I am upon Him for everything in my life.

There are many who are living in jealousy, always wanting what others have or have had. The sad part is most of us see only the good others have, never realizing the heartaches their lives may have born or may be bearing. James 4:1–3 says, "What causes fights and quarrels among you? Don't they come from desires that battle within you? You want something but don't get it. You kill and covet, but you cannot have what you want. You quarrel and fight. You do not have, because you do not ask God. When you ask, you do not receive, because you ask with wrong motives, that you may spend what you get on your pleasures." We need to consider the balance once again, in evaluating accumulation of wealth on earth:

Wealth on Earth

Rich in money, material items   Poor in money, material items
(Off Balance)   (Off Balance)
Focus on wealth   Focus on wealth
Focus on the Lord
(Balanced)

Two things I ask of you, O Lord;
Do not refuse me before I die:

Keep falsehood and lies far from me;
Give me neither poverty nor riches,
but give me only my daily bread.
Otherwise, I may have too much
and disown you and say, 'Who is the Lord?'
Or I may become poor and steal,
and so dishonor the name of my God.
Proverbs 30:7–9

Often, people, in their jealousy, try to place guilt upon others because they perceive that others have what they themselves desire. The Lord does not want us doing that. Instead, He tells us to come to Him, and He will provide all, even those missing needs and desires from the past. I know. He has certainly done it for me. Granted, it has taken a long time, but He has given me tremendous blessings. In 1990 and 1991, He promised restoration and a renewal of my youth, like the eagles, and He has been faithful. He has also restored these missing pieces:

Grandpas: I never had any—Gordon's Grandpa
   Irv and our neighbor Bill
Sports: I was too frightened to try out in junior
   high and high schools—watching Eric and
   Sarabeth
Reading again: one of my favorite pastimes from
   my youth
Walking again: something I loved when I was
   growing up—time in nature
Time by a pasture: something I loved on my
   walk—Sarabeth's horse riding
Time talking to Judy: something we spent hours
   doing growing up
Times shared with Mary Lou: reminders of past
   sharing with sisters and friends

Having pets: reminders of growing up with dogs
and my neighbor's cats

The more the Lord has healed inside me, the more of the old uplifting feelings from my childhood have begun to resurface. Now along with memories of carefree days are coming more frequently those feelings that I experienced then. With so much pain for ever so long, those wonderful impressions that were buried inside have been gladly welcomed. The Lord has not only restored good for bad but He has also brought joyful emotions with those memories.

After suffering for the longest time, I had come to believe the Lord had for us only a life of pain and suffering, the lot Adam and Eve chose (the same I would have chosen if here before them). But one summer day, as I sat outside and absorbed the beauty, the realization came that the Lord meant for life to be enjoyed. "I have come that they may have life, and have it to the full" (John 10:10b). His plan is to bless us, living in close relationship with Him, thankful for His blessings:

Sights: beauty of all nature
Sounds: birds/water/breeze/music
Smells: flowers/earth/trees/food
Tastes: so many foods and drinks
Touches: breezes / loving touches within a family

Not only has the Lord put both needs and desires within us, but He has put equal attraction into others that we might all enjoy life and love. He made us want to give love and to receive it. Just as He made a cat with soft fur, which we wish to pet, it also loves to be petted and responds. As He put the yearning into a husband to touch his wife, she also has been given the longing to be touched and responds. It is supposed to be a joy to live and love.

One day, an older man, a carryout at the grocery store, shared that we have so much in our country and are all spoiled. I left there agreeing and feeling guilty to be so blessed. But as I drove away, I heard distinctly, "You cannot be spoiled if you are thankful." The Lord intended for life to be good. Our enemy wants us to feel guilty for our blessings. "For everything God created is good, and nothing is to be rejected if it is received with thanksgiving, because it is consecrated by the word of God and prayer" (1 Timothy 4:4, 5). The Lord desires first for us to come to Him and accept His most wonderful and free gift of salvation and then to daily come to know Him better. Then He begins to heal us and to "restore to us the years the locust have eaten" (Joel 2:25a) so that eventually we can say, "Surely goodness and love will follow me all the days of my life, and I will dwell in the house of the Lord forever" (Psalms 23:6).

CHAPTER 15

The Greenhouse Or God's Presence

L ooking down from the kitchen table, I could now see a replenished area, a dream for any gardener. Enclosed in the same beautiful glass as throughout the house, this retreat was filled with green and flowering plants in abundance. Each corner was girded by strong wooden pillars, and, just as in entering a greenhouse, the first step brought the fresh scent of earth and growing things. There was this also: as we descended the steps, a little fountain, splashing joy, bubbled below us. The steps and path were of moist, packed earth so that all around it too had the feel of a rain forest. Here in this room were two colorful birds sweetly singing and butterflies also flitting here and there. It is one place that continually beckons—complete contentment and refreshment, joy and peace.

****

For a man is a slave to whatever has mastered him.
—2 Peter 2:19b

Did you know that we were made in such a way to become addicted? We usually think of addiction in a negative way, but it can easily apply to positive things as well. The negative seems to come to mind first—drugs, alcohol, pornography, gambling—but there are also addictions to such positives as work, sports, sex, eating, shopping,

194

cell phones, Internet, and TV (huge ones in our society). Not only can we become addicted, we all have some addiction.

What is your addiction? What does the word even mean? The dictionary describes the verb *addict* as devoting ourselves to something obsessively.[1] The original Latin word *addictus* means to be enslaved.[2] Do you know that the Lord wants us to be addicted? In fact, He intended for us to be.

What characterizes an addiction? It begins innocently, something we do that brings pleasure and may even be difficult, so we repeat it until we are unable to live without it. At first, it makes us feel good. Pretty soon, that pleasure begins to dominate our thoughts and desires. That is all that we want, and we may do anything for it. This is most easily seen with drug addicts, who crave their drug to the extent of stealing and/or murdering, anything to obtain what their bodies are craving. They cannot resist. It has become all consuming. The sad part of most addictions is that they eventually lead to being so absorbed with ourselves, that we hurt others, either by neglect or a more blatant injury. They also always have negative side effects for the addicted himself.

So you may ask, why would God want us addicted? I have come to realize that the Lord does indeed want us addicted—to Him. Anyone who knows the Lord and has practiced being in His Presence will tell you it is the most peaceful and joyful place in the world. Jesus said, "Peace I leave with you; my peace I give you. I do not give to you as the world gives. Do not let your hearts be troubled and do not be afraid" (John 14:27). There also is no joy like it. "…in thy presence *is* fullness of joy; at thy right hand *there are* pleasures for evermore" (Psalms 16:11b, KJV). The more time spent in the Lord's Presence, the more is desired so that soon we are hooked. It gives meaning to the scripture "Pray continually" (1 Thessalonians 5:17). It is like first love, when it is hard to wait to be with the beloved. We count the days, hours, minutes when we are apart. And that is how it becomes with the Lord. We cannot wait to be near Him, to be close to Him, but it begins with practicing daily being in His Presence, resting in His arms, laying our heads on His shoulder, being close. As we experience that joy and peace, we begin to long for those times more and more. Every spare minute we desire to return, and the best part is there are no side effects, not to others or ourselves. It actually draws us closer to others, with the Lord among us.

The Lord is calling each of us to become addicted to Him. Is this not amazing? The Lord of the whole universe wants to be with us all the time! What could be better? Truly, this is good news!

CHAPTER 16

The Sunken Living Room Or Hearing from the Lord

Down from the kitchen to the west, wooden stairs descended to a cozy living room. Before the stairs was a wooden landing, wide enough for a day bed on the south end, with a door to the outside beyond it. The south wall was a huge glass window with a round stained glass in the center. Up high on the west wall were windows to let in glorious afternoon light, and under those were shelves containing more books! The north wall was wood paneling, and a fireplace graced the southwest corner of the room. This room had more pieces of the furniture, a couch and chairs, I had seen in the upstairs room on my first visit. Only now the old, ugly coverings were replaced by soft leather of a warm and soft brown color. The chairs in the kitchen had been similar, as were the couch and chairs in front of the fireplace of the great room. This was a warm and welcoming room.

****

For God does speak—now one way, now another—
though man may not perceive it.

—Job 33:14

While the Lord was on earth, He often spoke using parables, which are stories of everyday life that illustrate spiritual truths. Many seem confusing because our understanding is dependent on knowing the culture and everyday life of the Jewish people at that time. Some stories are more universal, such as the one about God caring for flowers and birds (Luke 12:22–31) and, therefore, more easily understood. I have found that He now uses parables from life today to teach us also.

One area I want to address involves something difficult for most of us: learning to hear and understand what the Lord is saying. Jesus said His sheep know His voice and follow Him (John 10:4, 27). Once we have been born again, we become His sheep and can hear His voice. It can, however, still be confusing if we are unsure we have heard Him or what He many be saying.

Being a people-pleaser most of my life, all that others have spoken to me through the years has been taken very much to heart. I have always second-guessed my own thoughts as others shared theirs. With the deaths of our three children, people began sharing their beliefs. That was unsettling, especially when condemning words came. It was not until my second depression in 1989 that I earnestly began to ask the Lord, "What are *You* saying to me?" That is when the Lord began to show me many truths and helped me understand what had happened to us and the plans He had for our future. In the midst of that, He also revealed His beautiful character—His comfort, encouragement, understanding, and lack of condemnation. It is important for all of us to hear from the Lord. If we only talk to Him, not expecting Him to respond, we are missing the best part! When I first became a Christian, I was encouraged to read the Bible and a devotional book daily. Those have been lifelines through the years, as the Lord has been teaching me to hear His voice in other ways also.

This area of hearing from the Lord can be the source of much pain. There are churches who do not believe that the Lord speaks to us at all today except through the Bible in a more general way, not personally. For a person who is struggling with hearing from the

Lord, there may be feelings of condemnation, either from (1) those who teach that God does not speak to us personally or (2) those who believe He does and who express His words to him. Both positions can be perplexing.

Regarding the first, Jesus said His sheep know His voice and follow Him (John 10:4, 27). John 8:47a also says the same: "He who belongs to God hears what God is saying." Obviously, to have a true relationship with someone, there has to be communication. If we alone speak to the Lord and do not expect an answer, we do not have a very close relationship. Also, from experience, I have come to know that the Lord does speak in a personal way.

As others share experiences, we often feel we must not be real Christians or simply do not have much faith. Having gone through this soul-searching for a long time, I can finally say, "Yes, I am a true believer, and I have learned to hear His voice." Below are answers that have helped me.

1. We are often so busy it is hard for the Lord to get our attention. He may be speaking constantly, but we do not hear because we are not quiet before Him. We rush through prayers and readings and hurry off, not taking time to hear what He is saying. It seems that the times in my life I have been most needy, especially during my two deep depressions, when I was desperate to be in the Lord's Presence, have been the times I have heard the Lord best. Those times have been the ones when I sought the Lord with all my heart, 1983 and 1989, and He answered me (Daniel 2:22, Psalms 25:14, Psalms 119:10, 11). I began to write that those were the times He has spoken most, but I changed my mind, knowing the Lord is often speaking even when we are unaware. We need to take time to hear by practicing being in His Presence daily. Some of us workaholics have to be slowed down with trials so that we can learn to hear Him. We need to follow Mary's example and sit at His feet as

we follow Martha's example of working also (Luke 10:38–42). We can learn to continually be aware of His Presence, even as we work throughout our day, "praying constantly" (1 Thessalonians 5:17) and thinking on what is good and pure, the only One (Philippians 4:8). "Fix your thoughts on Jesus" (Hebrews 3:1b).

2. We may have the misconception that we will hear Him in our heads. I believe that this can come but later on, usually after we have come to hear His voice in other ways. Our pastor said that the Lord uses many different voices, but His message will always be the same, repeated many times as confirmation. If we look at what we have been reading in our Bible and/or our devotionals, we can actually find a common word, especially if we have been seeking the Lord for specific answers in some area in which we are struggling, either for understanding or for guidance.

3. Another hindrance can be our emotions. When we are upset, it can cloud our minds, keeping us from hearing. It is only in calmness that a message may come.

4. Another obstacle may be a reluctance to hear from the Lord, fearing deception by the devil. This is a legitimate concern. However, being surrounded by numerous dangers in our everyday lives—using electricity, gas, cars, fire, even water—we do not cease to use them because of their intrinsic dangers. Their benefits far outweigh their risks. Nevertheless, we have had to learn to use them safely. In the same way, if we seek the Lord, He will teach us the safe way to hear and follow Him. I have found one caution essential: to always ask the Lord if the word I have heard is truly from Him. If so, He will repeat it in other ways. If not, it could be our enemy, parading as "an angel of light" (2 Corinthians 11:14). If there is no verification, I can be certain it was not from Him.

A final word of caution: it is important not only to ask Him to help us to hear and understand but also to have His written Word, the Bible, as our compass. It is the filter through which we must pass every word we believe we have heard. If anything contradicts what has been written there, it is not from the Lord, because the Lord does not change (Malachi 3:6a), and neither do His words. Many have deceived and been deceived due to this error. Religion involves trying to become good enough and do enough work to be accepted by the Lord. The Bible teaches that our salvation does not come from those self-efforts but through the free gift of God (Romans 6:23). Cults come about when one person says that he alone has the Word of God and that others have to follow what he says. The fallacy of that is evident when we remember that Jesus said that *all of us* who know Him hear from Him, and in fact, the Bible is the Lord's Word, revealed to many people over the course of time. True Christianity is God's gift of salvation and the subsequent loving relationship that continues throughout our life, not self-efforts or man-made rules to earn salvation.

Throughout this book, I have shared my experiences in seeking the Lord's answers to questions I have had. At the beginning of my journey, it was rare for me to hear Him. After our seven years of intense pain and seeking the Lord, my hearing became clearer. Also at times in my life when I have had more alone time, specifically once the kids went to school full-time, more words came (1990/1991, 1999–now). They have come through many sources, first of all, the Bible, but also through other books, movies, people, retreats, dreams, songs, and experiences. This book is the sharing of those treasures that I hold dear and that have indeed kept me going, His words of Life.

In conclusion, if you have also struggled with hearing from the Lord, please do not condemn yourself wondering if you could truly be a Christian because you feel you have never heard from the Lord. Do not fear something is wrong with you. Instead, ask the Lord to help you to hear Him, because He is speaking and does care. His words bring encouragement and joy. "The words that I have spoken to you are spirit and they are life" (John 6:63b). "At that time Jesus said, 'I praise you, Father, Lord of heaven and earth, because you have hidden these things from the wise and learned, and revealed them to little children'" (Matthew 11:25).

CHAPTER 17

The Secret Attic Room
Or Faith and Promises

Leaving the sunken living room, I was reentering the kitchen when my Lord stopped me. Near the kitchen door to the outside on the west wall was a built-in china cabinet. When My Lord pushed against the wood on the side near the steps, a secret panel was disclosed, exposing a hidden ladder and opening in the ceiling. He then beckoned me to ascend into the secret room above. Of course, this was more of what my heart had always desired, the invisible and unknown.

No one can guess the joy of seeing a hidden room for the first time. Not only hidden, but also long awaited, even sending out muffled calls daily to the soul. I cannot begin to tell you the deep feelings in my heart as the Lord revealed this most sacred place. And oh, for me to share it now will only be most disappointing to you, because you can never know until you visit your own secret place and room just what it means—how indeed humbling, thrilling, and exalting it is all at the same time. I guarantee my description will not excite you as what was before us was most simple—a wood-paneled room, small and devoid of any furnishings, except big sky-blue padded cushions, and a corner fireplace. Although the wood of the east and north walls and floor were oiled to an exquisite shine and engraved with tiny rainbows, that was not the amazing part. What *was* amazing was the view: two huge windows facing out to the south wall of rock and to the western sloping lawn and lake, and beyond, the giant waterfall that provided constant and soothing background music. From outside, this room is hidden, the windows a reflective covering that appears textured, only clear inside. No one could know the wonder inside, and I previously had no inkling myself. From here, my Lord has revealed hidden wonders, unknown dreams and paths to their fulfillment.

****

> The Lord is faithful to all his promises and
> loving toward all he has made.
> —Psalms 145:13b

> Let us hold unswervingly to the hope we
> profess, for he who promised is faithful.
> —Hebrews 10:23

Two post notes concerning hearing from the Lord have to do with faith and promises. The first involves faith. I have heard of people condemned for not receiving healing or for having bad happen in their lives, even feeling condemned by some in our pain. The idea bothered me until the Lord showed me Romans 10:17, which states, "Consequently, faith comes from hearing the message, and the message is heard through the word of Christ."

I now realize that thinking the Lord will heal or do anything for us is presumption or assumption on our part unless He has spoken to us personally. We can continue to pray and hope, trusting in His goodness and love, but we cannot exercise our faith until the Lord has spoken He intends to do something. Then we can choose to believe, to have faith, or not. Before then, if we claim certain scriptures that are not legitimate promises, we are being as Satan in the tempting of Jesus (Luke 4), taking a scripture and using it, thinking we are stepping out in faith, when we are testing God, and if not testing Him, at least telling Him we know better than He does what is best. Often God has a reason for allowing a person to stay in a certain position. His word may be "Wait," not necessarily "No." To condemn that person is to place a time limit on God's work or to assume that we know better. Anyone who has waited for God's deliverance knows it always comes in His timing, not ours. Also, it may not be the best God has for that individual. God chose not to heal Paul. Instead, He told him, "My grace is sufficient for you, for my power is made perfect in weakness" (2 Corinthians 12:9a). Also we have to hear a word before we can hold on to it. Unless the Lord has said and verified He will do something, we are walking on shaky ground to believe it. Many have been condemned for lack of faith who should be commended for not presuming on God.

To me, there is a distinct difference between faith and trust. Faith believes what we have heard, whereas trust involves a surrendering of our lives to God, believing in His goodness and good purposes, despite what we may see. "And we know that in all things God works for the good of those who have been called according to his purpose" (Romans 8:28). The Lord gave me two wonderful illustrations of this trust. The first involves Sarabeth. For the longest time, she wanted a dog and pestered her dad for one. Neither he nor I were excited about it and had already gone through the pestering with Eric, who was appeased with a cat instead. Although Gordon continued to deny her request, she was persistent, like the widow in the story Jesus told (Luke 18:1–8). Finally, Gordon said, "Maybe." Well, Sarabeth told everyone at preschool she was getting a dog, and that spring she did indeed get one. After hearing "Maybe," she exercised her faith, believing and waiting.

The second example is with that very dog, Sally. Often we had food around her, and she, like most dogs, came and sat at our feet with pleading eyes. It is like the story of the Canaanite woman who told Jesus even dogs ate crumbs from their master's table (Matthew 15:21–28). These are good illustrations of trust. Both Sarabeth and

Sally trusted the love of the person to whom they turned. They believed not only that he was able to grant the request but also loved them enough to do it.

I see another biblical illustration of this in the story of the lepers (Luke 17:11–19). They trusted the Lord enough to ask for healing, obviously believing He could do it and wanted to. I have often wondered if I would have been like one of the nine who did not return to thank Jesus, not because ungratefulness, but because of legalism, believing that *not* to go to the priest and show myself would have been disobedience and have reneged the healing. That shows lack of trust and understanding. Realizing Jesus was kind enough to heal him took away any fear the tenth man had of thanking Him. It is knowing and trusting in the goodness, kindness, and love of the Healer.

What then is the answer to the scripture, "Ask and it will be given to you; seek and you will find; knock and the door will be opened to you. For everyone who asks receives; he who seeks find; and to him who knocks, the door will be opened" (Matthew 7:7)? I believe that we do receive with every prayer request. The Lord says "Yes" or "Yes, but wait" or "No." If "Yes" or "Yes, but wait," of course we eventually receive what we have asked for. If He says "No," however, we will still receive, because His "No" is only as a loving Parent, knowing our desire would not be good. In this case, He brings something better. So with any request, we are guaranteed the ultimate best.

We have to consider God's will, trusting that He does indeed have the most excellent plan. We also have to know that His timing is just right. Answers to prayer, especially huge prayers, often take time. The answer may already be in heaven, but the Lord has to deliver it here through the agency of time. Please be encouraged if you have been one of the condemned. Know the Lord does care. Seek Him. Often His answer is not "No" but "Wait." That has been the case for me numerous times, but there are also times He has said "No," as with Eric playing basketball his last two years of high school and also of my sister Judy and her family moving here. Though sad in both instances, I am certain, having known my Lord for a long time and through numerous trials, He had a good reason.

As shared earlier, there are times when the Lord does give us definite promises, often followed by a period of waiting. There are many examples in the Bible—Noah, Abraham, Joseph, Moses, Hannah, Elizabeth, Mary, and many others. In each instance, the Lord gave a promise, resulting in faith being exercised through times of waiting and obeying the Lord's leading.

This is the way the Lord wants to deal with us today, giving promises for our future. Our faith is developed and strengthened as we wait to see Him perform whatever He has pledged, even in the face of impossible odds. The Lord encouraged me about promises when he revealed the following. To us, promises appear as shadows, which are different with the changing light of the day. From our perspective, they seem to change, but actually, each new circumstance does nothing to change the reality of the promise. The truth is that the object that casts the shadow stays steady. It does not move or change. Promises are the same. They are not shadows of the object, but the objects themselves. Once given by the Lord, we can count on their fulfillment. "The law is only a shadow of the good things that are coming—not the realities themselves" (Hebrews 10:1a).

God is not a man, that he should lie, nor a son
of man, that he should change his mind.
Does he speak and then not act? Does he promise and not fulfill?
—Numbers 23:19

Blessed is she who has believed that what the
Lord has said to her will be accomplished.
—Luke 1:45

So keep up your courage, men, for I have faith in
God that it will happen just as he told me.
—Acts 27:25

The rainbow is God's ultimate sign of keeping His promises. If you have a word from the Lord, hang on to it because our God is faithful and will do just as He promised. When Satan tempts us to disbelieve, we need to run to Jesus and ask, "Lord, did You not speak to me?" He will answer, most often with confirmation of the original word. Take heart! He is faithful to His promises.

CHAPTER 18

The Porch Or Puzzles

O nce down the ladder, we headed to the door in the kitchen, which led to the covered outside porch. All its damaged wood had now been replaced, but not as before, with ordinary slats. Instead, small pieces of many kinds of wood formed pretty patterns, one of a sun, a rose, a rainbow, a heart, and other meaningful pictures. It was obvious much care had been taken to fit each piece, providing something precious in the process. In the corner was a round table with a mosaic top and in front of the window was a swing. Below, a rock pathway descended to the stream. A peaceful getaway.

****

Now we see but a poor reflection; then we shall see face to face.
Now I know in part; then I shall know
fully, even as I am fully known.
—1 Corinthians 13:12

As mentioned earlier, I do not like puzzles! Oh, not easy kid puzzles that can be put together in a short time, but the big small-pieced puzzles that require much time and are generally a slow process. To me, they seem overwhelming. I much prefer projects quickly accomplished with immediate rewards. Once again, evidence of an extremely impatient person! But guess what? God has been teaching me to accept puzzles, even if I still do not like them.

From the beginning of my Christian life, the Lord's most consistent word has been *wait*. He has been teaching me how to live a little at a time so as not to become overwhelmed. It has been challenging not to dwell on the whole picture, all to be done, and instead focus on the small parts that compose the complete picture. Like house remodeling, puzzles involve time and cannot be rushed. Eventually all the pieces fit together to form the picture on the cover, the Lord's ultimate plan.

Probably the Lord's most profound way of teaching me this concept came through years of grief. Going through grief and depression does teach us to live a little at a time, the reason being we have no choice. We are not able to do more. Living through those times can only be accomplished by living right now, this minute. It is too wearing to look far ahead or even into the following week or next day. The old saying "Live a day at a time" becomes especially significant to those experiencing grief. We have had to learn to live a second at a time because we were so overloaded physically, mentally, and spiritually that we could not make plans. We get through right now and often, with difficulty. The Lord did ingrain this principle into me because even now, years later, I am unable to plan far ahead, instead living a bit at a time, which is all I can handle. For those who feel more in control of their lives, I am probably a source of frustration, but in the back of my mind, the knowledge that our best-laid plans often fail is a constant reminder. "Many are the plans in a man's heart but it is the Lord's purpose that prevails" (Proverbs 19:21). We have experienced many foiled plans. So we have come to hold those plans more loosely, placing them instead into God's hands, knowing we definitely are not in control and can only do our tiny part.

This principle of puzzles affects not only projects and plans but also many other areas of our lives. One that has brought much frustration to me personally is in the area of change. There are certain habits that have plagued me, which I have begged the Lord to remove. In my impatience, there has been the definite hope that He would answer with a streak of lightning and an immediately new and improved me, something that certainly would have seemed to be His will also. Unfortunately He did not answer that quickly, instead allowing me to struggle through years of trying to deal with anger, using my self-efforts, before He provided the answer, as it turned out an easy solution.

In the same way, He is now teaching me about self-respect and has shown me specific areas in which to practice. Once again, this puzzle concept is frustrating and seems monumental, as all I can see is the whole area in need of change. It is like my second depression, feeling trapped in a huge sand pit, where climbing out becomes an exhausting and frustrating endeavor. That is how all change seems, monumental and impossible, as if there will never come a time of victory. It is a slow process. But do you know how the Lord helped me out of the pit of depression? With little steps, resting on Him, knowing He would bring me out. He slowly revealed comforting and encouraging steps, recorded previously. Slowly, ever so slowly, He pulled me out. It was not me panicking to find a way out, though that was a huge desire and temptation. It was only Him, His grace, love, strength, and wisdom. In all change, it helps to remember that God is performing the work while we do our little part with His guidance. When we slip, and we will slip, because our part usually takes all we have, we need to remember that He is still in control and not all is lost.

This is also the story of my home, remodeled a room at a time—the story of my pregnancies, my ulcers, and Sarabeth's stomach problems—all we have to learn in school, in sports, in life, and some things we have to relearn, the bad habits that somehow crept inside too. It is all the same, a puzzle in which we must trust the Lord and do our little part, waiting for Him to accomplish His big work. Eventually, we can look at the whole and say, "I understand. I can now see that it is complete."

Sometimes, in the process, we need to step back and view the whole picture and see what God has already accomplished. Otherwise, we can bog down on pieces that continually seem not to fit. It helps to get a glimpse of what has been done as we look to the goal.

This book has been a definite area of practice regarding puzzles. The desire to write has been consistent and intense, and I always hate to put it up for later. As John 7:38 states, "Whoever believes in me, as the Scripture has said, streams of living water will flow from within him." Unfortunately, there has been little time to devote to it, only a couple mornings a week. At first, there were thrill and compulsion, then realization of the immensity of the undertaking, then many distractions and fears of leaving out important lessons or not explaining well, but piece by piece, I have continued and hopefully, will one day see the final result. The Lord merely wants me to continue and not give up. And one day I can say, "Thank You, sweet Jesus! What seemed a huge mountain has now become a resting spot for my soul!" If you also struggle with puzzles, be encouraged. A day does arrive when each puzzle is completed, with great relief and a sense of accomplishment. Do not give up!

We all begin our lives with a box of puzzle pieces that has our picture on the front. Most of us soon find that we need the Lord's help to put it together. One day, when the final piece is set, the day He calls us Home, the picture on the front will have appeared, but instead of our own picture, there will be the reflection of Jesus! How kind is our Lord! "And we, who with unveiled faces all reflect the Lord's glory, are being transformed into his likeness with ever-increasing glory, which comes from the Lord, who is the Spirit" (2 Corinthians 3:18).

****

Why Did This Happen to Us?

My journey years were some of the most painful and confusing of my life. When Gordon and I attended the Compassionate Friends National Convention, the keynote speaker shared his experience of seeking answers to the why of his daughter's death. He said it is not that God does not want to answer our questions. It is that we are incapable of understanding. It is something far beyond our mortal comprehension.

That is the same answer the Lord gave to Job (Job 40, 41). Though it may seem like the Lord was upset with Job, I do not think so. I have found He is exceptionally patient in our sincere questioning and searching. What He was saying to Job (and us) is, "How can you understand? You have not created the world. You do not know how it works. How can you expect to understand these extremely hard circumstances?" We cannot. There are questions that will not be answered in their entirety until we pass on. We simply do not have the capacity to understand. But our loving Lord does not leave us without answers. He began preparing my heart years ahead for what He knew was coming into my life, most of all by giving me *Hind's Feet on High Places*. After much soul-searching and years of analyzing, I believe the Lord has provided three comforting answers for now until I can see the whole picture in heaven. These are themes of *Hind's Feet* also.[1]

1. When I was born into the family of God, I was extremely wounded and sick. Ezekiel 16:4–8 clearly explains where I was: "On the day you were born your cord was not cut, nor were you washed with water to make you clean, nor were you rubbed with salt or wrapped in cloth. No one looked on you with pity or had compassion enough to do any of these things for you. Rather, you were thrown out into the open field, for on the day you were born you were despised. Then I passed by and saw you kicking about in your blood, and as you lay there in your blood I said to you, 'Live!' I made you grow like a plant of the field. You grew up and developed and

became the most beautiful of jewels. Your breasts were formed and your hair grew, you who were naked and bare. Later I passed by, and when I looked at you and saw that you were old enough for love, I spread the corner of my garment over you and covered your naked-ness. I gave you my solemn oath and entered into a covenant with you, declares the Sovereign Lord, and you became mine."

Truly, if the Lord had not rescued me, I would have soon died, through suicide, sickness, accidents, or disease. My pain was intense. Like Much-Afraid, I felt self-conscious about my obvious inadequacies, especially around other Christians.

Unfortunately, although we *do* become new creatures when we ask the Lord into our hearts, we are still wounded from our pasts. Nancy Missler explains this clearly in her book *Be Ye Transformed.* She says we receive a new spirit, a new heart, and a new will when we are reborn.[2] Unfortunately, our souls and bodies remain the same. That is where healing is required. The Lord, like a trained surgeon, knew that surgery was needed to bring healing to me. When one of us has a severe, life-threatening injury or sickness, surgery is often the only answer. Do we consider the surgeon cruel and heartless when he hurts us further, bringing more pain into our lives? No, because we can see his ultimate goal: to bring healing. Our recovery time may be long and slow, but it is ultimately to bring health long-term. The Lord showed me that He had to do massive surgeries on me, which were incredibly painful and brought long-suffering, so much so that I was certain I would die anyway. But the Lord is faithful. Instead, "I will not die but live, and will proclaim what the Lord has done" (Psalms 118:17). Although the Lord accepts us exactly as we are, His heart is not content until He is able to bring healing to us in all areas. He understands and comforts us in our pain, but that very understanding will not allow Him to leave us in such a despairing state. He loves us too much.

2. Through all the surgeries and recovery, 1983–1990, seven years of intense pain, the Lord showed Himself not only to be my surgeon and healer but also as my nurse, counselor, and best friend.

He took my broken heart and mended it with utmost care and spent all the recovery time with me, constantly at my beck and call, easing every pain, comforting and encouraging, listening, and sharing. All the pain He allowed has drawn me closer to Him, and I can say with my whole heart the Lord is my dearest friend, my husband, my lover, my all. Through the journey, I have come to see His deep, deep love for me and know it is for all of us. Not only can extreme circumstances lead us closer to Him, but they also help to develop balance in our characters, with Jesus at our centers.

3. As in *Hind's Feet*, when Much-Afraid's journey led to the Kingdom of Love and her subsequent healing, my journey led to the same place, one of restoration. Following that, she (and I) found the Kingdom of Love our permanent home, a place to return after times of ministering to others. We are comforted to comfort others. "Praise be to the God and Father of our Lord Jesus Christ, the Father of compassion and the God of all comfort, who comforts us in all our troubles, so that we can comfort those in any trouble with the comfort we ourselves have received from God. For just as the sufferings of Christ flow over into our lives, so also through Christ our comfort overflows" (2 Corinthians 1:3–5).

The Lord's desire is for us to be whole, in Him, for not only ourselves, but also that we can help others who are suffering. When we are broken, all our energies go into surviving daily. We need His touch before we can help others. A perfect example of this was apparent years ago as I returned from walking Sarabeth to school. A neighbor had her sprinklers running, and one of the heads was broken, its water shooting into the air and pouring into the gutter, eventually hurrying down the drain. All of its energy was wasted. The life-giving water was not going to the grass, helping it grow, but going down the drain, helping no one. Its original purpose, to sustain the grass, was defeated. The following week, I noticed the sprinkler head had been repaired, but now another was broken, exhibiting the same problem. This is a good illustration of the church. We all enter the Kingdom of God wounded, some of us worse than others. God, in His great wisdom and mercy, works to make us whole—for Him, for ourselves, and for others. In the process, we become closer to Him, knowing He understands our weaknesses and therefore no longer feeling unworthy of His love. Then we begin to feel better and have renewed energy. Finally, we can reach out to others who are wounded, with the great news of the Lord and the kindness He has shown to us.

In ending this chapter, I need to share this final word of encouragement from the Lord. Through the years, the thought occurred occasionally to my mind that the Lord had brought these hard trials because of my disobedience in marrying a non-Christian. As shared before, I also feared He was punishing me for yelling at Eric. Though I hoped and prayed it was not true, those thoughts would resurface, never totally disappearing from my mind. With His answers, recorded above, these accusations subsided a great deal. Just recently, the Lord brought more understanding.

He showed me that His forgiveness was given right from the beginning in each instance, and He was never punishing me. But there were natural consequences the Lord desired for me not to have to endure. With Gordon, these included fearing for his salvation, going to cell group and church alone or taking the kids by myself, and never being able to share spiritually with one I loved. With Eric, the natural consequences were alienation from my son.

When Eric was in elementary school, *Choose Your Own Adventure* books were popular. Throughout each book, there were choices given for where the storyline would go. A chapter would end with questions, and the continuing page given, depending upon the reader's answers, so that more than one story could be found within the one book.[3]

In this same way, God respects us, letting us make choices, and sometimes we make faulty ones, but He does not give up on us as we struggle through the natural consequences, and He does not punish us. He is there to love us through it all. You may ask, "Why then does He not remove those consequences?" Three reasons come to my mind: (1) we often learn best through those results, (2) we often seek the Lord more in our consequences, and (3) He knows that anything placed in His hands can be changed for good. "And we know that in all things God works for the good of those who love him, who have been called according to his purpose" (Romans 8:28).

There is much pain in the world, and many times God gets the blame, when in reality it is often the result of our own poor choices. God made the world with consequences physically, mentally, and spiritually. If we choose to jump off a cliff, ignoring the physical law of gravity, we may die. That, however, is not God's fault but our own. There are other sources of heartache also—sickness, accidents, natural disasters—that come from living in an imperfect world. The enemy initiates many of these occurrences, because he hates all people, both believers and unbelievers, God's creation.

In the Old Testament, the Lord dealt with the Israelites with rules and punishment. Once Jesus came and died, this old covenant was replaced with a better one, a covenant not just for the Hebrews but also for all of us. This new arrangement is by the Spirit, not by the law, so that punishment for sin has been abolished for those of us who have the Spirit living inside. We have a protective covering, while those who do not are more susceptible to the enemy's attacks.

God is forever a gentleman. He does not force us to love Him or to move into His kingdom. Even once we are part of His family, He will not initiate healing (our homes remodeled) without our consent. When an individual or nation rejects Him, He withdraws, not out of revenge, but out of deep love, the foundation being respect, giving us free will, the freedom to make our own choices. He says He is at the door gently knocking, but He will never force His way inside.

Although those who do not have His Spirit inside are more vulnerable to the enemy's assaults, even we Christians will experience pain, God will allow it, when we seek healing from Him, acting first as a surgeon and dearest Friend, drawing us close and teaching us compassion for the hurting. Because we are now living in God's time of grace and mercy, I do not believe He brings evil upon anyone, believer or unbeliever; that is the result of a faulty world and our enemy's tactics. The Lord is ever waiting (and wanting) our permission to come and help. Revelation says that in the end, the Lord will send disasters to earth, but I believe, out of compassion, it will be His last attempt to draw people to Him before the world ends. Many cannot believe a loving God would allow terrible events. That is in itself proof He is a loving God. He sees eternity and knows our suffering here will be much less than suffering for all eternity.

The Bible teaches of the Father disciplining his son in love. "Our fathers disciplined us for a little while as they thought best, but God disciplines us for our good, that we may share in his holiness" (Hebrews. 12:10). When we come into His family, He works as a doctor to heal us, then as a parent, with understanding and encouragement, teaching His young. Finally, He works as a teacher, with many lessons and tests along the way, always, always in love.

CHAPTER 19

The Swimming Pool and Jacuzzi Or God's Will

From inside, the great room looked out to the west. A door near the stairwell led to a most tranquil place. My first quick glimpse had come from peering through the arched metal gate outside. Now we entered from the glass door inside the house. I was surprised it had escaped my notice on the day of viewing the renewed great room for the first time. Perhaps that room itself was simply so overpowering. Once we walked out onto the stone patio, a tier of steps led to a big pool. On the far northwest corner, at the top of the steps was another Jacuzzi. All this was surrounded by a rock wall, into which were embedded horizontal strips of glass, looking out to the west upon the sloping lawn, quiet lake, and far below, the valley. We have visited the lake on many occasions, resting on its waters in a little boat. Halfway up the slope is a precious glass-enclosed gazebo, a wonderful place to view sunsets over the lake. To the north is the quiet and protective forest. How peaceful!

****

Commit your way to the Lord; trust in him
and he will do this: He will make your

righteousness shine like the dawn, the justice
of your cause like the noonday sun.
—Psalms 37:5–6

Do not be anxious about anything, but in
everything, by prayer and petition,
with thanksgiving, present your requests
to God. And the peace of God,
which transcends all understanding,
will guard your hearts and your minds in Christ Jesus.
—Philippians 4:6–7

Although those of us who are Christians understand that we have given our lives to God and have asked Him to come live within us, it is often a difficult lesson to give up some treasured plan, dream, or hope and our self-efforts to attain these. Thankfully, God does live within us and helps us change so that we are able to accept His will. There have been many experiences of this in my life, mostly involving God's timing: (1) my prayer for a husband, (2) our prayer for a house, (3) our prayer for children, and (4) my daily plans, accepting God's alternatives.

I have come to know through much waiting that when we give a need, desire, concern to God and sincerely leave it with Him, accepting whatever decision His may be, we come to know peace inside, and that is also when God begins to work on our behalf. When the Lord brought me to the point of accepting Eric as our only living child, thanking Him for him and acknowledging we may have no other children, I found peace and comfort in the Lord. Then He began to work. That does not mean that He always gives us what we desire. He may say no, but often He is saying to wait. He delights to answer our prayers, but it is often not in our timing, and sometimes the fulfillment would not be for our best. We have to know and remember that whatever He says, He always has our greatest interest in mind. As I reflect upon some of my past prayers, I can see the reason and sincerely thank the Lord for his wisdom in denying them. He is not trying to thwart or deny us. As we give to Him our desires, needs, concerns, leaving them in His hands, He does help us to let loose and to be at peace, accepting His will.

Having experienced years of drought, as Colorado (and many other states) hurt for water, with less runoff from winter snows and scant rain, there have been many fires throughout our state. This has helped me to understand God's ways, as I was thinking how many of us travel, often in the winter, and always with a prayer that we will not have bad weather or roads. What occurred to me was that if everyone prayed that prayer in the winter as they traveled over the mountain passes and if the Lord agreed with each one, there would be no more storms or water from them. In that respect, it is obvious that not all our prayers are wise. The drought is a good example, a helpful lesson, showing why God may not grant our every request. We need storms and the moisture they provide.

I have recorded below some of the desires I have relinquished to the Lord in the past. At first, most involved much self-effort. After experiencing many failures, I gave my desires to the Lord, waiting for Him to act, which finally led to their fulfillment.

1. My husband, Gordon, 1976
2. Our home, 1981
3. Healing of depression, 1983–1984
4. Birth of Eric after my first miscarriage, 1985
5. Gordon's salvation, 1987
6. Healing of ulcer and depression, 1989
7. Birth of Sarabeth after Matthew's death and my second miscarriage, 1992
8. Healing of Sarabeth's stomach, 1997
9. Ministry after my first attempt in 1989, 2001–2003

CHAPTER 20

The Sunken Garden
Or My Father's Acceptance

Although I had often viewed this enchanted respite from a distance, it was to be one of the last places my Lord took me. He has since shown me many ways down into my sanctuary. The one I have nearly always taken, however, has a most unique entrance. The towering cottonwood tree reaches its limbs so high that from the little stream on the east side of the house, no one would guess its trunk actually descends to the bottom of the garden. On our first visit, we sat in the homemade tree house right below the stream. Many times since, after resting in the tree, we have dropped into the garden by way of wooden slats nailed to the trunk, so reminiscent of happy childhood escapades!

This garden is huge, and even now, I have to admit I have not seen all of it. It is precious, nonetheless. Most of the bottom feeds numerous fruit trees: peach, pear, cherry, apple, lemons, and limes. Its slopes contain various types of vines and shrubbery: woodbine, grapes, clematis, lilacs, magnolias, gardenias, and honeysuckle. Though I named some, it is by no means all it encompasses.

The south side is an enticing one for me, as it grows delightful flowers of all colors, textures, and kinds. What is most precious is that the seeds from all these have come from prayers my Lord has sown for me. Oh, how glorious to see them bloom forever.

The northeast corner has a beautiful lake, though not nearly as large as the one below the house on the west side. A stream falls from above into its far corner. To the south is a hidden alcove with a bench. This is a most precious sanctuary, filled with joy and acceptance, ever welcoming!

****

For we are God's workmanship, created in
Christ Jesus to do good works,
which God prepared in advance for us to do.
—Ephesians 2:10

In order to see the Lord in His true perspective and to understand our relationship with Him and how He views us, it is important to examine our past relationship with our human parents. This can be difficult for some, not wanting to place blame upon their parents. Therefore, it is imperative to ask the Lord to reveal what He wants to show us, what would help in examining our past.

When Sarabeth began first grade, I once again had full days alone, the first time since Eric started first grade, a year before Sarabeth was born. This need for alone time has been strong and consistent for me. The winter following Sarabeth's entrance into first grade, the Lord began to reveal the many misconceptions I had learned as a child and by which I was still living, unspoken rules that had me bound by guilt and fear of punishment and/or ridicule.

As we grow up, most of us view our fathers with special wonder, especially little girls. What an awesome job God has given to dads. They are the ultimate example of what our Heavenly Father is like! Although none of us want to be held to such high standards, it is nevertheless the way that most children develop a picture of the Father. Those whose fathers were close to them and spent time with them, disciplining with encouragement also, will have a healthy and true picture of Him. For those of us who had fathers who were mostly distant and showed little approval and/or consistent anger toward us, we may have a marred, unhealthy, and untrue picture of the Heavenly Father.

It has taken the Lord to reveal misconceptions from my youth, falsehoods that became written law inside me. One example is the fact that my dad thought me lazy and many times told me so. I grew up believing that I was but trying to prove that I was not. Unfortunately, the desire to prove ourselves may last our whole lives, unless we allow the Lord to take those areas and bring truth to us in place of the lies. The Lord helped me to realize the root of my dad's remarks and of my own behavior. He showed me that when Dad would ask for help, my response was always one of reluctance. Dad judged that to be laziness. The truth is that I did not wish to help, not due to laziness, but because I feared his criticism and anger and chose to avoid those situations.

Another area with which I have struggled is concerning college. Through the years, I sensed disappointment from my dad that I did not continue working after I had our kids. This engendered many feelings of shame, guilt, and condemnation inside me, knowing he helped with the cost of four years of my college. I have also been upset, thinking I should have returned to a higher-paying job every summer to contribute more to the payment of college. Another source of guilt was not having work-study, which would have at least provided spending money. Recently, the Lord began removing this load from my shoulders by showing me the following:

1. I did help with college by
   A. working every summer,
   B. paying for my school clothes and other needed items and also my summer spending,
   C. staying out of school for a year to work and buy my own car,
   D. working hard to get good grades and scholarships each year, and

E. taking our savings, once I quit working, and returning to Dad part of what he paid.

2. The Lord led me on my particular path, because
   A. He wanted me to work at the Christian book store for two summers to build a firm foundation, and
   B. my desire to stay home with our kids was in fact His desire also.

Seeing this situation from the Lord's perspective has lifted away bitter feelings from the past. I am grateful to Him for revealing this truth, which has removed the weight of guilt I was carrying.

The Lord has also disclosed other areas where I had believed lies. He had me write down the fallacy, followed by the truth of His word, what it says about Him. Now when the harsh rules of the past that have bound me try to resurface inside, engendering feelings of guilt, fear, condemnation, and worthlessness, I am able to renew my mind with the truth that the Lord has shown. I am not worthless. I can indeed do good things. In fact, God does not want us to criticize ourselves or each other (His children) because He is our Creator. When we demean ourselves and/or others, we are, in truth, putting down God who made us and them! We all need to bear that in mind before we treat other people, even ourselves, unkindly. I do not mean that we cannot defend ourselves but am speaking more of people who wish to control, to the extent of trying to change others to suit themselves. We are each responsible for ourselves before God, not before others. As we understand that and accept the Father's love, we can begin to value and respect ourselves and others also.

At the age of forty-three, twenty-three years after becoming a Christian, I finally came to understand these words of Jesus: "Don't you know me, Philip, even after I have been among you such a long time? Anyone who has seen me has seen the Father" (John 14:9 a–b). My eyes have been opened to see that the Father has the same loving character as His precious Son, whom I have come to know better through years of trial. The most amazing part is that not only does He accept me but He is even pleased with me! No longer do I need to cringe in fear with each thought of Him but feel instead His warmth and love, as tender as His Son's.

Coming to see our Father in the true light was a dramatic about-face for me. I have heard people share that the Father turned away from Jesus in His death because He could not stand to see our horrendous sins that Jesus carried. From what I now know of our Father, I do not accept that. I believe Jesus's words, asking why His Father had abandoned Him, came as a human response to intense suffering, the feeling of being deserted, when in reality His Father was there with Him through it all. If the Father did indeed turn His back, I believe it was because His tender heart could not bear the pain of seeing His Son suffering, knowing also that He was able to save Him but could not.

It is important to delve into the source of the lies we may have accepted from our past and let the Lord instead unveil His truth, the only truth, to us. "Then you will know the truth, and the truth will set you free" (John 8:32). It is freeing to finally understand and accept the Lord's words and to learn to reject those past untruths as they resurface. These may have come not only from parents but also from previous influences—other family, friends, school, culture, and even church. To those people who struggle with looking back, I only want to say that the road to healing begins there, not to blame anyone, but to find healing. What we all need to realize is that we live in a flawed world, with imperfect people, so none of us had perfect parents and none of us will ever be a perfect parent. There is only one of them: our Heavenly Father.

Our job as parents is to point our children to that Perfect Parent, not to be flawless ourselves. We are to lead them to the Lord and are best able to do that as we become more balanced, healed people in our own lives. Then as that happens, we can raise our children more fairly, not simply passing on the same lies to our own kids but instead learning to treat them as the Lord treats us, neither harshly nor leniently. Even if we eventually find this balance, however, we will still make mistakes, which is good. Our kids need to understand that we are not perfect. And although many of us probably went through grade school believing our parents were, usually adolescence is a time of disproving that and realizing our mistake, and all theirs! It is also a growing time for a whole family as a child seeks to understand life for himself and not blindly from his parents' perspective.

What happens to kids who do not live under a balance? There seem to be two extremes, both of which are detrimental, because they produce a warped view of who we are and who our Heavenly Father is. The first extreme occurs when a child is raised too harshly. That child is characterized by the following: (1) he feels sinful and guilty, worthless, all the time, (2) he feels that nothing he does is ever good enough, and (3) he sees others as excelling in all they do and therefore better than him, not understanding God gave him talents also. Although this person can easily see his need of God, he will continually struggle with seeing his own worth and feeling the Father's acceptance. The second extreme, the exact opposite, occurs when a child is raised too leniently. This child usually feels (1) he cannot sin and does no wrong, he is infallible, which is a lie ("If we claim to be without sin, we deceive ourselves and the truth is not in us" [1 John 1:8]), (2) all that he does is good and should be praised, and (3) others never do quite as much or as well as he does.

Although I most identify with the first example and know the pain of that life, it almost seems that this second kind of person is more to be pitied, because the lies he has believed often keep him from even seeing his need for God. He is self-sufficient and therefore not only able to care for himself but certain that he needs to control others' lives as well. He essentially becomes a Pharisee, more of which is said in a following chapter. "For nothing is impossible with God" (Luke 1:37), but it is much more difficult for the Lord to help this kind of person than the first, because he will not come to Him. That is why Jesus wept and said, "O, Jerusalem, Jerusalem, you who kill the prophets and stone those sent to you, how often I have longed to gather your children together, as a hen gathers her chicks under her wings, but you were not willing" (Matthew 23:37).

For me, the time of seeing our Father in a true light was essentially the same experience that Jesus had at His baptism. It was a time of knowing the Father's approval and acceptance. For Jesus, it was immediately followed by the Holy Spirit driving Him into the desert, where He was tempted by the devil for forty days (Luke 4:1-2).

After the Father's revelation of His love for me in January of 2000, another event happened in March that followed the same pattern as Jesus's. At that time, I began taking antibiotics for an infection. Unfortunately, they immediately bothered my stomach, but I rationalized that it was short-term medication and figured that I should stick it out. Surely in that much time not enough damage could be done that I could not fix it. Unfortunately, those pills aggravated the ulcer from my freshman year of college, which had recurred after my second miscarriage and taking iron tablets. When I returned to the doctor, this time in need of medicine for my stomach, the drug he prescribed began to affect me in the same way as that given in 1989, making me groggy and confused. Remembering the subsequent depression that occurred then, I was especially concerned about taking any more of the medicine. Mary Lou and Judy both prayed, after which I decided to consult the chiropractor who had taken care of our kids. He gave me supplements, which began to make a difference immediately. But there was no warning of what a slow process the healing was to be. By December, I was better but still unable to eat many foods. After Christmas and splurging on foods I had been avoiding, my stomach was much worse. I returned to our doctor in January of 2001. Once again, I tried a similar medication, only to find the same side effects.

It was at that point I began to seek the Lord diligently, believing He had shown me that He was going to bring healing. Yet now I was extremely sick again, unable to eat most foods. It was confusing. What was the Lord doing? After struggling one particular day and resting in bed, He revealed the following, the analogy of my experience to the story of Jesus and His baptism and His subsequent temptation time afterward. Just as Jesus had known the approval of His Father and was then led into the desert by the Holy Spirit to be tempted, so I was following the same path. He then reminded me that Jesus's time of temptation was followed by His ministry. In the same way, He was preparing me for the ministry He had planned. I was thankful and amazed at this revelation but totally unprepared for what followed: He wanted me to write a book about our experiences and all He has done. "Write in a book all the words I have spoken to you" (Jeremiah 30:2b).

As I studied Jesus's temptation time (Luke 4), I began to understand that He was tempted in three areas: (1) physically, (2) mentally, and (3) spiritually. These three areas comprise who we are. Satan left no place untouched. The first area involved Jesus's physical health. He had gone without food for a long time and was extremely weak, the point at which His enemy came to tempt Him to turn stones to bread. He was tempting Him to use His own self-efforts. The second area involved Jesus's mental health, His desire to be accepted and affirmed by others. Once again, His enemy came offering glory from the world if He would only bow down to him. He was appealing to Him to seek help from someone else. The third area was spiritual, a temptation to test His Father, to ask for proof of His Father's love. Because help was prolonged, Satan saw the perfect opportunity to tempt Jesus in His weakness. He had invited Him to use His own self-efforts or those of others. When those plans failed, he urged Him to at least make sure His Father still cared. After all, why was it taking so long? Maybe He had forgotten or maybe Jesus had misunderstood. Of course, Jesus did not give in but remained firm, after which the Father sent angels to minister to Him.

In the same way, the Father began to show me I was going through a similar temptation time. With my physical, I thought I could fix it myself, and then I turned frantically to others. He told me that He wanted me to go back to taking supplements from the chiropractor and wait patiently for His timing in my healing. He then showed me that I was also being tempted in the mental area. After having read the book about self-esteem, I read *The Birth Order Book*.[1] From that, I was able to see, as a middle child, my tendency to be a people-pleaser and appease everyone, especially firstborns in my life. The Lord was calling me to stand up to them and do what He desired, no longer trying to win their acceptance. Lastly, He revealed that Satan wanted me to doubt His words the previous January, that He does indeed love me and also accepts and approves of me. In all these areas, the Father wants us to be as Jesus was, dependent upon Him for all of our needs, physical, mental, and spiritual, to learn to live with Him as our only Source. We are not to depend upon our own efforts or those of others, wanting them to save us, and we are not to test the Lord's love. The Father will provide all these needs in His time. He wants to see if we will trust, though the way is long, with few signs that those needs will ever be fulfilled. Will we continue to believe the Father's words?

That same year, 2001, the Lord used the video, *Joseph, King of Dreams* to speak to me.[2] We had bought it for Sarabeth for Christmas 2000, not realizing the Lord had a message for me. After watching it many times, the analogy of Joseph's life to Jesus's became clear. In fact, it would seem that Joseph's life was prophetic of the Savior that was to come.

Joseph	Jesus
Special child to his parents	Promised to His parents
Long awaited	Long-awaited Savior
Not accepted by his brothers	Not accepted by the Jewish leaders
Father's approval	Baptism, approval of His Father
Plans for his future, revealed through dreams	Plans He knew from His Father
Time of temptation	Time of temptation
Sold into Egypt / life in prison	Desert time / garden time before being sold to Jewish leaders

Others delivered	Barabbas released
He was kept in prison	Jesus sentenced to death
Deliverance	Deliverance
1) From hard slave labor	1) From temptation time
To work inside	Jesus's ministry begins
2) From prison, Joseph's	2) From the grave,
ministry begins	
Bringing physical	Bringing spiritual salvation to all
salvation to all	
Confrontation with brothers	Confrontation with Jewish brothers
Followed by forgiveness	Followed by forgiveness— on the cross
Provided physical salvation—	Provided spiritual salvation—
for Egypt	for Jews
And his Jewish family	And for the rest of the world

Seeing this analogy was good because it illustrates the pattern we are all to follow in our lives. Once we come to know the Father's love, we are led into a time of temptation while we wait for His deliverance followed by the ministry He has planned for us. We are then called to forgive those in our past, reaching out to them and others with the good news of our Savior. The disciples also experienced this: coming to know the Father through Jesus, followed by a time of not understanding and temptation when Jesus was killed. With Jesus's resurrection and subsequent appearance, there was deliverance, followed by forgiveness and ministry to others.

Once again, in January of 2002, still struggling and feeling weak, the Lord reminded me of Jesus's temptation time, this time allowing me to see it from Jesus's perspective. All that is recorded is Jesus's final answers to Satan, which had always seemed spoken easily. I had assumed it must not have been that difficult for Him.

After all, He is the Son of God. But the Lord brought two thoughts to mind: (1) we do not know what Jesus suffered during those forty days because it is not recorded and (2) Jesus was a human being, just as we are, and was weak in His humanness, as we are.

In referring to the dictionary, the word *tempt* means generally to entice someone to do wrong, to make it appear inviting or attractive, usually with the promise of a reward.[3] The very nature of temptation is that it involves struggle. Jesus's time of temptation was the same, extremely difficult for Him, as challenging as any we have ever suffered. Because of this, Jesus is compassionate toward us in our weaknesses. He went through His own time of intense pain. Hebrews 2:18 says, "Because he himself suffered when he was tempted, he is able to help those who are being tempted."

Satan has used the same ploy since the beginning of time, with Adam and Eve and Abraham and Sarah and many others. He tries to make us doubt the love of our Father and be impatient in waiting for His timing. We all go through this, the point being to finally say as Job did, "Though he slay me, yet will I trust in Him" (Job 13:15a). We need to come to the point of accepting that even if the Lord has deceived us all along, we will still hang onto Him and trust in Him. It is the word of Shadrach, Meshach, and Abednego as they were being thrown into the fiery furnace: "O Nebuchadnezzar, we do not need to defend ourselves before you in this matter. If we are thrown into the blazing furnace, the God we serve is able to save us from it, and he will rescue us from your hand, O king. But even if he does not, we want you to know, O king, that we will not serve your gods or worship the image of gold you have set up" (Daniel 3:16–18). I believe although it is not recorded, Jesus Himself faced the possibility of His own death, first of all, in the desert.

Because we all go through these times, we need to follow Jesus's example, which means that we need to consider how He successfully defeated His enemy. I think His success came from remembering two things about His enemy and two things about His Father. Concerning His enemy, (1) he has always been a liar and a deceiver, and (2) all his motives are for his own glory. Concerning His Father, (1) He has always been truthful and faithful, and (2) He loves Jesus so much that He only allows what is for His best. You might say, "How could Jesus's death have been for His good?" All I can say is that He agreed to die for us judging the joy of being reconciled with us, whom He loves so much, to be worth more to Him than any pain He had to experience. In that, He showed that He could take even horrible death over the thought of losing us. When we realize this, we also understand how stupid it is to rebel against Him, thinking He is trying to harm us. In light of this, how can we ever again question His love?

Like Jesus, we will succeed in defeating the enemy in the same way He did, by realizing what He realized: the lies of the enemy and the truth of the Father and His deep love for us. Like Jesus, the Father will help us through, which means we need to realize that He never punishes us, venting His anger in frustration and revenge. Instead, He is our teacher and our advocate. He is on our side, teaching us patiently, as we do with our children who are learning to walk, excited when there is progress, encouraging when there is failure, and extreme celebration at completion. "There is no fear in love. But perfect love drives out fear, because fear has to do with punishment. The man who fears is not made perfect in love" (1 John 4:18). "Therefore he is able to save completely those who come to God through him, because he always lives to intercede for them" (Hebrews 7:25).

Through my time of temptation, the Lord has shown me the differences between the ministry I was trying to do in my own strength in 1989 and this new ministry.

In 1989, with physical temptation, my trust was solely in the doctors, even though my body was telling me something different. I was trusting them to bring healing, instead of depending totally on the Lord and His guidance.

With mental temptation, I was still seeking approval and acceptance from others, especially at church and Compassionate Friends. Although my motivation to help others one-on-one was sincere, there was also a deep need for approval and acceptance. I was seeking approval and acceptance from man instead of the Lord.

With spiritual temptation, I felt abandoned by the Lord, sure of His disappointment and anger, gauged from perceptions from others. I did not see my Father in His true light. "Woe to those who go down to Egypt for help, who rely on horses, who trust in the multitude of their chariots and in the great strength of their horsemen, but do not look to the Holy One of Israel, or seek help from the Lord" (Isaiah 31:1).

Now, with physical temptation, although I wavered, especially at first, my desire has been to leave my health totally in the Lord's hands all these years, trusting in Him and His guidance and timing. After so many years of running to the doctor with chronic problems, for which there were often no answers, I am finally understanding. All along, the Lord has been calling me to turn to Him first of all, trusting that He will provide the answers, sometimes through doctors, sometimes through chiropractors, sometimes by other means, but always through His guidance and in His timing.

With mental temptation, I have been learning to stand up to people from my past and present, who have previously led me, with no resistance on my part. The Lord has revealed to me my need to stop people-pleasing and my need to please Him alone, letting Him lead me and receiving His approval and acceptance.

With spiritual temptation, I have come to know that even if the Lord has deceived me, there is no other path worth following. I have found nothing that even comes close to my life with the Lord. This is the best life I have ever had, and I do not intend to turn my back on it. It is the parable of the man who found treasure in a field and sold all he had to buy the field (Matthew 13:44). I have learned to trust His love and to know that He does have the best in mind, even as I wait for His timing.

In review, the plan of ministry the Lord has given follows a distinct pattern, similar to the path our Savior took: a time of realizing and accepting the love of the Father, followed by subsequent testing in all three areas of life—physical, mental, and spiritual. In this testing, He desires that we leave behind our own self-efforts and seeking help from others. Instead, He wants us to turn to Him for all the answers, even if it requires a long time of waiting, which tries us in ways that cannot be expressed. He wants us to *know* He is working wonders for us.

What happened in 1989 was needful in order for me to follow the footsteps of Much-Afraid: her death to the desire to be loved (dying with Jesus), followed by rebirth (a glorious resurrection), living life with the Lord in His High Places, and performing the work and purpose He had planned from the beginning. "For we are God's workmanship, created in Christ Jesus to do good works, which God prepared in advance for us to do" (Ephesians 2:10).

The Bible relates many examples of suffering, temptations, pain, all resulting in better days. When the testing is over, the Lord brings good: Job found restoration, Joseph was given both ministry and restoration, and Jesus, more than any, knew the joy of bringing salvation to us.

My spiritual college years were fall of 1995 through spring of 1999, followed by graduate school from 1999 through 2003, with this book being my thesis at my heavenly school. The Lord gave me the gift of compassion at birth and fine-tuned it through years of grief, finally revealing it all to me in college. The Lord brought spring years to us, 1990–1997, followed by our summer years, 1997–2004, with the promise of fruit appearing at the harvest time in the fall, and into the winter. We wait in joyful expectation! Our Lord is infinitely kind and compassionate, our loving example!

One final note concerning the writing of this book, the ministry I believe the Lord has given to me. In the course of writing, I have returned to the Lord many times for confirmation about continuing. In the summer of 2001, Judy gave me the book *Classic Christianity* by Bob George.[4] After reading it, I felt encouraged, as it was definitely a confirmation that what I was writing had also been heard by others; but I also questioned the Lord, "Is there really a need for my story?" Again, in the summer of 2002, after reading two other books by Bob George, *Grace Stories*[5] and *Growing in Grace*,[6] and two Mary Lou had given me by Chuck and Nancy Missler, *The Way of Agape*[7] and *Be Ye Transformed*,[8] I again asked the Lord what need there was for my story. To which He seemed to say, "Keep writing!" The beginning of 2003, Mary Lou lent me the book *The Purpose Driven Life* by Rick Warren.[9] For the third time, I felt a confirmation, but also the same questioning. That is when I felt the Lord say, "The books you have read were written from the authors' experiences. Your story is also written from your experiences, but it is the lab write-up." I had to laugh! God chose me to do the lab write-up? Me, who hated all labs. Me, who was too squeamish to dissect my frog in biology. Me, who was too afraid to light my Bunsen burner in chemistry. Me, whose lab experiments resulted in little or no conclusions. God chose me to do the lab write-up, which resulted in the same conclusions as those so well written by others! Truly, He does have a sense of humor. It is wonderful to see how the Lord can take our weaknesses and use them for His own glory! I am amazed and thankful to Him!

CHAPTER 21

The Fences Or Protection from Judgment

We have often walked the perimeter of my Secret Place, and though much of it borders the kingdom, some does not. A fence marks my land so that none may enter unless they come by the gates that bear my name. My Lord has made the fences and gates such that no one can trespass. They are able, however, to call across the fences and/or gates, which can be encouraging, a time for connecting with friends. There are those, however, who are not friends and cannot possibly belong, nor is it their desire. Their only purpose is to destroy what the Lord has provided for me. There are times I rebuke their unkind remarks, but my Lord has an even better solution.

There are, within my property, various escapes strategically placed near the borders so that when enemies come to call and torment, I can make a quick and secret get away in times of urgent need. The Lord has revealed these entrances a bit at a time, the first one being shortly after I had begun living full-time in my private home. We had gone quite a way from the house and were nearing a far border, when He led me to a set of steps, which descended into the grass and a wooden door beyond. Inside was a tunnel with lights and a damp earthen floor. It did not take long to reach its end, and how I wondered, where had it taken us? My Lord opened the door to the most appropriate room, the grief room, of course the best place to be rid of false words and filled with peace! I have since been shown other escapes, which help, as the unwelcome voices are immediately silenced. I am thankful to know and use my secret tunnels.

****

> But avoid foolish controversies and genealogies
> and arguments and quarrels
> about the law, because these are unprofitable and useless.
> —Titus 3:9

> But you—who are you to judge your neighbor?
> —James 4:12b

After speaking with people from various churches through the years, it seems the biggest source of judgment comes from donning our masks. This is done daily in public, but no masks are as deceptive and harmful as those for church. None of us wants to appear unspiritual or lacking faith, and we certainly do not want anyone to know how much we are struggling at home within our own families. So, we pretend to be super spiritual, with no problems. "We have it all together." And many are fooled. How often have we been shocked to hear of couples we thought were close getting a divorce! In fact, statistics show the divorce rate just as high in the church as outside of it.

When we hide behind masks, we learn to look good, to do and say the right things, so no one will suspect the truth. After a while, we even begin to fool ourselves, believing we are that good. It is at that point that judgment of others becomes increasingly easy. After all, we look good and can legitimately condemn those who do not, which also leads to competition, the Pharisee attitude.

Within small groups, people seem especially prone to be guarded, with masks up, probably for three reasons: (1) they do not want people to judge them, (2) they do not want hurtful remarks made to them, and (3) they are afraid what they share may not be in confidence but spread through the church. All are legitimate concerns. Gordon never would attend cell group because of a bad experience in high school. After asking for prayer for his shoulder, news filtered back to his football coach, with negative results. His trust of those groups has been weak ever since. Others have shared how their words were used against them. From that perspective, masks seem essential for survival.

The sad part about masks, however, is not even that they lead to judging others harshly but that they do not allow God to work in us, to heal our own lives and hearts. We may fool others, and even ourselves, but we cannot fool the Lord. I have observed when we judge others most harshly, thinking ourselves more spiritual, we still have control of most of our lives. It is only when we surrender, relinquishing our control, that the Lord can begin to work, the beginning of the journey to the High Places. Pain, and the subsequent honesty resulting from it, is the path on the way to healing.

When I attended church and cell group, my mask was mostly down, for two reasons: (1) I have never been an actress. I have always been me, extremely shy and self-conscious in public until I become more comfortable. And (2) My emotions were too close to the surface in my many sufferings to be able to hide them. Like Job, I was broken and honest before man and God, and all three of the above concerns touched me because I was humble, with my main motivation to find healing and become what God desired. Because of that, I also went through humiliation, with some people judging me, making hurtful comments, and sharing my story. But at the same time, God honored my honesty and did indeed bring healing to me. He has done so much in my life, as I have been open before Him. "Humble yourselves before the Lord, and he will lift you up" (James 4:10).

I believe God's heart for people in the church is to drop their masks, enabling Him to heal and make them what He intends. The only way small groups can work is for all members to share honestly and humbly. When we are vulnerable, there are usually two reactions: (1) some are uncomfortable, because of pride, while (2) others, who are also suffering, are comforted they are not alone. The function of the church, I believe, is to foster honesty, because we are all in intense battle and need one another's support and comfort in order to make it out alive. Often, however, the only way for this to occur is through heartache, where masks are no longer useful or practical.

I have found there is a balance, however, in sharing, as mentioned in the chapter on emotions. Being in public after painful events can be devastating, as emotions come so easily. That is why those in the Old Testament who were suffering were *alone*, covered in dust and ashes, a time away from others. We need to be able to be vulnerable in a safe place.

Eric once wrote a report about John Wooden. While reading through it, one quote caught my attention: it said to pay more attention to your character than your reputation. Our character is what we are, while our reputation is only what others think we are.[1] While Jesus was on earth, He was simply Himself, unconcerned about what others thought of Him. He knew who He was in relation to His Father. Even as He ministered, there were those who said, "Isn't this Mary's son?" (Mark 6:3b). Having grown up in a small town, I feel certain some added this tidbit: "And he wasn't even conceived in wedlock!" Those choice morsels seem to spread quickly. Was God concerned with how that looked? No, because He knew the truth: Mary's child was His Son. We need to do right in God's sight despite how it may look to others, our need be only our character, who we are before God, not our reputation, who man thinks we are. "If God is for us, who can be against us?" (Romans 8:31b).

In my Christian life, my reputation is extremely tarnished. My health problems are certainly ones Christians are not supposed to experience: ulcers three times and deep depressions two times. Yet in my life, I can see how the Lord has used those trying times to heal my insides and teach me and, most of all, greatest of all, to draw me closer to Him. We need not be concerned about our reputation. Jesus was not worried about His. There are Christians today who would probably have condemned Jesus's emotions, even in the garden before His arrest. We need to understand His humanity and our own in order to learn His compassion for others and ourselves. He came as a human and did not want to suffer any more than we do. Yet He loves us and knew how important His mission was. No wonder His suffering was so intense.

To those in the church who look down on others, either new Christians or those with many and great needs, the message is, you need to examine your own hearts. Jesus came to help the sick, not those who are well, and to seek the lost, not those who know the way. All of us are sick and lost, with recurrent sin and areas of need in our lives. The Lord will continue to work on us until the day He takes us Home. How much more rewarding to help Him than to condemn His work. We all need to cease being judges, learning to be as Jesus, comforters and healers.

Another source of judgment comes from living the lie of legalism. When living this way, we expect perfection from others and ourselves and judge accordingly. A favorite scripture of many Christians seems to be, "Instead, speaking the truth in love, we will in all things grow up into him who is the Head, that is Christ" (Ephesians 4:15). What many fail to see in that verse is the word *love*. We have taken the scripture to mean we have free license to point out others' faults whenever we want and can pat ourselves on the back afterward, thinking we have surely done something wonderful, even something God would commend, when most often we have created a wounded person and another place in the church for division. Another interpretation of this scripture could be truthfulness about *our own struggles*, alluded to in this scripture: "Therefore each of you must put off falsehood and speak truthfully to his neighbor, for we are all members of one body" (verse 25).

Too often, the truth that is spoken does not even involve spiritual problems but everyday trials. A good example is in the area of babies and toddlers. Often people make an issue about four areas of development: sleeping through the night, weaning, walking, and potty training. Those whose children learned these skills early let the rest of us know our children should be farther along. It is fine to give advice when a person has asked for it, but often a new parent may only be sharing frustration, hoping for encouragement. Instead, a barrage of unwelcome words makes matters worse.

My experience in each area, once again, involved the Lord having me wait. Neither Eric nor Sarabeth slept through the night until they were fifteen months old, but both were big babies (eight pounds, two ounces, and nine pounds, six ounces, respectively) and breastfed. Eric was weaned at fifteen months, and Sarabeth later. Eric walked at about a year, but Sarabeth did not start walking until eighteen months. They may not have learned these skills early, but both faced major situations they were surviving daily. Eric was dealing with the deaths of Matthew and our fourth child and the turmoil we all experienced afterward. Sarabeth had major stomach problems from the start. During those times of struggle, there was a constant feeling of failure. These other areas only intensified that. I did not need anyone else pointing it out. Thankfully, the Lord has helped me to see the profound effect of all our struggles back then and to view those days more realistically. When a family is barely surviving each day, the thought of adding any new challenge is not even considered.

It is easy to judge others when we are outside of the pot looking in. Our perspective changes dramatically once we are in the boiling pot ourselves! ("Walk a mile in my shoes.") A great example of this concerns me. I remember the many times, before I had kids, when I said or thought, "My children will never act like that." It did not take long before I found out how right I was. There were a number of situations where my children acted even worse!

Today, families are under great amounts of stress. I do have good news for those of you who are now in the midst of one of these frustrating baby/toddler times, an encouragement. Eric and Sarabeth are now grown up, and guess what? Both are sleeping through the night, weaned, potty-trained, and walking just fine! If you compare them to early sleepers, weaned, potty-trained, and walkers, I doubt you would find much difference. It does not necessarily mean children who develop skills early are brilliant but that Mom and Dad want others to think their kid is exceptional so they can pride themselves on a job well done. What they may want to remember is that there may be other areas of their lives that are not so under control, other areas where there is need for growth. Most definitely, they also have some need of change, something that may not come so easily.

For this very reason, Jesus spoke these words, "Why do you look at the speck of sawdust in your brother's eye and pay no attention to the plank in your own eye?... You hypocrite, first take the plank out of your own eye, and then you will see clearly to remove the speck from your brother's eye" (Matthew 7:3, 5). Most people who quote the earlier scripture of speaking the truth in love seem to forget this one. If we consider what Jesus was saying and are honest with ourselves, each of us has to admit that not only are we unable to remove the speck from our brother's eye but we cannot even remove the plank from our own. Our Lord alone is able to change us, as we continually remain in Him (John 15:4a). He lives within us to guide and change us. If we could grasp this, there would be fewer wounded people in the church because there would be less judgment.

So how should the first scripture be applied? Hopefully sparingly, only in critical situations. If someone is headed off a cliff, yes, talk to him. But God says, "Speak the truth in love." Anyone who genuinely cares about a person will have been seeking God beforehand, already have been praying for the person. That is the key. Seek God first, and then act only as He shows you. Usually a person has to be fairly close to someone before sharing in this way. Then it is more apt to be done in love. There may also be times when a pastor or another leader may have to confront someone. But it is all to be done with the person's best interest at heart, not thinking, "God is going to punish you because you are breaking His law!" which is condemnation. Instead, "I am worried because you are going down a path the

Lord has warned is treacherous and a trap of the enemy. I don't want you to get hurt." That is love, the love God has for all of us.

I have heard there are lists of criteria to determine spiritual maturity. This seems a trick of the enemy, because such judging only leads to one of two conclusions, recorded below.

Judging Spiritual Maturity

Many criteria met	(Balanced)	Few criteria met
(Off Balance)	My focus is on the Lord	(Off Balance)
I am spiritually mature	"Let us fix our eyes on Jesus,	I am worthless
Self is glorified	the author and perfecter of our faith ..."	Though downcast,
	(Hebrews 12:2a)	Self is still in the forefront
	Trusting Him to make me	
	What I am to be and show me what I am to do	
	God is glorified	

It is easy to see how focusing on self can make us off balance and easily cause hurt and division within the church. That is why we are not to judge, even ourselves. Paul did speak of judging one another in the church, but it was in regard to settling disputes (1 Corinthians 6:2). He also admonished the Corinthian church to confront a sinner among them, but to me, this would have been a job for the leadership, not everyone else.

I end this chapter with excerpts from three thought-provoking scriptures. How much love the church could give if we would rid ourselves of judging, both others and ourselves!

Jesus straightened up and asked her, "Woman, where are they? Has no one condemned you?" "No one, sir," she said. "Then neither do I condemn you," Jesus declared. "Go now and leave your life of sin."

—John 8:10–11

"Neither this man nor his parents sinned,"
said Jesus, "but this happened
so that the work of God might be displayed in his life."
—John 9:3

Accept him whose faith is weak, without passing
judgment on disputable matters.
—Romans 14:1

****

Be still before the Lord and wait patiently for him; do not fret
when men succeed in their ways, when they carry out their
wicked schemes. Refrain from anger and turn from wrath;
do not fret—it leads only to evil. For evil men will be cut
off, but those who hope in the Lord will inherit the land.
—Psalms 37:7–9

"Do not take revenge, my friends, but leave
room for God's wrath, for it is written:
'It is mine to avenge; I will repay,' says the Lord."
—Romans 12:19

Pharisees surround us every day, though not necessarily in churches as in Jesus's day. Looking at the characteristics of the Pharisee, however, we soon see the same evident in some of the people around us—in school, sports, government, jobs, and even church. What are these characteristics?

1. He feels he is without sin and does no wrong.
2. He feels he is to be commended for all the good he does.
3. He feels that no one else can accomplish what he can.

Because of these beliefs, which cause pride, these further characteristics also begin to emerge:

1. He needs to be in control of himself and others (as he does no wrong).
2. He desires all of the glory (for all the good he does).

It is impossible for him to see his need for Jesus, because in order to follow Jesus, we have to

1. give up control of ourselves to Him, and
2. let our lives give glory to God, not ourselves.

All the above characteristics give the Pharisee a sense of superiority, power, and an insatiable desire to control others. He essentially feels perfect and is God in his own eyes. Therefore, he feels threatened by others who he views as wanting his position. The Pharisees of Jesus's day were so blinded by these lies they could not even see the miracles Jesus performed and feel the awe that others, who were more humble, did. Other characteristics of the Pharisee include deception (never allowing others to see him in his true light) and punishment toward those who do not do what he desires. He is also quick to criticize others but easily offended himself. Jesus's description of the Pharisees and the teachers of the law is given in Matthew 23, an even more extensive assessment.

This same type of Pharisee survived the years and is still with us today. They are the ones who try (and usually succeed) to push to the top at any cost, to be first, to be praised and glorified and treated with honor. In the meantime, they consider no one else, in their attempts to have all their own way. One of the most obvious examples of this type of person is seen in the political arena, not that all are like this, but many. Power and money can quickly consume a Pharisee, who has no regard for the common man. "For such people are not serving our Lord Christ, but their own appetites. By smooth talk and flattery they deceive the minds of naive people" (Romans 16:18). "Their hearts are callous and unfeeling" (Psalms 119:70a).

That is the exact picture of life in Jesus's day. The religious leaders were powerful and expected the praise and honor of the common man. Yet they had no concern themselves to help this common man. But Jesus "did not come to be served, but to serve, and to give his life as a ransom for many" (Matthew 20:28). He came humbly, although He is God, who could have demanded praise and honor for Himself. He honestly deserves it. Yet He provides a perfect example of how we are to treat both ourselves (the common man) and those Pharisees who surround us today. We are to follow Him, respecting ourselves and others in the process. (1) He did not seek out the Pharisees, although they were surrounding Him, and (2) He answered them with wisdom. (3) Meanwhile, He was focused on accomplishing the work His Father had sent him to do: to find and heal the sick and hurting until the time of His ultimate sacrifice for us. We are called to follow His example.

The Lord brought two scriptures regarding our response to Pharisees: "Answer a fool according to his folly, or he will be wise in his own eyes" (Proverbs 26:5), and "Do not answer a fool according to his folly, or you will become like him yourself" (Proverbs 26:4). At first glance, these adjacent verses appear contradictory, but, in seeking the Lord, I feel this is His response.

1. The first scripture is saying we need to answer a fool as he would us, not remaining silent. Otherwise, he begins to think to himself, "I am so wise, they are unable to even respond to me."

2. The second scripture refers to responding to the person in a vindictive manner in order for revenge. In that case, if we follow his example, we will become like him, which the Lord does not want. He reserves the right to vengeance, probably for two reasons:

A. He knows it hurts us to dwell on an offense and the subsequent plans for revenge.

B. He knows we would probably not treat the person in a loving way. The Lord's heart is *always* for the benefit of each of us (even our enemies), for our best, for our good. Our motivation most often is rooted in a desire for our enemy to suffer as we have. God, however, is just and compassionate and wants well for all of us.

Some people may respond that not only are we not to show revenge to our enemies but we are called to love them, which is true. Once again, Jesus is our example. He loves us all and shows that love through respect. He respects Himself, not changing who He is to please others. Yet He also respects others' opinions of Him by not forcing them to love Him in return. That is true love: free will. Though His greatest desire is for all of us to know Him and love Him, He never pushes us into that choice. In the same way, we are not to be people-pleasers, as was my tendency. We need to love and respect ourselves, not trying to change ourselves to please others; and we need to love and respect others, not pushing them to change and to accept us. We are not to be discouraged by those around us, though it is easy to do. Instead, we are to do as Jesus did, leaving their lives to our just and compassionate Father. "When they hurled their insults at him, he did not retaliate; when he suffered, he made no threats. Instead, he entrusted himself to him who judges justly" (1 Peter 2:23).

In the book of Job, we sense Job's discouragement with these people as he pours out his heart of pain. "Why do the wicked seem to succeed?" (Chapter 21). We can take encouragement from many sources, two of which are: the story of Mordecai and Haman in the book of Esther and the parable Jesus tells of Lazarus and the rich man. The first story, shared earlier, involves Haman, a powerful man in the government, essentially second in command to the king, who demands that all bow as he passes. When Mordecai, a Jew, refuses,

Haman becomes obsessed with anger, first toward Mordecai, but then to all Jews. He finally determines to have them all killed. Thankfully, the Lord has other plans, brought about through Esther, Mordecai's niece and the king's new wife. After much prayer, she seeks help from the king, essentially risking her own life, which results in the death of Haman and the salvation of the Jewish people.

The second story is about a rich man who feels no compassion for the beggar at his feet (Luke 16:19–31). When both have died, the beggar goes to heaven, but the rich man to hell. In his extreme arrogance, the formerly rich man tells the angel to send the beggar to him with a drink of water. When refused, he wants someone sent to his brothers, who are still on earth, to warn them. The answer was: "If they do not listen to Moses and the Prophets, they will not be convinced even if someone rises from the dead" (verse 31). Both of these stories show that the Lord does, indeed, bring justice. The Pharisee will not forever rule the earth.

There is a saying, "It is not what you know but who you know." And though we may not have realized it, the truth is, even getting to heaven is political. The only way is through knowing Jesus. Yet it is different from politics we have come to know on earth in that His love and mercy exclude no one. He has invited us all, and there is no partiality. He, who accepts and loves us, will not leave us defenseless. The One we know is much more powerful and legitimately in control, unlike those who think they are. "You, dear children, are from God and have overcome them, because the one who is in you is greater than the one who is in the world" (1 John 4:4). The Lord's justice will be done. We need to do our part, trusting God to bring fairness, now or in the future.

Our family has seen consequences of politics in the area of high school sports. Our son, Eric, loved basketball. He started playing city league in fourth grade and continued all the way to his sophomore year. That year, he began to experience problems with his left shoulder and decided not to try out the following year. As it turned out, we were thankful to be free of the obvious problems the basketball program had been experiencing. During those years, we saw much in the way of politics, with certain parents pushing to make sure their kids were first, not caring who they had to push aside in the process. We were not the only parents to observe this but, like others, chose not to say anything for fear of hurting our son. It is the age-old story of the emperor with no clothing. All knew the truth but doubted themselves and feared the consequences, so we said nothing. Many boys quit due to the partiality. As parents, seldom around the coach and practices, we saw the obvious politics and realized that our kids were even more aware and subsequently discouraged.

For many years, I have heard how sports are good for kids but honestly have to say I wonder at the statement, unless it means they learn that life is political and how to deal with unfairness at a young age. Many parents became frustrated with the obvious partiality, but it seems that often natural consequences bring retribution. The varsity basketball team those years lost most of their games, with the few wins against teams in leagues below ours. To me, this shows that the boys were ever aware of the unfairness and never able to play as a team. "To show partiality is not good—yet a man will do wrong for a piece of bread" (Proverbs 28:21). The reason for this is that trust has not been built within the team and with the coach. Although a couple sets of parents influenced the coach, the team's success was jeopardized for those players. How sad, when high school should be a time for good memories. Few are going on to the big leagues. Why not have a great team instead?

Gordon and I were blessed to be part of a wonderful experience in high school, as our varsity football team took state our sophomore year. Gordon was especially blessed to be on the team. In all the years he played (sophomore through senior), their team only lost two games, and in the playoffs! They had excellent teams those years. Unlike what we have seen recently, there seemed to be less politics then but respect instead. The parents were not influencing the coach, and he had full say, which produced trust and a true team, obviously necessary ingredients for a winning program.

We can be encouraged that those who appear to be most in control of their lives and others will, one day, maybe sooner than we realize, find consequences for their unfairness and control! We were surprised, but not unhappy, when we heard that the coach was no longer involved with the program.

On that note, I need to say that, although I feel angry at Pharisees, especially special interest groups attempting to control the government and schools, there is another area I have needed to consider. That is, the followers of those leaders. Most of the leaders will probably never humble themselves and find the Truth, just as most of the Pharisees did not in Jesus's day, but many of their followers may. We need to have compassion for those caught in traps, not of their own making.

The similarities between us as believers and those who disagree with us are striking. I am not saying there are not people trying to harm us as Christians, because there certainly are, but there are also those who are merely followers and caught in a web of lies, honest and sincere in their beliefs. We can be earnest yet also deceived. Paul is the perfect example. He wholeheartedly believed he was doing what God wanted in killing Christians. But then he saw the Light and understood the truth, and his life was forever changed. Have not most of us Christians followed his same path? We need to be willing to reach out with the love of Jesus to those who are like we once were (2 Corinthians 1:3–5). That is Jesus's example and our calling, going to the sick, as we also deal with those who are "well."

Before concluding this chapter, I need to bring up one final point, something especially close to my heart, as it is another area in which we have battled. Perhaps the saddest part about Pharisees is that they are not only adults. Those who are children can be especially cruel. There have always been bullies in school, but their occurrence seems to have increased since we were young, as can be seen in the rise in violence, in elementary, middle, and high schools. One source of this is that we no longer teach respect for those in authority.

Kids no longer fear the principals as we did. The consequences now for bullying are not what they used to be. When we were in junior high school, no one wanted to go to the principal's office because he had a thick paddle, which he used not to kill anyone but to get his point across. Of course, that is not politically acceptable nowadays. Instead, we choose to talk to bullies, trying to change their behaviors in this way. Unfortunately, bullies are masters of talk. They will always win at that game. Most need strong consequences in order to see a behavior change. Suspension for physical violence is probably most welcome to a bully, who does not always enjoy school to begin with. The saddest part is the victim because he is taught to use words to defend himself. But with continued bullying, there may come a day when the victim may react in a wrong way, and at that point, he ends up being the one in trouble.

Unfortunately, our society does not agree on how to deal with bullies, as seen in the disunity throughout our country, regarding the war in Iraq. When I read stories of the people oppressed there by the ultimate bully, my heart went out to them. There are times victims need help from those who are stronger and more powerful. "You rescue the poor from those who are too strong for them, the poor and needy from those who rob them" (Psalms 35:10b). How unfortunate if we, as Americans, have become so fat in our many blessings that we no longer feel pain and compassion for others who are genuinely hurting. How many of us in that same situation would not be exceedingly grateful to be rescued from our tormentor and think the longest time well worth the effort? I believe that we in America, who have been so richly and kindly blessed, may yet find understanding for those who are hurting, as we may suffer tremendously in the days to come at the hands of these bullies, who we think can be swayed by kind words. Meanwhile, they are planning our demise! The Bible says that even Jesus learned obedience from what He suffered, though He never sinned. "Although he was a son, he learned obedience from what he suffered" (Hebrews 5:8). That is how we *all* learn. When consequences are removed for unacceptable behavior, we never learn to obey.

This is fresh in my heart because of many problems experienced in this area with Sarabeth in elementary school. The year of 2003–2004 was an especially difficult one, with the culmination before spring break, when I learned Sarabeth had lied to a friend, the principal, and me also, saying a certain boy, who has bullied her all year, had hit her. It turned out he did not hit her but spoke cruelly again after numerous times since the fall, when she first had befriended him as he was a new kid in school. I have to humbly admit that after a long time of dealing with the stress, my temper flared in talking to the principal, both on the phone, when I defended my daughter (before finding out that she had, indeed, lied) and again when we went into her office the following day. The school had been aware he hit her the previous fall, and we had hoped the problem was resolved. Although he had not hit her again, he had continued to torment her verbally. In discussing this with the principal, she encouraged us to work on Sarabeth being more assertive and possibly even taking karate classes. Meanwhile, the school was working with the boy to help him talk nicer. The future scenario we feared was Sarabeth defending herself with karate and then still in trouble.

Though initially defending our daughter, we did initiate consequences for lying, and I did much soul-searching, questioning myself and my daughter. What she did was wrong, and she did suffer consequences. Most of all, that trust was broken. I was encouraged, however, remembering good remarks she had received from teachers about her behavior, both to us personally and on report cards. I realize my daughter is not perfect but also that others had seen her behavior was usually good. That was my encouragement, which I believed came from the Lord, as I sought the truth in the whole incident. Since then, there have been other parents, who encountered the same problem, most who have taught their kids to treat others kindly, which obviously does not work in this society. A couple mothers decided to pull their kids out and homeschool them because of constant bullying. Another indication this is a widespread problem in schools is the fact our elementary school implemented a program years ago aimed at teaching kids to treat each other better. The fact that schools now have to implement lockdowns is also not positive.

We did hear that the boy who tormented Sarabeth throughout her fourth-grade school year was suspended weeks after the latest problem with Sarabeth for consistently telling his teacher and student teacher no. Although a relief, I also experienced an unexpected sadness for both him and his family, thinking of the pain ahead of them if he does not learn to obey. My feelings most definitely had to be from the Lord, as I had been extremely upset earlier. Before school was out for summer, he was seeing the school counselor and trying to be nicer to Sarabeth.

Personally, I believe the increase in bullies in our society is due to three problems: (1) lack of respect for others and ourselves, (2) too many kids in daycare for the providers to teach them kindness, (3) much anger in kids, who are yearning for the attention of their parents, with no response. From personal experience, I know this inattention breeds hurt and rebellion.

In closing, Pharisees are definitely one of the biggest trials of our lives. The Pharisee's desire to control everyone and everything obviously causes much turmoil in the lives of those of us who are trying to live what we believe. Thankfully, we have Jesus's understanding and example of how to deal with those people. And most importantly, we can go to Him with our frustrations, knowing He understands and stands with us in our pain. We can also be uplifted, knowing that the Pharisees will not always succeed. The Lord is just, and the way He made the world produces natural consequences for those who choose to bully others. He will not always remain silent. And, we can know that His judgment will be right, administered with compassion, giving the Pharisee a chance to turn to Him, that he might be changed also. In the meantime, let us not give up hope. The Lord is still ultimately in control! And that is Good News! "The wicked freely strut about when what is vile is honored among men" (Psalms 12:8). "When the foundations are being destroyed, what can the righteous do? The Lord is in his holy temple; the Lord is on his heavenly throne" (Psalms 11:3–4b). "If this is so, then the Lord knows how to rescue godly men from trials and to hold the unrighteous for the day of judgment, while continuing their punishment" (2 Peter 2:9).

CHAPTER 22

The Invitation
Or a Place for Every...One
A Window to the Greatest
Adventure—Rebirth

T here is a defined path leading into my Lord's kingdom, and all are welcome. The Lord is waiting to reveal this to you personally and to receive your permission to move your house here also, with renovation and restoration following, a most wonderful experience.

****

He who dwells in the shelter of the Most High
will rest in the shadow of the Almighty.

—Psalms 91:1

The first part of this book gave the history of my life through spring: my journey. The second part is what the Lord has revealed through it: my house. With that in mind, know that not intentionally but naturally, there has been some repetition. At this point, I feel I need to share about the turning point in my life, the point at which my true life and journey began. That was in the spring of 1976, when I turned to the Lord and asked Him to come into my life. At that point, I was born spiritually. Jesus told Nicodemus that he must be born again, and Nicodemus, like most of us, struggled with understanding exactly what that means. Today there are many terms describing this experience: finding the Lord, being saved, accepting Jesus as Lord and Savior, asking the Lord into our lives or hearts, giving our lives to the Lord, coming to know the Lord, committing ourselves to the Lord, becoming a Christian. All of these mean the same thing as Jesus's description of being born again. Below I want to share both the reason for being born again and the process.

To fully understand the reason, we need to return to the time of Adam and Eve. When God created them, He placed them in a beautiful garden. At that point, the world was perfect—the perfect place God created, with no sin, sickness, or suffering. He gave Adam and Eve control over all plants and animals, but the most obvious blessing was that they walked and talked with Him daily. The only command He gave was not to eat of the fruit of the tree of knowledge of good and evil, and that, if they did, "they would surely die" (Genesis 2:17b). At first, they obeyed, avoiding the tree, but as with each of us since, Satan came to deceive them, saying that eating from the tree would not make them die but would make them like God, knowing good from evil. The temptation was strong, and Eve first, followed by Adam, chose to disobey God, which is sin. At that point, three events occurred: (1) they did indeed know right from wrong, and therefore, tried to hide from God (our natural tendency when we sin); (2) they did indeed die, not physically, but spiritually, and they were also put out of the garden, but most sadly, and importantly, out of daily abiding and communion with God; and (3) they brought sin, sickness, suffering, and physical death into the world.

From that point on, man has been born spiritually dead, separated from God (because of sin, Isaiah 59:2) and prone to sin throughout our whole lives. God is just, allowing natural consequences, but He is also merciful. In His mercy, He provided a means of covering sin. The people back then continually had to sacrifice unblemished animals, whose blood covered their sins, thus meeting God's requirement for justice. Throughout the Old Testament, this was performed by the Jewish people and was occurring when Jesus came to earth. Once Jesus came and died, He became the unblemished lamb, voluntarily dying, not to cover our sins, but to take them away. For "all have sinned and fall short of the glory of God" (Romans 3:23). Only a sinless man dying could take away the sins of the whole world. There is only One: Jesus. Therefore, His death took away all of our many sins, not just covering them. It is a one-time sacrifice that cleanses us forever—that is, once we have accepted that gift that Jesus has freely given (Hebrews 7 and 9).

Because of this, Jesus's death paved the way for us to be reconciled to God. Our sins no longer separate us from Him. They have all been paid for by Jesus. We can once again walk and talk and live in fellowship with God, and, even more wonderfully, when we accept Jesus's gift to us, His Holy Spirit comes to live inside us, helping us to become and do all that He desires. In this way, all three of the devastating events that occurred with Adam and Eve's sin no longer bind us once we have been born again. (1) We still know right from wrong and sometimes sin, but now those sins are paid for, so that we are righteous in God's sight. We also have the Lord's very Spirit inside us, taking away our desire to sin. (2) We are no longer spiritually dead, because God's Spirit lives within us, and fellowship with Him has been restored in the renewed garden, a Secret Place, for each of us to commune with Him. (3) Although we continue to experience sickness, suffering, and physical death, the Lord has promised to stay with us through it all, helping us through every trial and eventually to His ultimate garden, heaven, a place where He brings all who have this new life, all who have been born again. Our bodies will die, but our spirits will live on. To those who are born again, the Lord has given eternal life, which He says, "That they may know you, the only true God, and Jesus Christ, whom you have sent" (John 17:3). That is the reason that Jesus spoke of our need to be born again. We are all born physically, but we each need to be born spiritually also.

Now, the next logical question after "Why do we need to be born again?" is "How are we born again?" The New Testament says we need (1) to acknowledge and confess that we are sinners; (2) to repent, which means desiring, and being willing, to forsake our sins; and (3) to believe that Jesus died for us, accept His death personally, and invite Him inside. At this point, we are cleansed of sin and reconciled with God, resulting in the Holy Spirit coming to live within our hearts and a new home made for us in heaven, a most amazing experience, at which time Jesus's Presence becomes real.

After that, one needs to be prepared to encounter resistance from many sources, which is the way Satan works. In my experience, he often told me that because I was not like other Christians, I could not have been born again. Another tactic is to bring dissenting issues from various churches. For me, I encountered those who believed that water baptism is essential to being born again. Because of their insistence, I conceded to a water baptism. However, as I have grown older, I no longer believe this is true. John the Baptist said, "I baptize you with water. But one more powerful than I will come, the thongs of whose sandals I am not worthy to untie. He will baptize you with the Holy Spirit and with fire" (Luke 3:16). Also the thief on the cross, as recorded in Luke 23:39–43, had no baptism, yet Jesus acknowledged that he would be in heaven with Him that day. There are other examples in the book of Acts where people received the Holy Spirit without a water baptism. I believe water baptism was Jesus's physical illustration, pointing to the baptism of the Holy Spirit that He promised to send once He went to heaven. It also seemed to be a public acknowledgment of a changed heart.

Once we are born again, the Holy Spirit lives within us "to will and to act according to his good purpose" (Philippians 2:13b). At this point, we need to seek Him daily, learning to be aware of His Presence and to commune with Him. We learn to pour out our hearts to Him (Psalms 62:8), as we also learn to listen and understand what He is speaking to us. That is our responsibility (and the greatest blessing of our lives). It is then the Lord's responsibility to work within us and through us to change and empower us to do what He desires. "I am the vine; you are the branches. If a man remains in me, and I in him, he will bear much fruit; apart from me, you can do nothing" (John 15:5). In this life alone do we find true fulfillment.

We will all live on forever, some blessed with life with the Lord in heaven, pure joy, while others will be damned with suffering in hell, away from the Presence of the Lord. We have a choice. Why does God not let all of us go to heaven, especially if it is not based on behavior or works? Because heaven will allow no evil, and until we have the Spirit of God living in us, we are prone to evil. It takes God living in us to make us right and to help us to do what He desires. He respects us and enters only upon our request. He does not force Himself upon anyone. The essence of heaven is being with our loving Lord. Those who reject Him would not find joy, even in heaven!

This book is not intended to be a self-help book but rather a description of how the Lord has worked in my life and helped me to understand the remodeling He has made to my house. Although all of us have homes with similar rooms, the design, layout, and furnishings are unique so that not all of what I have shared may apply to you personally. There are rooms that are universal to all houses with purposes the same for everyone. In those instances, the insights the Lord has provided to me may help. But as I said earlier, we each have to seek the Lord ourselves to hear what He is saying to us personally about our own homes. The only advice I would give is above: to be born again and to grow daily closer to the Lord, our truest Friend. "But seek first his kingdom and his righteousness, and all these things will be given to you as well" (Matthew 6:33). I do not believe that our real lives begin until we are born again. I would urge those who have not yet made the decision to do so now.

I would also add that what I shared here is what the Lord showed me personally for me so that not everyone will identify. Those with personalities that are different from mine, which include the following: an introvert, shy, quiet, middle child, people-pleaser, or those with circumstances different from mine, which have included a

Catholic background and many years of sorrow and grief, may disagree with some or all that I relate. But there may also be those with similarities that will find consolation and renewed hope. That is my prayer. Whichever person you may be, however, whether you identify or not, you need to seek the Lord yourself. The things I shared are what I believe the Lord has shown me, but each person has to seek the Lord himself to find out what God would say to him personally. The Lord is the only authentic counselor, because He alone knows each of our lives, our whole lives, past and present, and how He made us. He alone can lead us to become and do all that He planned from the beginning.

In closing, I want to share the following. One day in the summer, on a walk with the Lord, I felt Him ask me, "Has the journey been easy?" to which I responded, "Oh, no, Lord!" "Has it been long?" "Very!" "Has it been worth it?" "Oh, Lord, more than words can say! More than I can express!" I do not kid you, and, as you can well see from the first part of this book, this has been a difficult journey for me. The Lord tells us to "count the cost" of following Him before we sign up (Luke 14:28–33). But I would also say that my life is so full now with depth, meaning, and purpose. There is hope, joy, and peace with Jesus that was never there before. "I have come that they may have life, and have it to the full" (John 10:10b). He has shown me a full and abundant life.

One more thought is helpful. When we enter the kingdom, we enter as not only babies, children of God, but also another truth is that we have received a new heart. In the physical analogy, someone must die in order for someone needing a transplant to live. In the spiritual, we can see the analogy: Jesus died for us, so that we could receive new hearts, His heart within us. Our old hearts have been removed and His new one inserted. We need to be patient with ourselves in this process. Only remember, it takes a lifetime to grow into Jesus's heart.

****

God's Love Gives Every...One a Place in This World

> Moreover, no man knows when his hour will come: As fish
> are caught in a cruel net, or birds are taken in a snare, so men
> are trapped by evil times that fall unexpectedly upon them.
>
> —Ecclesiastes 9:12

As I come to the conclusion of this book, my prayer is that my original goals have been met: to give praise and thanksgiving to my Lord, to reveal His loving character that I have come to know, to provide comfort to the hurting and to be a voice for them, and to provide understanding to those in my past. Hopefully, through this book, the Lord's deep heart of love for us has been revealed.

With the anticipation of the new millennium and the Y2K fears in 1999, many of us began to dwell more on the End Times prophecies. Since the terrorist attacks in September of 2001, there has been even more talk of this, with many new books published. There seem to be signs all around us, pointing to the last days and the return of Jesus. For us Christians, this is a thrilling thought: to be rescued from the evil world and go to be with the Lord. But we also have a heart of love and compassion for those who do not yet know the Lord, wishing for them to be as we are, as does our loving Lord. "The Lord is not slow in keeping his promise as some understand slowness. He is patient with you, not wanting anyone to perish, but everyone to come to repentance" (2 Peter 3:9). The Lord's heart loves all of us, and He is waiting patiently, but one day He will come, and no one knows the day or the hour. "You also must be ready, because the Son of Man will come at an hour when you do not expect him" (Luke 12:40). It does not seem a coincidence that the *Left Behind* series[1] and *The Lord of the Rings* series,[2] both concerning end times, were released recently. To me, they are words from the Lord. "Yes, I am coming soon" (Revelation 22:20b).

With Eric having completed college long ago and Sara recently finishing, we have come to understand the financial process fairly well. Again, the Lord revealed an analogy. Colleges often offer scholarships: free money and/or benefits. Most often, they continue through the years with criteria, such as being a full-time student and keeping a certain grade point average. The key point about scholarships is that the recipient must accept them in order for activation.

In the same way, the Lord has offered us the ultimate scholarship: total coverage for undergraduate school (here on earth) and also for graduate school (in heaven). We are only responsible to accept it. If we choose not to do so, payment comes due at the end of the age. If we do accept the scholarship, we are automatically given many benefits: a constant professor, tutor, friend, and counselor to help us here on earth as He imparts many lessons to us and the promise of a home in heaven after this earthly school. Because He lives within us, He can work whenever He desires and He never gives up on us.

The end of the age will come, and it seems close even now. All of us must decide if we will accept the Lord's generous offer or try to pay off our debt ourselves when it comes due. Those of us who have Jesus as our friend get a free ticket out of this world before payment is due (the Rapture). For those left behind, judgment will come, first during the Tribulation, followed by Jesus's return and subsequent requirement of payment. Unfortunately, whatever payment is offered will never be enough. Only Jesus's death provides the full payment for heaven. At this time, while there still is time, it would be good to consider if you want to accept the scholarship offered to each of us by a kind and loving God, who paid for it with His very life. Please do not wait too long, for the time is short. He will come soon to take us, His friends, home. Do not be one of those left behind.

Yet those days may be far away. Even so, we should all be ready for death each day. Gordon and I never dreamed Matthew would die when he did. In fact, Gordon did not rush home at first, even after receiving the message, because he thought it was concerning his grandpa. None of us could have fathomed that Matthew would die five days before Grandpa!

Probably few people who boarded planes or entered the World Trade Center on September 11 had any premonition their lives would end that day. We simply do not know. Jesus tells the story of the rich man who had so much hay he was having bigger barns built, his only concern with this life. But Jesus also tells us that this man was called by death that very night (Luke 12:13–21). What was Jesus's advice given through the parable of the ten virgins? He told us to be ready. He was referring to the end times, but we need to be ready daily. We do not know when He will come to take us—whether it is through sickness, accidents, or the rapture, none of us knows. What did the five faithful virgins do? They held their lamps with the oil, which provided light and heat to those around them as they waited patiently for their bridegroom. The oil is God's Spirit. If Jesus lives inside of you, you will have enough oil. Hold your lamp filled with oil and wait expectantly, for He will come to take each one of us one day.

Jesus said, "Here I am! I stand at the door and knock. If anyone hears my voice and opens the door, I will come in and eat with him, and he with me" (Revelation 3:20). His desire is for the response of an opened door, welcoming Him inside. If you have not done so, know that it is time, and He is calling *you!* "Lord, I acknowledge my guilt, all my sins in my life, and ask for Your forgiveness. I accept Your death for me and ask You to come live within me, which alone makes me righteous and acceptable to You." Satan will try to convince you this is not real, but hang on and ask the Lord's help. The Lord knows your sincerity. Meanwhile, draw near to Him daily, speaking to Him and learning to hear His voice. He loves you immensely. He loves us all immensely. Let us all be waiting, holding our lamps high, as we say, even so, "Come, Lord Jesus" (Revelation 22:20c).

Epilogue

He who dwells in the shelter of the Most High
will rest in the shadow of the Almighty.
—Psalm 91:1

The things of earth will grow strangely dim …
(Lemmel, 1922)[1]

The more we view heaven, the more this earth, as full of beauty and pleasure as it may be, cannot compare. The Lord wants our thoughts on Him and our heavenly home so we will be prepared for the day we will go to live with Him forever. That is the only way I have found to cope with the difficult circumstances of life, retreating to my home with the Lord. He is all Joy and Peace and has a place for every one of us to live and rest with Him, being in His Presence. He has also taught me to daily plant my worries and fears in our flower garden, as He makes those seeds bloom into something beautiful. The streams there also provide cleansing daily from my sins. In addition, thanksgiving seems to flow in this special place. "Do not be anxious about anything, but in everything, by prayer and petition, with thanksgiving, present your requests to God. And the peace of God, which transcends all understanding, will guard your hearts and your minds in Christ Jesus" (Philippians 4:6–7). Psalm 23 is often quoted at death, referring to the valley of the shadow of death, but what comfort to find that place while still living on earth and struggling with problems here!

When I was in elementary school, a favorite oral report for me (because I was so focused on it and therefore, not as self-conscious) was reviewing mystery books, finishing with the following announcement, "If you want to know the rest, you will have to read the book yourself!" I have been "reading the book" and have summarized it for you. My Secret Place is real to me, and I would encourage anyone who wants to know more to do what we all need to do first no matter who shares or what they may share: "But seek first his kingdom and his righteousness, and all these things will be given to you as well" (Matthew 6:33). Seek the Lord, first of all, dwelling in His Presence daily, and see what wonders He will reveal to you. "No, we speak of God's secret wisdom, a wisdom that has been hidden and that God destined for our glory before time began" (1 Corinthians 2:7). "However, as it is written: "'No eye has seen, no ear has heard, no mind has conceived what God has prepared for those who love him'—'but God has revealed it to us by his Spirit'" (1 Corinthians 2:9–10a). May the Lord richly bless you.

Notes

Preface
1. Cowman, *Streams in the Desert*, 21-22.

Chapter 4
1. Hamilton, "Along the Road," 907.
2. Hurnard, *Hind's Feet on High Places*, 17-70.
3. Hurnard, *Hind's Feet*, 71-116.

Chapter 5
1. Hurnard, *Hind's Feet on High Places*, 117-169.
2. Hurnard, *Hind's Feet*, 170-180.
3. Russel, ed., *God Calling*, 67.
4. Hemans, "The Child's First Grief," 112.
5. Stevenson, "Footprints in the Sand."
6. Springer, *Within Heaven's Gates*.
7. Hurnard, 181-214.
8. Anderson, "Suffering a Loss," October 4, 1988.
9. Claypool, Keynote Address, 1989.

Chapter 6
1. Hurnard, *Hind's Feet on High Places*, 217-254.
2. Green and Hazard, *No Compromise: The Life Story of Keith Green*, 290.
3. Hurnard, *Hind's Feet*, 181-243.
4. Bluth, *The Land Before Time*.
5. Fox, *The Lion, the Witch, and the Wardrobe*.

6. Burnett, *The Secret Garden.*
7. Hibberd and Kingsriter, *Rough Roads and Rainbows.*
8. Springer, *Within Heaven's Gates.*
9. Burnett, *The Secret Garden.*
10. Burnett, *The Little Princess.*
11. Lewis, *The Silver Chair.*
12. Various Artists, *Love-a-Byes: Quiet Songs of God's Love.*

Chapter 8
1. Roemer, *Rudolph the Red-Nosed Reindeer.*
2. Jackson, *Color Me Beautiful.*
3. D'Adamo, *Eat Right 4 Your Type*, 89.
4. Ward, *Self-Esteem Gift from God*, 23-36.

Chapter 9
1. Leman, *The Birth Order Book*, 115-130.
2. Holt and Ketterman, *When You Feel Like Screaming! Help for Frustrated Mothers.*
3. Oliver and Wright, *When Anger Hits Home Taking Care of Your Anger Without Taking It Out on Your Family*, 248-249.
4. *American Heritage Dictionary of the English Language*, new college ed. (1976), s. v. "self-respect."
5. Kendrick, *Fireproof.*
6. Kendrick, *Courageous.*
7. Eastwood, *Bridges of Madison County.*
8. Leman, *Sex Begins in the Kitchen.*
9. *American Heritage*, s. v. "intimate."

Chapter 10
1. Cowman, *Streams in the Desert*, 392.
2. Graham, *The Holy Spirit*, 181-185.
3. Tolkein, *The Lord of the Rings* book series.
4. Jackson, *The Lord of the Rings* movie series.
5. Tolkein, *The Hobbit.*

6. Wilkinson, *The Dream Giver.*

Chapter 11
1. Holmes, *To Help You Through the Hurting,* 101.

Chapter 12
1. Missler and Missler, *The Way of Agape.*
2. Missler and Missler, *Be Ye Transformed, 181.*

Chapter 13
1. Zemenckis, *Cast Away.*
2. Johnston, *Honey I Shrunk the Kids.*
3. Dravecky, *A Joy I'd Never Known.*
4. *American Heritage Dictionary of the English Language,* new college ed. (1976), s. v. "premise."
5. *American Heritage,* s. v. "premises."

Chapter 15
1. *American Heritage Dictionary of the English Language,* new college ed. (1976), s. v. "addict."
2. *American Heritage,* s. v. "addictus."

Chapter 18
1. Hurnard, *Hind's Feet on High Places.*
2. Missler and Missler, *Be Ye Transformed,* 173-188.
3. Montgomery and Packard, *Choose Your Own Adventure* books.

Chapter 20
1. Leman, *The Birth Order Book.*
2. LaDuca and Ramirez. *Joseph King of Dreams.*
3. *American Heritage Dictionary of the English Language,* new college ed. (1976), s. v. "tempt."
4. George, *Classic Christianity.*

5. George, *Grace Stories*.
6. George, *Growing in Grace*.
7. Missler and Missler, *The Way of Agape*.
8. Missler and Missler, *Be Ye Transformed*.
9. Warren, *The Purpose Driven Life*.

Chapter 21
1. Wooden, *They Call Me Coach*, 68.

Chapter 22
1. La Haye and Jenkins, *The Left Behind* series.
2. Tolkein, *The Lord of the Rings* series.

Epilogue
1. Lemmel, "Turn Your Eyes Upon Jesus," in Baptist Hymnal 1991, #320.

Bibliography

American Heritage Dictionary of the English Language, new college ed. Boston, Massachusetts: Houghton Mifflin, 1969, 1970, 1971, 1973, 1975, 1976.

Anderson, Paula Massa. "Suffering a Loss: Couples need help after miscarriage." *Daily Sentinel*, (Grand Junction, Colorado). October 4, 1988, Westlife/ health.

Bluth, Don, dir. *The Land Before Time*. Motion picture. Los Angeles, California: Universal Studios, 1988. http://www.imdb.com/title/tt0095489/

Burnett, Frances Hodgson. *A Little Princess*. New York, New York: Harper Collins Children's Books, 1998. https://www.common-sensemedia.org/book-reviews/a-little-princess

———. *The Secret Garden*. New York, New York: Harper Collins Children's Books, 1911. https://www.commonsensemedia.org/book-reviews/the-secret-garden

Claypool, John. Keynote Address. Presentation at The National Compassionate Friends Conference, Tampa Bay, Florida, July 14, 1989.

Cowman, Mrs. Charles E. *Streams in the Desert*. Grand Rapids, Michigan: Zondervan Publishing House, 1997.

D' Adamo, Peter J. *Eat Right 4 Your Type*. New York, New York: G. P. Putnam's Sons, 1996.

Dravecky, Jan. *A Joy I'd Never Known*. Grand Rapids, Michigan: Zondervan Publishing Company, 1996. https://books.google.com/books/about/A_Joy_I_d_Never_Known.html?id=PQm4ZTheD_AC

Eastwood, Clint, dir. *The Bridges of Madison County*. Motion picture. London, England: Warner Brothers, and Universal City, California: Amblin Entertainment, and Carmel-by-the-Sea, California: Malpaso Productions, 1995. http://www.imdb.com/title/tt0112579/

Fox, Marilyn, dir. *The Lion, the Witch, and the Wardrobe*. TV series. London, England: British Broadcasting Corporation, and Pleasanton, California: Wonderworks, 1988.

George, Bob. *Classic Christianity*. Eugene, Oregon: Harvest House Publishers, 1989.

———. *Grace Stories*. Eugene, Oregon: Harvest House Publishers, 2000.

———. *Growing in Grace*. Eugene, Oregon: Harvest House Publishers, 1991.

Graham, Billy. *The Holy Spirit*. Waco, Texas: Word Books, 1978.

Green, Melody, and David Hazard. *No Compromise: The Life Story of Keith Green*. Chatsworth, California: The Sparrow Corporation, 1989.

Hamilton, Robert Browning. "Along the Road." In *Bartlett's Familiar Quotations*. 13th and Centennial ed. Boston, Massachusetts and Toronto, Canada: Little, Brown, and Company, 1955.

Hemans, Felicia. "The Child's First Grief." In *The Primary Standard Speaker*, edited by Epes Sargent. Philadelphia, Pennysylvania: Charles DeSilver, 1857. https://books.google.com/books?id=3vZaCo22gv8C&printsec=frontcover&source=gbs_ge_summary_r&cad=0#v=onepage&q&f=false

Hibbard, Ann, and Doug and Debbie Kingsriter. *Rough Roads and Rainbows*. Pomona, California: Focus on the Family, 1990.

Holmes, Marjorie. *To Help You Through the Hurting*. New York, New York: Bantam Books, Inc., 1983.

Holt, Pat and Grace Ketterman, M.D. *When You Feel Like Screaming!* Wheaton, Illinois: Harold Shaw Publishers, 1988.

Hurnard, Hannah. *Hind's Feet on High Places*. Wheaton, Illinois: Tyndale House Publishers, Inc., 1975.

Jackson, Carole. *Color Me Beautiful*. New York, New York: Ballantine Books, 1984.

Jackson, Peter, dir. *The Fellowship of the Ring*. Motion picture. Burbank, California: New Line Cinema, and Miramar, Wellington: WingNut Films, and Burkley, California: The Saul Zaentz Company, 2001. http://www.imdb.com/title/tt0120737/

———. *The Return of the King*. Motion picture. Burbank, California: New Line Cinema, and Miramar, Wellington: WingNut Films, and Burkley, California: The Saul Zaentz Company, 2003. http://www.imdb.com/title/tt0167260/

———. *The Two Towers*. Motion picture. Burbank, California: New Line Cinema, and Miramar, Wellington: WingNut Films, and Burkley, California: The Saul Zaentz Company, 2002. http://www.imdb.com/title/tt0167261/

Johnston, Joe, dir. *Honey, I Shrunk the Kids*. Motion picture. Burbank, California: Buena Vista Pictures, and Doric Productions, and Beverly Hills, California: Silver Screen Partners III, and Burbank, California: Walt Disney Pictures, 1989. http://www.imdb.com/title/tt0097523/

Kendrick, Alex, dir. *Courageous*. Motion picture. Tokyo, Japan: Tri Star Pictures, and Albany, Georgia: Sherwood Pictures, and Franklin, Tennessee: Provident Films, and Culver City, California: Affirm Films, 2011. http://www.imdb.com/title/tt1630036/

———. *Fireproof*. Motion picture. Los Angeles, California: Samuel Goldwyn films, and Culver City, California: Affirm Films, and Orange, California: Carmel Entertainment, and New York, New York: FortyFour Studios, and Franklin, Tennessee: Provident Films, and Albany, Georgia: Sherwood Pictures, 2008. http://www.imdb.com/title/tt1129423/

King James Bible. New York, New York: American Bible Society, 1611.

LaDuca, Rob and Robert C. Ramirez, dir. *Joseph King of Dreams*. Video. Glendale, California: DreamWorks Animation and

DreamWorks Home Entertainment, and Universal City, California: Universal Home Video, 2000. http://www.imdb.com/title/tt0264734/

LaHaye, Tim, and Jerry Jenkins. *The Left Behind Series*. Wheaton, Illinois: Tyndale Publishers, Inc., 1995-2010. https://www.thriftbooks.com/series/left-behind/37387/

Leman, Kevin. *Sex Begins in the Kitchen*. Grand Rapids, Michigan: Fleming H. Revell, 1981, 1992, 1999.

———. *The Birth Order Book*. New York, New York: Dell Publishing, 1985.

Lemmel, Helen. "Turn Your Eyes Upon Jesus." In *Baptist Hymnal 1991*, #320. Nashville, TN: Genevox, 1991. https://hymnary.org/text/o_soul_are_you_weary_and_troubled

Lewis, C. S. *The Silver Chair*. New York New York: Macmillan Publishing Company, 1953.

Missler, Chuck, and Nancy Missler. *Be Ye Transformed: Understanding God's Truth*. Coeur D'Alene, Idaho: Koinonia House, 1996, 1997, 1998, 1999.

———. *The Way of Agape: Understanding God's Love*. Coeur D'Alene, Idaho: Koinonia House, 1994, 1995, 1996, 1997, 1998, 1999, 2000.

Montgomery, R. A. and Edward Packard. *Choose Your Own Adventure Books*. New York, New York: Bantam Books, 1979-1998. http://www.edwardpackard.com/cyoa.php

Oliver, Gary Jackson and H. Norman Wright. *When Anger Hits Home: Taking Care of Your Anger Without Taking It Out on Your Family*. Chicago, Illinois: Moody Press, 1992.

Roemer, Larry, dir. *Rudolph the Red-Nosed Reindeer*. TV movie. Burbank, California: Rankin Bass Productions, and New York, New York: Videocraft International, and New York, New York: National Broadcasting Company (NBC), 1964. http://www.imdb.com/title/tt0058536/

Russel, A. J., ed. *God Calling*. Uhrichsville, Ohio: Barbour Publishing, Inc, 1954.

Springer, Rebecca. *Within Heaven's Gates*. Springdale, Pennsylvania: Whitaker House, 1984.

Stevenson, Mary. *The Official Footprints in the Sand Page*, 1984. www. footprints-inthe-sand.com/index.php?page=Poem/Poem.php

Tolkien, J. R. R. *The Fellowship of the Ring*. New York, New York: Ballantine Books, 1965.

———. *The Hobbit*. New York, New York: Ballantine Books, 1937, 1938, 1966.

———. *The Return of the King*. New York, New York: Ballantine Books, 1965.

———. *The Two Towers*. New York, New York: Ballantine Books, 1965.

Thompson, F. C. *The Thompson Chain Reference Bible-New International Version*. Indianapolis, Indiana: The B.B. Kirkbride Bible Company, Inc. and Grand Rapids, Michigan: The Zondervan Bible Publishers, 1973, 1978, 1983.

Various Artists. *Love-a-Byes: Quiet Songs of God's Love*. Audio Cassette. Brentwood, Tennessee: Brentwood Music, Inc., 1995.

Ward, Ruth McRoberts. *Self-Esteem Gift from God*. Macon, Georgia: Smyth & Helwys Publishing, Inc., 2000.

Warren, Rick. *The Purpose Driven Life*. Grand Rapids, Michigan: Zondervan, 2002.

Wilkinson, Bruce. *The Dream Giver*. Sisters, Oregon: Multnomah Publishers, Inc., 2003.

Wooden, John. *They Call Me Coach*. New York, New York: McGraw-Hill Education, 2004.

Zemenckis, Robert, dir. *Cast Away*. Motion picture. Los Angeles, California: Twentieth Century Fox, and Glendale, California: DreamWorks Pictures, and Novato, California: Image Movers, and Santa Monica, California: Playtone, 2000. http://www.imdb.com/title/tt00162222/

About the Author

Rose Gardunio grew up in Salida, Colorado, with her parents and four siblings: Fred, Mary Kay, Paula, and Judy. She has a bachelor's degree in math and computer science and worked for five years for a health maintenance organization before realizing her dream of becoming a mother and remaining at home to raise her children. She is the proud mom of two grown children, Eric (33) and Sarabeth (26). She and her husband, Gordon, reside in Grand Junction, Colorado, and were leaders of the Mesa County Chapter of The Compassionate Friends from 1989–1995. They have been married for thirty-nine years.